New Paths to Raymond Carver

New Paths to Raymond Carver

Critical Essays on His Life, Fiction, and Poetry

EDITED BY

Sandra Lee Kleppe
and Robert Miltner

The University of South Carolina Press

© 2008 University of South Carolina

Published by the University of South Carolina Press
Columbia, South Carolina 29208

www.sc.edu/uscpress

Manufactured in the United States of America

17 16 15 14 13 12 11 10 09 08   10 9 8 7 6 5 4 3 2 1

Library of Congress Cataloging-in-Publication Data

New paths to Raymond Carver : critical essays on his life, fiction, and poetry / edited by
  Sandra Lee Kleppe and Robert Miltner.
     p. cm.
  Includes bibliographical references and index.
  ISBN-13: 978-1-57003-724-5 (cloth : alk. paper)
  ISBN-10: 1-57003-724-8 (cloth : alk. paper)
  1. Carver, Raymond. I. Kleppe, Sandra Lee, 1964– II. Miltner, Robert, 1949–
  PS3553.A7894Z78 2008
  813'.54—dc22

                                                                    2007044236

This book was printed on Glatfelter Natures, a recycled paper with 50 percent
postconsumer waste content.

Contents

Kirk Nesset

Foreword

Given the meteoric rise of Raymond Carver in the early 1980s, and given his sustained relevance and popularity, it is not surprising that criticism keeps pouring forth on his work. Carver was identified early on as an innovator, and he was labeled the "godfather of literary minimalism," standing as he did at the head of a vanguard, alongside writers Tobias Wolff, Richard Ford, Ann Beattie, Bobbie Ann Mason, Amy Hempel, and others. He helped resuscitate the mostly moribund American short story and influenced entire generations of writers in the United States as well as across the globe. Carver's fiction was and continues to be anthologized universally, translated into dozens of languages; he has been called "the most important American fiction writer in the second half of the twentieth century" (Delaney, "Raymond Carver," 442) and "the most influential American short story writer since Ernest Hemingway" (Stull, "Prose as Architecture," 8). On the occasion of his death from cancer in 1988, the *London Times* called him "the American Chekhov," and the world reeled to see a writer of stature cut short in his prime.

A first wave of scholarly books arrived to lay the groundwork, addressing the fiction primarily—full-length studies by Arthur Saltzman, Randolph Runyon, Ewing Campbell, Adam Meyer, and me. They locate Carver in the tradition of American fiction, weighing the corpus volume by volume, exploring the oddness and darkness of each, or identifying the hope in "Hopelessville" (to borrow a word from one of Carver's first critics). They draw connections between and within stories, playing up the nuances of Carver's characteristically underplayed themes; and they note the influence of Sherwood Anderson, Anton Chekhov, John Cheever, and above all Ernest Hemingway, whose tendency toward leanness in prose Carver turned even leaner. Each book addresses in its way what Ted Solotaroff has called "those rusted-out marriages and stalled affairs and misfiring bar seductions and sprung friendships" (Stull and Carroll, *Remembering Ray*, 203). In addition, each addresses, more or less, the issue of "minimalism" in fiction—an issue that now seems soundly dead, not to mention passé, thanks in part to periodic bursts of "maximal" fiction from various quarters (William Vollman, Dave Eggers, and Jonathan Franzen come first to mind). In the meantime—concurrent with this first wave of books—more work by or about Carver surfaced in print. Two books of his uncollected writing appeared, as did *All of Us*, the collected poetry, and a new configuration of selected stories (commemorating Robert Altman's feature film *Short Cuts*, based on Carver's texts). A book of interviews was published as well, as were three volumes of memorabilia (*Remembering Ray, Carver Country,* and *Raymond Carver: An Oral Biography*). Most recently a pair of "casebooks" arrived on the scene, treating "Cathedral" and "Where I'm Calling From," respectively; also arriving recently is Arthur Bethea's *Technique and Sensibility in the Fiction and Poetry of Raymond Carver* (2001), which treats not just the fiction, as its title indicates, but the poetry too—treats it extensively, including a sixty-three-page "thematic guide" to Carver's corpus of poems. While Bethea's *Technique and Sensibility* presents insightful ideas regarding Carver's poetry at some length, *New Paths to Raymond Carver* offers multiple viewpoints, often on the same poems or collections, thus offering a dialogue on the poems.

In the spirit of Bethea's study, this collection of essays investigates Carver's prose and poetry alike. It insists that we look into the poetry comprehensively and deeply in order to examine it for what it does on its own, above and beyond its capacity (as much of the existing criticism demonstrates) for extending and flavoring discussions on prose. Not unlike the fiction, Carver's poetry is unadorned to the point of translucent, and it runs the gamut from early to late in terms of tone. The early books (*Near Klamath, Winter Insomnia, At Night the Salmon Move*) are spare and stark and elliptical, while the later books (*Where Water Comes Together with Other Water, Ultramarine, A New Path to the Waterfall*) are fuller and more optimistic, more strikingly and straightforwardly so than the late stories, which remain guarded even as they affirm. Early or late, the poems are crisp and direct and intense, and they operate typically in narrative mode; William Carlos Williams, Charles Bukowski, James Wright, and Theodore Roethke are preeminent in terms of influence. The bareness and plainness stem from Williams, of course, and from Bukowski, whose bluntness and edgy clarity often disarm and unsettle. From Roethke and Wright come Carver's lyrical reverberation and range, as well as his capacity for locating in various ways something enduring in the most innocuous moments or places or things. Carver's poems celebrate, as Stephen Dobyns observes, those "small occasions of fragile contentment, of time lived instead of passing" (Stull and Carroll, *Remembering Ray,* 111). Yet, like that of his forbears, Carver's lyricism tends to be muted, underplayed, understated. As Saltzman notes in that very first book, the Carver icebreaker: "Carver's poems seem designed to honor the landscape, not to dominate it with soaring language. The poet does not wish to disturb the poised moment, nor does he venture to compete with the remarkable. . . . This is poetry that takes notice but stands clear" (*Understanding Raymond Carver,* 165).

Highlighting moment after poised moment, Jo Angela Edwins discusses in this volume the function of the traditional elegy in English in relation to Carver, and to Carver's "grief poems" in particular. The menace and dread we encounter in the early poems fall away, Edwins observes, as Carver confronts that ultimate

menace: death, his own, which impends. As gestures of writing, Carver paradoxically accepts and defies mortality, the poems themselves at once adopting
and reconfiguring the tropes of traditional elegy. In the spirit of *Reading Raymond Carver*, which examines the relational aspects of the adjacencies and con-
tiguities within and between Carver's stories, Randolph Paul Runyon identifies
(in the next essay) the imagistic and thematic links between poems in *Ultramarine*, which in veiled ways often refer to each other and to the fact of their inter-
connectivity. The intricacies of *Ultramarine's* assembly, Runyon observes, recall
"dream-work as Freud describes it in *The Interpretation of Dreams*," given that
each poem "seems to find in its immediate predecessor remnants . . . to put into
a new context for its own dream." Equally fascinating, William W. Wright sees
each of Carver's poems as a "transitional object" in which speakers reflect, or
fall silent. Each poem employs a unique "vocabulary of affection" that celebrates presence in the face of disappointment, disaffection, dissolution, and
death. The recognition or recognitions each poem offers, however, are not necessarily redemptive. "If anything," Wright notes, "the fact that this vocabulary of
love does not rescue or redeem the objects and people at whom it is directed
makes the efforts on the part of the speakers of the poems all the more
poignant and focused."

Similarly, Robert Miltner observes in the poetry the burgeoning of recognition, and a kind of redemption, if qualified in that characteristically Carverian
way. Examining the poems Carver wrote at midcareer and after—after his "second life" began (a phrase Carver used to describe life after drinking)—Miltner
explores through a thematic/biographical lens the ways in which Carver
employs memory and the writerly act of transcribing memory as means to transcend his turbulent past. Carver rebuilt his life, Miltner explains, by "sifting
through the destruction and devastation" and by restructuring himself and his
life through "the creative self-discovery and catharsis of writing." In the last of
the essays addressing the poems, Sandra Lee Kleppe uncovers the figure of the
voyeur in Carver's verse, which until now has been addressed only with regard
to the stories. Kleppe places Carver's voyeurs in a long literary tradition, from
antiquity to the Renaissance and beyond, observing Carver's tendency to "create a persona who is simultaneously close and distant, present and absent,
active and passive." As a result, she contends, Carver "involves the writer, the
reader and the characters"—in the poems and stories alike—"in a mutual pact
of intimacy."

Essays on Carver's short stories have continued to proliferate in recent years,
as one might expect, and the seven essays gathered here evidence the range and
depth of such scholarship. Adjoining Sandra Kleppe's study on the persona-
voyeur is William Magrino's "American Voyeurism: Why Does Raymond Carver
Want Us to Watch?," which connects voyeurism in the stories to subjectivity
and Lacan's field of the gaze; the reader becomes a voyeur in the process,

Magrino argues, watching the watcher watch, as it were, "to gain knowledge as well as contemplate the source of that knowledge." In a similar vein, Abigail Bowers explores "voyeuristic empathy" in *Will You Please Be Quiet, Please?*, observing not only the degree to which Carver's figures measure their own lives to the lives and accomplishments of others but also the degree to which already disenfranchised characters become detached and further diminished. While such characters often seem poised for change, for positive movement or new possibility, they "are never aware of what this is, or how it can happen, so they stay stagnant in their lives."

On a more cultural-critical note, Marc Oxoby assesses "The Voluminous Impact of Television in the Fiction of Raymond Carver," suggesting that the impact of media is not only present but also pervasive in Carver, though less overtly than in certain postmodern writers. The role of television (an object that "appears in Carver's short stories with a frequency at least equal to that of alcohol and cigarettes") develops over the course of Carver's career, from its reflective role in the early stories to the complex, character-interactive medium featured in "Cathedral." The story implies, Oxoby observes, that "while television ought not be a substitute for human interaction, it can in some cases be an enabler." Tamas Dobozy argues, alternately, that Carver's stories are a record not only "of America's quotidian struggles" but also of an expression of, if not "a response to, larger, even international, political conflicts." Examining an early story minutely, Dobozy suggests that Carver's fiction is indeed political, though not overtly, as was the case with his postmodern contemporaries; "What Do You Do in San Francisco?" offers, in fact, a tacit critique of American cold-war policy, reflecting and embodying its paranoia and suspicion.

Weighing the later prose and poetry with certain biographical sources, Chad Wriglesworth creates a "necessary theoretical space for a spiritual reading" of Carver's life and work, comparing the phenomenological language of the Alcoholics Anonymous "Twelve Step" narrative to the language Carver employs in his work. Admittedly Wriglesworth notes, Alcoholics Anonymous is not the only narrative reflecting Carver's recovery, but since its "key stages" are present in the later texts, that rehabilitation as such "brought sense and order to a chaotic personal narrative." Also concerning transformation, movement from darkness to light, Paul Benedict Grant's "Laughter's Creature: The Humor of Raymond Carver" illuminates an often-neglected aspect of the work, the later fiction especially. Carver's humor, Grant writes—drawing insight from Freud—is "evasive, a way of distancing or displacing negative emotions, but it also has a heroic function in the sense of liberation." As an author and a human working hard to survive, and indeed one of "American literature's more improbable humorists," Carver uses humor to maneuver through "the difficult terrain of his own life and those he chose to depict." In the next essay, in a kind of Barthesian language analysis of Carver's last stories, Claire Fabre-Clark explores "The

Poetics of the Banal," particularly as it relates to Carver's use of clichés. The "density of verbal clichés," Fabre-Clark writes, "together with a restrained use of conventional imagery, leads to a denial of alterity, enabling the emergence of the banal." Consequently the stories unsettle the reader since they rely on modes of representation "based on literalness and repetition"—all the more so because the characters themselves, facing moments of dissociation, suddenly apprehend "a different kind of 'real,'" which seems to them "all the more threatening for being so familiar."

The pieces opening and closing this volume are not essays so much as reminiscences illuminating Carver in ways that tie the writing craft to his life, offering readers an even richer sense of the man. In the closing essay, "Bulletproof," William Kittredge, one of Carver's closest friends and a committed writer himself, we find an extended meditation on life and death, from Kittredge's first meeting with Carver in 1970 to the final visit in 1987, shortly after Carver's surgery for lung cancer. "Ray's best work," Kittredge writes, "continually suggests the need for attempting to keep decent toward one another while deep in our own consternations. His best stories are masterworks of usefulness; they lead us to imagine what it is like to be another person, which is the way we learn compassion." Opening the volume is Tess Gallagher's "False Sky," an introduction to the Japanese edition of *Ultramarine*, published here for the first time in English. She describes their working life together as writer-companions, illuminating both the poems and the process involved in their making. The new translation of *Ultramarine*, she observes, "brings to Japanese readers for the first time the raw spirit and life of Raymond Carver, for in his poems there is only a very thin membrane separating his life from his art." Gallagher's remarks about the poetry encapsulate much about Carver's achievement in general, the stories as well as the poems, so informed is it all by the life, those most difficult moments. "No one can read these poems," she notes—recalling the nightmare of Carver's alcoholism—"and not be aware that this poet has been to the bottom of the abyss, and that he has brought back the gifts of a survivor."

Carver's figures in turn are survivors, to use Gallagher's word, which makes them and the writing compelling, urgent, intense. "Their valor," Henry Carlile observes, addressing the fiction, "is that in a world without assurances, and without having much insight into their own characters, they persist" (Stull and Carroll, *Remembering Ray*, 160). Persistence in the darkness of uncertainty explains some of Carver's relevance and popularity today, not to mention the fascination he continues to offer critics of literature. The problems we face in the early twenty-first century make those we knew in the 1980s seem mild by comparison. The gap between the rich and the poor has widened considerably; we are prone now (as nations and a global community) to terror and fear, and to rigid conservatism founded on fear; natural disasters occur more and more frequently, compounding as greenhouse gases collect; corporate corruption is setting new milestones, records for new depths of greed; and adding insult to injury, fuel prices soar out of control. The bewilderment and helplessness of Carver's figures are more relevant now than in the 1980s because a larger swath of the population feels bewildered and helpless—and numbers continue to rise. Yet, as Kittredge observes, decency and compassion are key. They arise in Carver, and in the reader, from "useful" acts of the imagination, from the transmission and reception of stories and poems—gestures that activate empathy, then recognition, and then further acts of imagination, ideally, beyond reading and texts, where restoratives lie.

If Carver's stories chronicle "the endless losing war our good intentions wage against our circumstances and our nature," as Tobias Wolff suggests, then survival as such involves in large part recognizing war as the war that it is ("Appetite," 244). Critics have noted repeatedly that for Carver's figures, recognition often involves transcending silence, involves removing the shackles impeding the tongue, and moving (like Ralph or Leo in Carver's first volume of fiction) through incomprehension to something better—if not comprehension per se, then out of the dark into something less so, even if dim. In one of the first essays published on Carver, Kathleen Westfall Shute writes, "while we may be sure, as Raymond Carver appears to be, that the act of articulation is not, in and of itself, a panacea for the grief and staggering uncertainty to which we are heir, we are reminded in [his] tales that the word, honestly uttered, constitutes a beginning, some place from which to start" ("Finding the Words," 9). Right till the end, of course, Carver sought such beginnings, illustrated so keenly in those last honest poems "No Need" and "Gravy" and "Late Fragment," for instance. Each in its own way is an epitaph, a poem of transition and fulfillment and grace. In each case persistence means leaving life consciously, though unwillingly, and never quite giving up, even when survival is clearly no longer an option. "When hope is gone," Carver wrote in one of his last journal entries, "the ultimate sanity is to grasp at straws" (unpublished journal, cited in Gallagher, introduction to *A New Path to the Waterfall*, xviii). It is this special sanity that makes Carver the writer he is; he awakens the survivor in the reader, text after text, book after book, presenting his baffled voyeurs, posing blank settings of bottles and mumbling TVs, darkly comic at times, uniquely banal; he offers unadorned elegies and contiguous dreams, where dismay and affection and fear run hand in hand. As Tobias Wolff observed in an interview, Carver "has penetrated a secret about us and brought it to the light, and he does it again and again. You have to go to the water and drink. There's something pure and cool and honest in his vision of life, and the beauty of his language, its exactness, its cadences, and its music. People will go back to it again and again and again" (Halpert, *Raymond Carver*, 158–59).

This collection of essays evidences such perpetual return, shedding new light on the light Carver brought. There will be many such books, I predict. Carver's water is deep and wide, converging, as it must, with other water. It remains vital, turbulent, nourishing—and so much of it close to home.

Works Cited

Carlile, Henry. In *Remembering Ray*, ed. Stull and Carroll, 150–60.

Carver, Raymond. From an unpublished journal. Cited in Gallagher, introduction to Carver, *A New Path to the Waterfall*, xvii–xxxi.

Delaney, Bill. "Raymond Carver." In *Critical Survey of Short Fiction*, ed. Frank N. Magill, 442. Pasadena, Calif.: Salem, 1993.

Dobyns, Stephen. In *Remembering Ray*, ed. Stull and Carroll, 108–13.

Gallagher, Tess. Introduction to Carver, *A New Path to the Waterfall*. New York: Atlantic Monthly, 1989.

Halpert, Sam. *Raymond Carver: An Oral Biography*. Iowa City: University of Iowa Press, 1995.

Saltzman, Arthur M. *Understanding Raymond Carver*. Columbia: University of South Carolina Press, 1988.

Shute, Kathleen Westfall. "Finding the Words: The Struggle for Salvation in the Fiction of Raymond Carver." *Hollins Critic* 24, no. 5 (1987): 9.

Solotaroff, Ted. In *Remembering Ray*, ed. Stull and Carroll, 199–206.

Stull, William L. "Prose as Architecture: Two Interviews with Raymond Carver." *Clockwatch Review: A Journal of the Arts* 10 (1995–96): 8.

Stull, William L., and Maureen P. Carroll, eds. *Remembering Ray: A Composite Biography of Raymond Carver*. Santa Barbara, Calif.: Capra, 1993.

Wolff, Tobias. "Appetite." In *Remembering Ray*, ed. Stull and Carroll, 241–50.

———. In Halpert, *Raymond Carver*, 153–59.

———. "Raymond Carver Had His Cake and Ate It Too." *Esquire* (September 1989): 244.

Preface

Given Raymond Carver's status as one of the most important short-story writers of the twentieth century—translated into over twenty languages and taught in schools in America and abroad that include courses in the liberal arts, social sciences, and medical humanities—critical studies of his life and work have been surprisingly few. There are illuminating monographs on Carver's fiction career, some of which include considerations of his poetry; the contributors to this volume are aware of many of these, either because they are the authors (Kirk Nesset and Randolph Runyon) or because these studies are a must for any Carver scholar or enthusiast.[1]

The impetus behind this volume of essays was to provide a current critical anthology with multiple perspectives on Carver's life, fiction, and poetry. This book specifically addresses a double need in current Carver scholarship: updating critical inquiry on his career and assessing the full scope of his work. One particular focus was to present an extended consideration of Carver's poetry—especially his late poetry in *Where Water Comes Together with Other Water, Ultramarine*, and *A New Path to the Waterfall*—which has remained an understudied and undervalued part of Carver's literary production; the structuring of this volume reflects that concern. Therefore, the first six essays focus specifically on his poetic oeuvre. Readers keen on widening their perspectives on and appreciation of the fiction will discover an array of exciting new approaches—textual, comical, political, cultural, and spiritual—to the short stories in the second half of the book. Structurally the book opens and closes with essays by two people who were close to Carver, Tess Gallagher and William Kittredge, as we believe their insights as friends, intimates, and fellow writers are invaluable in providing commentary on both his life and his works.

New Paths to Raymond Carver: Critical Essays on His Life, Fiction, and Poetry is thus the first broad study to focus equally on Carver's fiction and his poetry.[2] Moreover, this collection, by offering diverse geographical and theoretical perspectives on Carver's work, opens an expanded dialogue by placing the views of American scholars in a rich international context—the contributors are both new and established scholars working in France, Canada, Norway, and the United States—as well as offering for the first time in English Tess Gallagher's introduction to the Japanese edition of *Ultramarine*, which was originally intended for a Japanese audience.

This volume is designed to appeal to a wide readership that transcends both national and academic boundaries: general readers, students of literature, and scholars who are preoccupied with the content, craft, and cultural significance of Carver's writings. Considering Carver's enormous impact on a whole generation of writers, short-story writers in particular and poets and novelists in general will have an interest in this book. Additionally researchers will benefit from the detailed discussions of Carver's poetry and its relationship to his fiction as presented in this collection. Raymond Carver can be placed in cultural contexts larger than the limits of working-class minimalism, as is evident from the linguistic, stylistic, political, cultural, gender, psychological, and aging studies that these essays explore.

Notes

1. Standard studies of Carver's work include Arthur Saltzman's *Understanding Raymond Carver* (1988), Randolph Paul Runyon's *Reading Raymond Carver* (1992), Ewing Campbell's *Raymond Carver: A Study of the Short Fiction* (1992), Kirk Nesset's *The Stories of Raymond Carver* (1995), and Adam Meyer's *Raymond Carver* (1995). Recent monographs include Arthur Bethea's *Technique and Sensibility in the Poetry and Fiction of Raymond Carver* (2001), which includes a substantial discussion of the poetry, and G. P. Lainsbury's *The Carver Chronotope: Contextualizing Raymond Carver* (2003).

2. While Bethea's *Technique and Sensibility in the Poetry and Fiction of Raymond Carver* presents insightful ideas regarding Carver's poetry at some length, *New Paths to Raymond Carver* comprises multiple viewpoints, often on the same poems or collections, thus offering a dialogue on the poems.

Acknowledgments

A book of this scope would not be possible without the assistance of many participants and supporters of this project. We are grateful to Carver's widow, Tess Gallagher, for permission to include "False Sky," which opens this volume and appears here for the first time in English. Additional gratitude is extended to William Kittredge, who responded enthusiastically to this anthology by offering to reprint a personal essay on Carver, "Bulletproof," which originally appeared in *Ploughshares* (Winter 1990–91).

Only one of the other twelve essays on Carver's fiction and poetry has appeared elsewhere, albeit in a slightly different version; Chad Wriglesworth's "Raymond Carver and Alcoholics Anonymous: A Narrative under the 'Surface of Things,'" which was first published in *Religion and the Arts* (2004), is reprinted here by permission of the author and the journal. The remaining essays, written for this collection or adapted from conference presentations, are included here for the first time. The editors are grateful for the confidence and patience extended by all of our contributors.

We are indebted to Kirk Nesset for accepting our invitation to take on the important task of writing an introduction to this book and for providing an informative overview of its contents. Readers interested in particular aspects of Carver's career can consult Kirk Nesset's substantial introduction for guidance.

In addition to contributing an illuminating essay on Carver's poetry, William W. Wright acted early in the project as our third and unacknowledged editor, providing critical commentary on several of the essays and guiding their authors through various phases of revisions. We are indebted to him for these efforts.

We would like to give special thanks to the Humanities Faculty, University of Tromsø, for granting subsidy funds to assist with the production of this book, thus helping make this project a reality.

We are also indebted to Davis Schneiderman of Lake Forest College for his suggestions on preparing manuscript proposals, as well as to Joanna Hildebrandt Craig of Kent State University Press for her invaluable advice on press procedures and protocols.

Furthermore, this project has been aided by Joseph Polack of the business office at Kent State University Stark for his assistance with processing the subsidy funds in the United States and by Jean Holyfield of Kent State University Stark for her support efforts and secretarial expertise. Thanks also to Lisa Vargas of Kent State University for offering her excellent eye at proofreading and for her detailed and thorough indexing.

We are ultimately indebted to the University of South Carolina Press for sharing our belief in the merit and importance of this book, especially Barry Blose, acquisitions editor, for his initial support and Linda Haines Fogle and Bill Adams, who shepherded us through the completion of the project.

Finally, we are indebted to the people at International Creative Management (ICM), who represent the Raymond Carver Estate, for assisting us with all copyright issues concerning the poetry career of Raymond Carver. Special thanks go to Emily Brotman at ICM for correspondence and assistance. All references to Carver poems are from *All of Us: The Collected Poems,* edited by William L. Stull, introduction by Tess Gallagher (New York: Knopf, 1998). All Carver poems quoted in this volume are by permission of ICM, copyright Tess Gallagher.

"False Sky," by Tess Gallagher, translated by Emiko Kuroda, was first published as the introduction to the Japanese edition of Raymond Carver's *Ultramarine* (Tokyo: Chuokoron-Sha, 1990) and is reprinted here by permission of the author.

"Bulletproof," by William Kittredge was first published in *Ploughshares* (Winter 1990–91) and is reprinted here by permission of the author.

"Raymond Carver and Alcoholics Anonymous: A Narrative under the 'Surface of Things,'" by Chad Wriglesworth was first published in *Religion and the Arts* (2004) and is reprinted here by permission of the author and the journal.

New Paths to Raymond Carver

False Sky

Introduction to the
Japanese Edition of *Ultramarine*

When Raymond Carver and I met the Japanese novelist Haruki Murakami, who had been translating Ray's short stories, it was the summer of 1985.[1] We were sitting in the house I had built in 1982 as a retreat, what I called our "Sky House." It is located on the Strait of Juan de Fuca in Washington State. This is the very place, in fact, where the poems which would become *Ultramarine* were being written at that time. Mr. Murakami had brought his wife, Yoko, an artist in stained glass works, and I served tea with smoked salmon which Ray and I had caught.

We sat surrounded by windows which overlooked a body of water twenty miles wide separating America from Canada. Eventually our talk about the strange popularity of Ray's stories in Japan brought us around to the idea that perhaps the Japanese people had suffered a collapse in their dreams which was similar to that of the struggling middle-class people of America. Perhaps there had been a certain corresponding humiliation before the facts of working-class life. In Reagan's America certainly it was, we acknowledged, harder and harder to accomplish the so-called American Dream simply by hard work. Maybe the resultant spiritual desolation of alcoholism was also mentioned. I can't recall now.

What remains of that afternoon is Ray's beautiful poem "Projectile" (146), [2] dedicated to Haruki Murakami. The poem centers around the element of chance, which had also been briefly mentioned by Mr. Murakami that afternoon as something Japanese readers connected with in Ray's writing. They understood that one minute things could be fine and then the next minute a life would have changed forever. In "Projectile" we also experience the agility of memory—how it can suddenly take us out of a room and put us into a speeding car back in our past. Yet the past is not really "back there" after all, it seems, but is threaded through the present.

Again and again in these poems we feel what Ray calls "the lightning speed of the past," a past so insistent that it is always intruding into the present, often causing a long and troubling shadow across our path. But that afternoon as we sat with our Japanese guest, the sun was shining and several huge tankers were slowly moving east toward Seattle through the strait. The tide was coming in, and we could hear the waves below the house in their ceaseless rushing forward into the beach, then pulling back again. We walked up onto the deck and took in the view of the Olympic Mountains to the south, which are situated behind the town.

Then I pointed out to Mr. Murakami a smudged place on the deck where several birds had met their deaths after striking a triangular window. They had seen the sky reflected and had thought they could fly through the glass. A silence fell over us. It was as if we were each implicated and in danger from a fate similar to those innocent deaths caused by false sky. In his life and in his work Raymond Carver was an enemy of false sky. At the same time, he respected our vulnerability to it and knew that we could be similarly mistaken in costly ways. Nonetheless, he tried to make his reflections on the past yield fresh passage and understanding. Part of this effort involved finding new terms for old pain. For instance, we see him approaching and reapproaching two of the most difficult figures of his life: his dissatisfied mother, who expected her son to make her happy; and his former wife, who tried to bind him to her by guilt and accusation. By reframing his relationship to them in several different poems, he seems able to appease their unquiet presences, at least for a while. But the tyranny of family has a long arm:

> My loved ones are thousands of miles away.
> But they're in this cottage too.
> In Ballindoon.
>> And in every hotel room I wake up in these days.
> ("The Schooldesk," 195)

In "Hope" (159) he gives the humiliating scenario of the ending of his first marriage:

> When I drove off, she and her boy-
> friend were changing the lock
> on the front door. They waved.
> I waved back to let them know
> I didn't think any the less
> of them.

Sitting in Sky House as I write this, I appreciate freshly how little separates one from the sea, the sky, and the view of gulls and eagles, how the light changes continually through the seven skylights. No wonder Ray began to address the sea as an intimate:

> I pulled up
> a chair. Sat for hours in front of the sea.

> . . . Nobody knows what happened to me
> out here, sea. Only you and I know.
> ("Sweet Light," 179)

The fact that the mood of the exterior world can shift suddenly in this part of the country coincides with the emotional world of Raymond Carver, in which one has the continual sense of a slate being wiped clean and of having to start freshly. In the afternoons there is that light which "slices the room in two" ("Scale," 192), and sometimes "there's a milky haze over the water," which corresponds to a state of mind in which the speaker of the poem can focus on turmoil only so long before it's best to come back to present matters, best to "open a door, go out."

This return to the moment emphasizes the continual sense in these poems of a mind in solitude locating what's essential, what it should care about. In "Simple" (215), one of my favorite poems, things are reduced to the immediate present, the pleasure of eating a bowl of raspberries:

> If I were dead,
> I remind myself, I wouldn't
> be eating them. It's not so simple.
> It is that simple.

This poem short-circuits all those dialectical sideshows of the mind and strands us in a pure moment of being. It is somehow strangely appropriate that the last thing my husband ate was a bowl of fresh raspberries sent by a neighbor who knew how he loved them—those raspberries dividing life and death.

A line in the book's last poem ("The Gift," 223) might work as a clue to the simplicity of the music these poems carry in English: "No snow in Palo Alto." If you say it aloud, it gives the natural assonance of English and you experience the way Americans often speak intimately in phrases rather than sentences. It's a music so subtle in its chameleon-like ability to blend into its surroundings that some American critics have said this isn't poetry at all. They can't hear it. The diction is closely tuned to American nuances of everyday speech. There is also frequent use of the colloquial word or phrase, as in the word "sorry" is also a southern word for indicating that someone is never going to amount to anything. "He's sorry," they'll say, consigning him to the hell of the hopeless. Ray and I both heard this word often in our childhoods since our parents were raised in the mid-south of Missouri and Arkansas, then migrated west during the post-Depression years of the late 1930s.

It occurs to me that I don't know if the humor of certain poems in this book which make Americans laugh will have a similar effect in Japanese, but I hope so. It's a humor which doesn't fully surface, I must warn you, unless the poems are read aloud. In my own anthology of such poems I would list "Earwigs"

(172), "The Mail" (148), "The Car" (151), "Where the Groceries Went" (176), "Nyquil" (173), "Jean's TV" (155), and "Union Street San Francisco, Summer 1975" (153). These poems are, in a sense, so honest and even grim that our human response is to laugh at pain presented in such uninhibited, inescapable scenarios. I remember Ray saying of Nyquil that he never actually drank this strongly alcoholic cough medicine, but that if he had noticed the high alcoholic content he surely would have drunk bottles of it in the desperation of his drinking years. When the man in his poem drinks cases of Listerine (a mouthwash) we laugh because it is just too ludicrous and crazy. Yet at the same time our hearts are full of human pity for such a man. The two things coexist then— hilarity and pity—that sense of there being no limit to what people will do in hunger or addiction.

In rereading "Limits" (161) I marveled again at Ray's ability to witness even the worst that one could know about humankind. In the poem he records a scene in which a wretched, wounded goose is kept in a barrel. Its desperate cries are used to entrap other geese, which are then shot by the farmer-hunter who has invented this little hell. In the world of Carver the message is that people will do anything to get what they want. There are no limits. Even betrayal has to be decoded and understood as loss, as hunger. The goose whose cries attract and betray is another emblem of false sky—those Bermuda Triangles of the spirit where the innocent become victims despite all their best intentions.

Behind the poems of this book I sense that "iron will" spoken of in "What You Need for Painting" (142). It was this iron will which drove Raymond Carver toward his art when virtually everything in his working-class life was against it. I recall that at the time he was trying to begin to write poetry again in September 1984, we were living three thousand miles away from Sky House in Syracuse, New York, because I was teaching there. Ray had been awarded a Harold and Mildred Strauss Living Award, which was to allow him to devote himself completely to his writing. This intention to free him for his writing had no meaning, however, for his relatives who continued to embroil him in the family dilemmas. I told Ray he should leave Syracuse, go back to Washington to Sky House. It was okay to make an escape. When he agreed, I got him the plane ticket and he flew west to spend several months in solitude. We would speak by telephone each evening, and he would often read me what he'd written. He was writing sometimes two poems a day. It was as Rilke describes when he received the inspiration of the *Dueno Elegies*—as if an angel sat on his shoulder.

I joined Ray at Thanksgiving, and it seemed everything had turned to poetry. Poetry was a wonderful contagion which ran through the house. I began to write again too. It became the occasion for Ray to write "The Gift" for me, the poem which closes the book so tenderly. We also took walks near Morse Creek, a small river which runs through this peaceful valley. I recalled those walks in rereading the poems and also Ray's love for the winter steelhead fishing in that river. I also noticed that whenever Ray stands near a river in his poems there seems to be a communion with forces which are mysterious and beyond our daylight understanding.

At that time, looking over what he'd written, I'd felt a chill up my spine when I read the ending of "The Cobweb" (145): "Before long, before anyone realizes, / I'll be gone from here." I tried not to invade, not to question him about why he'd written such a thing. Then I read, "Soon enough we'll rot under the earth. / No truth to this, just a fact" ("Bahia, Brazil," 185) and "We vanish soon enough. / Soon enough, eaten up" ("Its Course," 206). I treated this as poetry, something generated by the poet's generalized concern with mortality. I couldn't read it as the nearby fate of my beloved companion.

So often art is ahead of life, preparing us, consoling us, causing us to treasure this strange gift which can be taken away at any moment. There is a story here in these poems, a narrative of a man assessing his past while at the same time he cherishes the moment and anticipates his own death.

As usual when he finished a book, Ray asked me to choose a title and to give the poems an order. In doing this I tried to emphasize the back-and-forth movement between his old alcoholic life and his new life of sobriety and productive work. *Ultramarine* moves toward a sense of spiritual equanimity, as in "The Debate" (206), where the poet realizes that whatever he decides to do with his day, he'll live; it will be okay. His delight at being alive and able to walk across a plowed field teeming with bugs had to be placed late in the book. He'd had a change of feeling about the earth in "The Fields" (218): "So what if the worms come sooner or later?" He seemed more at peace with the processes of living and dying.

I had chosen *Ultramarine* as the title of the book for its blue intensity and its relation to the sea. I had not yet come across the wonderful epigraph by the Irish writer Derek Mahon, a friend of mine from my time living in Belfast, Northern Ireland. I recall lying in bed one morning reading Mahon's *Antarctica* and calling out to Ray, "Come here! Come here! You won't believe what I've found!" He came to sit on the edge of the bed, and I read the passage aloud to him. He thought it was amazingly right. It suited the tone and the inner motivations of the book. I also looked up the meaning of the color ultramarine in the dictionary and found that it meant "coming from beyond the sea." This meaning comes from the fact that the semiprecious bluestone lapis had to be shipped from Turkey and Afghanistan. I also found that the color had spiritual significance.

Ray was the ultimate realist; yet there were strains of the surreal and even of the highly romantic at either end of his spectrum. He had survived a false sky through the mercy of powers which he acknowledged were beyond him. Someone in an interview asked him if he was religious, and he'd answered, "No," then added, "but I have to believe in the possibility of miracles and of resurrection."

We must necessarily broaden our idea of what a realist is when we enter the world of Carver. It is not someone willing to believe only in what can be seen. Nor is it a wholly pragmatic view of life. He was a gambler: "I gambled and lost, sure. Then gambled some more, / and won" ("The Fields," 218). What can I say? I fell in love with the gambler in him and with his iron will and with his tenderness which informed all he did. Emiko Kuroda, in her translation of Raymond Carver's poems, brings to Japanese readers for the first time the raw spirit and life of Raymond Carver, for in his poems there is only a very thin membrane separating his life from his art.

I admit it was hard, harder than I'd imagined it would be, to reread this book of poems Ray began writing only five years before his death. The book forced me back into the daily tenderness of our years together and into individual memories of times spent working on these poems with Ray. It was as if Ray's meditations on death in *Ultramarine* had finally allowed me, at least in an imaginative sense, to cross over into that silent place he now inhabited. The book had been my passage, my delayed entrance. The effort of penetrating that silence took a physical toll as well as a psychic one. I became feverish and started to lose sleep and to feel so intimately in touch with my absent husband that I began writing poems again to him, poems which left me exhausted and shaken. It soon became clear to my doctor that I had contracted pneumonia. I was put on a course of medication and was confined to my bed, where I reread this book for a third time. This time, finishing it, I felt refreshed and as if a great weight had been lifted from me. I said to myself, "Good. If he had to die so early, at least he knew all this."

No one can now read these poems, I think, and not be aware that this poet has been to the bottom of the abyss, and that he has brought back the gifts of a survivor. Ray's abyss was a ten-year eclipse into the hell of alcoholism, a hell from which he was just emerging when we met in 1977. Speaking about that time on a trip to London we made in 1985, he told an interviewer, "I was out of control, almost as good as dead. . . . My life was a wasteland. I destroyed everything I touched." The scars and ongoing reassessment of that past are made palpable here. We are in the company of one who has suffered great humiliation and spiritual pain and yet has been ennobled and purified, even beautifully simplified by that process. We are not offered this experience in any rarefied, transcendent form, but in terms that are as matter-of-fact and accessible as daylight.

It is possible that death is also a kind of false sky. We can't fly through it, but there may be other kinds of transport. Raymond Carver has found a way, through his writing, to at least evade his disappearance. He is even able to enter a new life in Japanese, a language he never spoke, a life with readers from a culture he was on the way to greeting when his life was stopped short. We had been scheduled to fly to Japan in the fall of 1987, but to our great disappointment his illness made itself known and the trip had to be canceled. Ray had looked forward very much to meeting the Japanese readers of his short stories. At least that intention, that happy meeting, finds another possibility through the gracious empathies and attention of Emiko Kuroda toward his poems.

Notes

1. This essay was first published as the introduction to the Japanese edition of Raymond Carver's *Ultramarine*, trans. Emiko Kuroda (Tokyo: Chuokoron-Sha, 1990).

2. All references to Carver poems are from *All of Us: The Collected Poems*, ed. William L. Stull, introduction by Tess Gallagher (New York: Knopf, 1998), reprinted by permission of Tess Gallagher.

Jo Angela Edwins

Sleeping and Waking

Raymond Carver's Late Poetry of Loss

> I want sleep to come and go, smoothly.
> Like passing out of the door of one car
> into another. And then to wake up![1]

Much has been written on the pervasive sense of "menace" in Raymond Carver texts. Referring primarily to fiction in his influential essay "On Writing," Carver insists, "I think a little menace is fine to have in a story. For one thing, it's good for the circulation. There has to be a sense that something is imminent, that certain things are in relentless motion" (17). In her introduction to *Carver Country*, Tess Gallagher states that a "current of benign menace seemed to pervade Ray's fictionalized world at its inception" (8). Graham Clarke claims that "Carver's early death in itself suggests something of the very ambience of his fiction and makes clear how pervasive the continuing fear and anxiety of death (and cancer) is to the lives he depicts" ("Investing the Glimpse," 100). However, Clarke's conclusion—that "death frames Carver's world and suggests an underlying nothingness" (100)—overstates the darkness of Carver's oeuvre, disregarding the increased hopefulness apparent in his later fiction and much of his poetry. Despite the fact that Carver's fame rests chiefly in his reputation as a fiction writer, he was a prolific poet who valued highly his work in that genre; as he told an interviewer shortly before his death, "When I'm writing poems, I don't know if I'll ever write a short story again, I feel incapable of it, because the poetry is so much with me" (Moffet, "*PW* Interviews," 241). Nevertheless, Clarke's reading of Carver does emphasize his acknowledged obsession (he disliked the word "theme") with loss and its personal ramifications, a subject to which he became reconciled most completely through his poetry.

Paradoxically, indeed almost ironically, Carver's later poetry confronting his cancer diagnoses and his impending death proves noticeably less menacing than his earlier writings. This essay thus aims to demonstrate the ways in which Raymond Carver's later poetry of loss, illness, and death in his final poetry collection, *A New Path to the Waterfall*, pivots on linguistic and situational contradiction—that is, the ways in which Carver unites rather than cleaves the concepts of living and dying, of hope and loss. Similarly some of the finest poems that deal with the approach of his death question the efficacy of language as a productive tool for defying annihilation and for expressing inexpressible emotions associated with illness, death, and grief, despite the fact that language and poetry are consistently evoked as vital ingredients of emotional redemption in the face of death. Several poems likewise highlight the paradoxical power of romantic love both to defy death and to make death's imminence all the more painful—even as love, like death, carries with it the risk of annihilating the lovers' individuality.

The paradoxical qualities of Carver's poetry enact the contradictions inherent in various theories of elegiac art. Peter M. Sacks, author of the pivotal study *The English Elegy*, argues that a crucial task for elegiac poets involves a "reluctant resubmission to the constraints of language" in the face of extreme loss (xiii). The poet Tess Gallagher, Carver's life partner for the last ten years of his life, wrote the influential essay "The Poem as a Reservoir for Grief" three years before his death. Here, Gallagher describes poetry's capacity to allow readers and writers to extend beyond "release of sufferings" to achieve a deeper understanding of loss that expresses both physical and psychological responses to bereavement (103). Gallagher asserts that, in a postmodern world that values quick recovery from the past to allow movement through the present toward the short-term future, the experience of mourning and loss is sacrificed to the relentless "now." Poetry, however, resists such tunnel vision, offering instead individualized spiritual release: "In such a [present-focused] world, poems allow a strictly private access to the grief-handling process, or, on another level, poems may bring one's own losses into communion with other deaths and mythic elements which enlarge the view of the solitary death. . . . one might open the book of poems in order, through experiencing loss, to arrive at an approach to one's particular grief and thereby transform that grief" (104). Indeed, Carver's poetry is not only paradoxical in its simultaneous embrace and rejection of language in describing loss experiences but likewise demonstrates the need of the grieving individual to connect his own loss to the many personal and collective losses that came before.

Part of the reason for the increasing hopefulness in Carver's later poetry lies in his highly publicized struggles with near-fatal alcoholism in the years before Gallagher and he began their close association. Carver was hospitalized four times for acute alcoholism in late 1976 and early 1977 before finally quitting his drinking for good on June 2, 1977, a date he referred to as "the line of demarcation" in his life (Weber, "Raymond Carver," 43). Gallagher asserts in her introduction to *Carver Country* that "Ray's sobriety was the single most empowering element of his life during our time together. Without that, nothing would have been possible" (13). When Carver had been sober for ten years, he was diagnosed with lung cancer in 1987. Within less than a year Carver would undergo surgery to remove two-thirds of his lung, would be diagnosed with brain cancer, and would face the recurrence of lung cancer approximately eight months after his lung operation before dying peacefully at home on August 2, 1988. Partly because of his sense that he had cheated death once by surviving severe alcoholism, Carver appeared capable of confronting these serious bouts with cancer with greater hopefulness. This sense of gratitude and optimism is perhaps best captured in his late poem "Gravy" (292).

Poems such as "Gravy" highlight the work of language as a process for expressing the inexpressible and for allowing the poet to impose order on the chaotic experience of terminal illness. "Gravy" and similar Carver poems ground the speaker's hope not in a cosmic vision of literary or spiritual immortality; rather, these poems describe Carver's hope for a future beyond death as emanating from his faith in his friends' memories of him as an integral part of their lives. "Gravy" tells a brief story of the response of a recovering alcoholic to a diagnosis of terminal illness: "No other word will do. For that's what it was. Gravy. / Gravy, these past ten years." The poem is not merely about its subject's experience but about finding the words to describe that experience. Carver's diction throughout the poem appears, as it does throughout most of his poems and short stories, highly colloquial, bordering on the cliché, indicative not of sloppy composition but rather of an attempt to access extraordinary experience through ordinary language. In "Gravy," Carver describes his post-alcoholic life as blissful because of its hard-won simplicity: "Alive, sober, working, loving and / being loved by a good woman." What many other men might take for granted, the poet suggests, seems nothing short of miraculous to the subject of the poem, who once before faced a death sentence because of alcoholism:

> Eleven years
> ago he was told he had six months to live
> at the rate he was going. And he was going
> nowhere but down. So he changed his ways
> somehow. He quit drinking! And the rest?
> After that it was all gravy

Communication drives the plot behind the poem. What is spoken here is, simultaneously and paradoxically, imperative and inconsequential. After he was "told" he had six months to live as an alcoholic, the subject "changed his ways / somehow. He quit drinking!" The essentials of the doctor's words are less important in this poem than the fact that those words spurred the subject to act—evidenced by Carver's well-placed exclamation mark. The horrible particulars of brain cancer are reduced to a vague and relatively benign assessment of the patient's condition as "some things that were breaking down and / building up inside his head." Much more important is the patient's reaction, gratitude for his life of sobriety, which enabled him not only to live but also to work and to speak to friends grieving over their imminent loss. Thus, the subject's "luck"—a ubiquitous force in Carver writings—resides not only in his ability to cheat death once and survive "ten years longer than I or anyone / expected," but also in his ability to tell his story, to express a message affirming the life and creativity his last ten years of sobriety afforded him. As Harold Schweizer notes about the poem, "In 'Gravy' the poet becomes his own survivor, so to speak. . . . [the poem] is a retrospective, redemptive self-completion by which life acquires the structure and meaning of a closed narrative" ("The Very Short Stories," 127).

Much less exuberant in tone than "Gravy," "Another Mystery" (255) finds Carver contemplating his own death by recalling the deaths of his father and his grandfather. In its linkage of Carver's death to those of his ancestors, "Another Mystery" parallels other Carver poems about his father, who died in 1967.[2] The poem begins with the speaker's memory of "that time I tagged along with my dad to the dry cleaners," shortly before his grandfather's funeral, when his father shows him the black suit in a plastic bag he had picked up and says:

> "This is the suit your grandpa
> is going to leave the world in." What on earth
> could he be talking about? I wondered.

Once more, the word—his father's telling him it is his grandfather's burial suit—and the gesture—his own touching of the plastic—offer themselves as differing strategies for accessing the experience of loss, though neither appears at all effective at this point in the poem. Confused by his father's reference to the grandfather's impending death, the young Carver apparently does not further question his father in the hopes that more words can clarify his understanding of the situation; rather, he resorts to the physical, the tangible, in an effort to comprehend what his father means. The boy's touch of the "slippery lapel of that coat / that was going away" like his grandfather offered no answers since the physical loss that would trigger such emotional loss had not yet taken place. His grandfather, like the burial suit, had not yet been fully lost to the boy. Death was indeed "just another mystery" that words could not solve.

The second stanza of "Another Mystery" describes the funeral of Carver's father. Again, the word—what his father's smile seems to say—and the gesture —Carver's touching of his father's hands and face—act as separate methods for examining and coping with the loss experience. Once more, both strategies prove inadequate, for "we knew better. He was dead, / wasn't he? What else could go wrong?" As the boy in the first stanza attempts to glean the meaning of his father's words through the physical gesture of touching the suit, so the young man in the second stanza attaches a verbal meaning that he knows to be a lie—*Don't worry, it's / not as bad as it looks* (Carver's emphasis)—to the physical spectacle of his father's dead body arranged awkwardly for viewing. Carver's grotesque description of his father's corpse reflects the young man's horror at the moment but does little to dignify or to soothe the pain of his loss. Still, the son attempts a final connection as he touches his father's hand and cheek, the few parts of his father which have apparently not been altered or garishly dressed after his death. However, the touch proves largely comfortless, as the only sensation the speaker recalls is "Cold." Despite his more intimate dealings with loss as a young adult, death here remains a mystery for the speaker.

The final stanza, however, features a literal and figurative breakthrough for the speaker, who achieves some release from the pain of his earlier losses by contemplating the nearness of his own death when he "picked up [his] own suit / from the dry cleaners," held it up in the sunlight, then

> tore a hole through the plastic to the other side. Took one of
> the empty sleeves between my fingers and held it—
> the rough, palpable fabric.
> I reached through to the other side.

Death, in the first two stanzas a frightening and confusing separation, becomes a less anxious prospect when the speaker imagines his own death and recognizes within it a physical loss that does not necessarily translate into a spiritual severing of ties with loved ones. The memories that Carver refers to as "clutter" that he "reeled up . . . from the depths" in the first line of the passage actually survive longer than any physical emblem of loss. It takes a moment for the speaker to muster the courage to make the deceptively simple gesture of tearing a hole in the plastic to touch "the other side," but once he does so, he realizes that the suit (presumably the suit he will be buried in) is nothing more than "rough, palpable fabric" subject to decay but, in itself, no longer a representation of menace to the speaker. Approaching his own death, the speaker acknowledges its inevitability and begins to conquer his fears, to solve the mystery as much as he can while still alive. The poem keeps alive through memory, individual and collective, the people and events that are no longer materially a part of the present. As such, "Another Mystery" demonstrates well Gallagher's view of poetry as a link among multiple past and future losses, creating a space where "the conscious and the unconscious experiences of the speaker and the reader are enabled to meet" ("The Poem as a Reservoir," 103).

The poems of the final two sections of A New Path to the Waterfall approach most directly Carver's recognition of his impending death, as well as the simultaneous sadness he feels at leaving behind his new, productive life with Tess Gallagher. These poems tend to vacillate in form between brief lyrics addressed to or directly concerning Gallagher and her grief and longer poems that relate a story important to Carver's and Gallagher's coming to terms with his physical decline. Among the longer ones of this group is "Wake Up" (287). The setting of the poem echoes its ominous subject as the speaker and his companion tour the dungeon of Zurich's Kyborg Castle. After scanning the various torture devices that litter the room, noting as well the crucifix hanging ironically on the wall, the speaker is drawn to the chopping block, where he cannot resist the temptation to lie down in the spot where prisoners were positioned for execution. In doing so, the speaker acknowledges a death wish that he believes all humans share:

> Who hasn't ever wanted to stick his neck out without fear
> of consequence? Who hasn't wanted to lay his life on the line,
> then draw back at the last minute?

The poem is saturated with oppositions: past and present, woman and man ("the North Pole and the South"), excitement and calm, life and death. The speaker's choice to rest his neck on the block results from his sense that he, like most people, views dying as the ultimate act of living, and he hopes to gain some awareness by mimicking the moment of his own death without fear that it will actually take place at this particular time. Not violent, as were those of the prisoners, his imagined death descends upon him as a kind of "drift[ing] off" to sleep, made possible in part by the fact that the threat of death he imagines is exactly that—imagined.

However, the presence of his companion intrudes on his calm: "Wake up, she says, and I do, turn my head over to see / her standing above me with her arms raised." In contrast to the speaker's relatively peaceful contemplation of his death in the previous stanza, the entrance of his companion into this mock drama raises the stakes, enhances the menace involved in the scene. Romantic partnership, as Carver writings often show, can prove both emotionally deadening and emotionally enlivening. In either case, as "Wake Up" suggests, the presence of a romantic other can make the prospect of death all the more insufferable, as death may either cap an emotionally desolate life or cut short an emotionally enriched one. The reader is returned to the conflict between words, in this case the "prayer forming in [his] throat," and gestures as means of communicating emotions relating to loss as his prayer is silenced by the feel of "flesh against my flesh as the sharp / wedge of her hand comes down unswervingly." The erotic yet threatening overtones of the passage are balanced somewhat by the vaguely comic atmosphere of the scene, but the poem demonstrates that the power of emotional involvement with another, if strong enough to revive, may also be strong enough to kill. The final lines of the poem underscore this point even as they suggest the possibility of redemption as the couple "walk into the next corridor / needing the light. And outside then, in the open, needing more." Once more, the physical gesture sustains the couple's emotions in the wake of the threat of death and separation; neither partner speaks as they leave the dungeon, but instead a "smile and my arm going / around her hips" become for the speaker the best comfort they can manage. Their togetherness, if potentially threatening individually, also provides an avenue for survival as they guide each other to "the open" and its comforting light.

"What the Doctor Said" (289), which centers on the effects on the speaker of his cancer diagnosis, also explores the strengths and limitations of language in the face of death. The doctor's words are given precedence in the poem; the phrase "he said" is repeated seven times, while the phrase "I said" appears only three times. Interestingly the first two-thirds of the poem reads like an unpunctuated transcription of a grimly comic dialogue:

> He said it doesn't look good
> he said it looks bad in fact real bad
> he said I counted thirty-two of them on one lung before
> I quit counting them
> I said I'm glad I wouldn't want to know
> about any more being there than that

The speaker attempts to deflect the fatal diagnosis with humor, so that the doctor acts primarily as a straight-man figure to whom the speaker responds with darkly funny punch lines tinged with desperation. Prayer, thwarted in "Wake Up," recurs in "What the Doctor Said," this time as the physician's suggestion to the speaker for a last-ditch effort at survival. The prayer image hinges on the capacity of language to evoke change ("let yourself *ask* for help"; "stop and *ask* for understanding"—italics added), but the speaker has placed little stock in the power of prayer to achieve wished-for results in the past. Despite his plans to "start today," his intention is less an affirmation of faith than an otherwise helpless attempt to achieve healing. Nevertheless, if the speaker—or at least his urge to survive—is to be taken at all seriously, he never fully rejects the potential for hope translated into words to do him good. Once more, language's usefulness is potentially powerful and seriously suspect, paradoxical and impossible to avoid. It is significant as well that the evocation of the spiritual and the capacity for renewal in this poem rest in the image of the waterfall ("let yourself ask for help / when you come to a waterfall"), as this is the central metaphor of the title of Carver's last collection. As in countless vegetation myths undergirding elegiac verse, the water image evokes the life cycle and is suggestive of the restorative powers of all living things. Despite his much-publicized realism, Carver in much of his poetry places great emphasis on the power of nature to renew and sustain. Whatever the comic overtones of the poem, the prayer scene described in "What the Doctor Said" is not merely held up for ridicule but likely contained for Carver a genuine possibility for redemption.

The speaker does recognize that words are not utterly powerless, as his response to the doctor's words indicates. Again paradoxically, words in this passage prove both powerful and ineffectual. The doctor's words in the early lines of the poem create such a marked impact on the speaker that he at last loses the capacity to speak meaningfully or to comprehend the last words the doctor spoke ("he said something else / I didn't catch"). After the speaker learns he will die soon, the doctor's words are both so frightening and so ultimately unimportant that he does not ask the doctor to repeat them and does not want to "fully digest" them. Suddenly communication halts between the speaker and the doctor, as both men "just looked" at each other in silence. Plunged as he is into the chaos of anticipating his own imminent death, the speaker's words and gestures prove meaningless, losing even the wit that characterized his initial denial-induced responses to the doctor's diagnosis. By the end of the poem, the speaker's words become something of a formality ("I may have even thanked him habit being so strong"), ironically rendered so by the force of the doctor's statement.

As its title suggests, "Proposal" (290) explores the verbal power of the marriage vow in the face of death, as the poem describes Carver and Gallagher's decision to marry shortly after the diagnosis of his lung cancer recurrence in June 1988. The opening stanza depicts the proposal scene as a mutual choice to confirm in words and ceremony the couple's decade-long commitment. Interestingly their long-standing intimacy renders words almost unnecessary, as the first three lines show:

I ask her and then she asks me. We each
accept. There's no back and forth about it. After nearly eleven years
together, we know our minds and more.

As is characteristic of Carver, the scene he describes demonstrates that realistic detail—the "ordinary"—is given precedence over romantic visions of how such an experience should be conducted. The long description of the Bette Davis movie that "unspools" as fireplace flames are "dancing / menacingly in the background" underscores the contrast between the precision of the ordinary moment and the stylized romantic ideal, of which Carver is routinely suspicious. Even within the "glamorous black and white," finely crafted world of Hollywood, life rarely proves emotionally black and white, as is illustrated by Carver's final lines as well as the film scene he describes. "Menace" pervades—in life, in film, in poetry. The paradox of the final lines is multilayered. As "Wake Up" suggests, romantic partnerships, for all their tenderness, are "entanglements." As "lovely" as intimate involvement can be, death always waits in the wings—metaphorically, when emotional conflicts can cause relationships to die, or literally, when one member of the couple succumbs to disease or sudden death. The final phrase—"In such a world / to be true"—can be read as a wish to defy irrational despair and "bad luck" by a commitment to an individual or a life purpose, but it can likewise be read as a lament, as if such a commitment were ideal but impossible. Carver, however, does not clarify what he means by "such a world" or by the equally problematic "true." Language here—like the emotional and physical pain the poem's subject involves—is in many ways inscrutable.

The poem returns the reader to another diagnosis scene, and once more the efficacy of language at such a moment proves a central issue. Communication

among the doctor, Carver, and Gallagher is hollow, largely because of the doctor's inability to read and understand the human reaction to the impact of his
words. Despite Carver's statement that he was "doing his best" to spare the couple pain, the doctor's references to Carver's body as a "shell" and his "going on"
and "hardly skipping a beat" demonstrate his insensitivity to the multiple possible interpretations of his words and to the shock the couple feel. Gallagher
could have been speaking of the doctor in Carver's poem when she explained
how the chief aim of the "business present" is to "act upon language and consequently upon our lives" by "driv[ing] out the ambiguity of language which is
the life blood of grief feeling and of poem making and reading" ("The Poem as
a Reservoir," 106). Far less sensitive than even the somewhat comical doctor figure of "What the Doctor Said," the doctor of "Proposal" reduces Elisabeth
Kübler-Ross's hypotheses and other stage theories of grief to their worst and
least useful form: a rigid schematic through which all individuals are expected
to pass in similar fashion.[3] Little wonder, then, that the speaker—an expert at
the art of language—finds himself so confused as to wonder momentarily at the
voice of his ten-year life companion. The doctor's handling of the act of telling
renders words far less beneficially powerful than they might have been at such
a traumatic moment.

Nevertheless, as in "Gravy," the doctor's words and the meaning behind them
have a serious impact on the couple. After their visit to the doctor, they begin
the task of mapping out how best to use the time left to them. Again, the
"word" figures prominently in their adjustment to the way time is "pressing
down / on us like a vise, squeezing out hope." The "everlasting," when faced as
a part of the couple's reality rather than merely a concept, creates a sense of
urgency similar to the carpe-diem atmosphere of other Carver poems in the
collection. Again, Carver's dark humor both distances and intensifies the mag-
nitude of the emotional struggle the couple face. The wit of the passage,
though, is balanced by the tenderness resulting from the honesty of "let[ting] it
all reach full meaning." Once more the gesture, the "[holding] on to each other,"
proves as necessary as the decision to exchange vows. The choice to marry in
Reno is prompted in part by the time constraints the couple feel pressing on
them since the terminal diagnosis; as a later passage of "Proposal" states about
Reno weddings, "No waiting period. Just 'I do.' And 'I do.'" Such a choice also
reflects Carver's love for the experience of the ordinary individual; according to
Gallagher, he affectionately referred to their Reno marriage ceremony as "a high
tacky affair" (introduction to *A New Path*, xxi). Thus, in yet another paradoxical
act, the couple agree to reshape a grief-charged ending into the celebration of
a beginning, as the poem's final passage illustrates with its references to dice,
roulette wheels, and slot machines. Carver's concluding image—"that suite
we'd engaged for"—suggests both a beginning and an ending, both the honeymoon suite of the newly married and the inevitable human passage into death.

By choosing to marry in the face of terminal illness, the couple gamble for time against an unavoidable fate, figured appropriately as "the muffled sound of dice" and the ominous "click of the wheel." The phrase "one more, one more chance" well describes the hope that many of Carver's characters cling to, and the couple in "Proposal" find themselves seizing the life left to them as the only hope remaining when, again paradoxically, "there's no more hope."

In "Cherish" (292), the speaker relishes the little time left to him to refer to his mate as his wife. "Cherish" immediately follows "Proposal" in the collection, an appropriate placement given its subject. The speaker of "Cherish" watches his wife through a window as she clips roses carefully in her garden. He realizes that she seems already "more alone in the world / than I had known," and he views her tending to the roses as a rite of endurance, helping her cope with a situation that words cannot adequately convey. "She won't / look up, not now," he thinks. "She's alone / with roses and with something else I can only think, not / say." The speaker, reciting to himself the names, taken from traditional wedding vows, of the rose bushes given to the couple as a wedding gift— "Love, Honor, Cherish"—is moved to "[Say] it then, against / what comes: *wife*, while I can" (Carver's emphasis). Here words and gestures combine to ward off the emotional sting of impending death. The speaker revels in the sensual odor of the rose and its symbolic "promise" of life and hope. He draws his mate physically close in a gesture evocative of the "holding on" to each other that gave them strength in "Proposal." The word "wife" with all its liveliness and promise is finally enacted "against / what comes."

Perhaps the most poignant poem in *A New Path*, "No Need" (293), features the speaker bidding good-bye to his loved one as he reluctantly accepts the inevitability of their separation. The opening lines, if mildly playful, nevertheless betray Carver's subdued frustration over losing his newfound life of renewal, creativity, and mutual love:

> I see an empty place at the table.
> Whose? Who else's? Who am I kidding?

Through the opening lines, Carver previews his own physical absence from Gallagher's future. Drawing on the traditional mythic symbol of the boat poised to take him from life to death, Carver speaks in the voice of a spouse embarking on a long voyage that will separate him from his mate, and in asking through the poem that Gallagher "remember" him and their lives together, he ensures that memory will take place by inscribing it as part of his literary legacy. The next passage then moves away from verbal or symbolic good-byes to images of physical farewells:

> We shall not meet again in this life,
> so kiss me goodbye now. Here, kiss me again.
> Once more. There. That's enough.

Despite the speaker's repeated urgings to his wife to "let [him] go," his similarly repeated request for one last kiss reveals that he does not wish to leave her behind any more than she wishes to be left. Ultimately, however, neither has a choice, and neither the physical nor the verbal gesture is strong enough to prevent the speaker's physical death. The physical act of the final kisses and the verbal act of the poem describing them become the nearest the couple's love can approach to immortality "in this life." In the introduction to *A New Path*, Gallagher notes that she unconsciously enacted the dramatic scene of "No Need" on the night before Carver's death, a fact that contributes additional poignancy to the poem's effect on Carver's readers:

> The three kisses which had been meant as "Good night" had, at the time, carried the possibility that Ray would not wake up again. "Don't be afraid," I'd said. "Just go into your sleep now" and, finally, "I love you"—to which he answered, "I love you too. You get some sleep now." He never opened his eyes again, and at 6:20 the next morning he stopped breathing. (xxvi)

The final poem in *A New Path* serves as the inscription on the gravestone that separates Carver's grave from the plot where Gallagher intends to be buried next to him. "Late Fragment" (294) continues the expression of gratitude that threads through much of Carver's poetry. Written as a dialogue of sorts—appropriate for a writer who valued communication as the central function of literature—it captures in epitaphic brevity Carver's assessment of his life and work as he neared his death. In "Late Fragment" an unidentified voice asks the speaker if he managed to "get what [he] wanted from this life, even so"; the speaker insists, "I did." "And what did you want?" the voice asks. Not surprisingly, the speaker's desire involves translating emotional experience into words; he responds, "To call myself beloved, to feel myself / beloved on the earth." The fact that Carver wished to be remembered as a person who could call himself and others "beloved" challenges the validity of the frequent readings of his works as emphasizing only the menace that plagues the human condition. Both Carver's literary legacy and his readers would be better served if we recognize the complexities of theme and of emotion that permeate his poetry and prose.

Notes

1. Raymond Carver, "Tomorrow," 816. All references to Carver poems are from *All of Us: The Collected Poems*, ed. William L. Stull, introduction by Tess Gallagher (New York: Knopf, 1998), reprinted by permission of Tess Gallagher.

2. Other Carver poems dealing with his father's loss include "My Dad's Wallet," in *All of Us: The Collected Poems*, ed. William L. Stull (New York: Vintage Contemporaries, 2000), previously published in *Where Water Comes Together with Other Water* (New York: Random House, 1985); "Photograph of My Father in His Twenty-Second Year," in *All of Us: The Collected Poems*, ed. William L. Stull (New York: Vintage Contemporaries, 2000), previously published in *Fires: Essays, Poems, Stories* (New York: Vintage Contemporaries,

1989); and "The Sturgeon," in *All of Us: The Collected Poems*, ed. William L. Stull (New York: Vintage Contemporaries, 2000), previously published in *A New Path to the Waterfall* (New York: Atlantic Monthly, 1989). See also Carver's essay "My Father's Life," in *Fires: Essays, Poems, Stories*.

3. In her important book *On Death and Dying* (New York: Macmillan, 1969), Elisabeth Kübler-Ross identifies five grief stages: denial and isolation, anger, bargaining, depression, and acceptance. Significantly Kübler-Ross never advocates viewing these stages as always experienced sequentially and acknowledges individual variations in each person's experience of grief, a point which later grief theorists have emphasized even more forcefully. See also Beth L. Rodgers and Kathleen V. Cowles, "The Concept of Grief: An Analysis of Classical and Contemporary Thought," *Death Studies* 1991): 443–581; Margaret Stroebe, "Coping with Bereavement: A Review of the Grief Work Hypothesis," *Omega* 26, no. 1 (1992–93): 19–42; and Wolfgang Stroebe and Margaret S. Stroebe, *Bereavement and Health: The Psychological and Physical Consequences of Partner Loss* (New York: Cambridge University Press, 1987).

Works Cited

Carver, Raymond. *All of Us: The Collected Poems*, ed. William L. Stull, introduction by Tess Gallagher. New York: Knopf, 1998.

———. *Carver Country: The World of Raymond Carver*. Introduction by Tess Gallagher. Photography by Bob Adelman. New York: Charles Scribner's Sons, 1990.

———. *A New Path to the Waterfall*. New York: Atlantic Monthly, 1989.

———. "On Writing." In Raymond Carver, *Fires: Essays, Poems, Stories*, 13–18. Santa Barbara, Calif.: Capra, 1983.

Clarke, Graham. "Investing the Glimpse: Raymond Carver and the Syntax of Silence." In *The New American Writing: Essays on American Literature since 1970*, ed. Graham Clarke, 99–122. New York: St. Martin's Press, 1990.

Gallagher, Tess. "Carver Country." Introduction in Carver, *Carver Country*, 8–19.

———. Introduction. In Carver, *A New Path to the Waterfall*, xvii–xxxi.

———. "The Poem as a Reservoir for Grief." In Tess Gallagher, *A Concert of Tenses: Essays on Poetry*, 103–17. Ann Arbor: University of Michigan Press, 1986.

Kübler-Ross, Elisabeth. *On Death and Dying*. New York: Macmillan, 1969.

Moffet, Penelope. "*PW* Interviews Raymond Carver." In *Conversations with Raymond Carver*, ed. Marshall Bruce Gentry and William L. Stull, 238–42. Jackson: University Press of Mississippi, 1990.

Sacks, Peter M. *The English Elegy: Studies in the Genre from Spenser to Yeats*. Baltimore: Johns Hopkins University Press, 1985.

Schweizer, Harold. "The Very Short Stories of Raymond Carver." *College Literature* 21, no. 2 (1994): 126–31.

Weber, Bruce. "Raymond Carver: A Chronicler of Blue-Collar Despair." *New York Times Magazine*, June 24, 1984, 36–50.

Randolph Paul Runyon

"It's like, but not like, a dream"

On Reading *Ultramarine*

In *Reading Raymond Carver,* I argue that the reader of *Will You Please Be Quiet, Please?, What We Talk about When We Talk about Love,* and *Cathedral* can profit by paying attention to the ways in which each story recycles elements from the story before. In the conclusion to that study I assert that Carver's poetic sequence *Ultramarine* "displays an integration that rivals that of the three major story collections . . . in which each poem repeats turns of phrase from its imme- diate predecessor and surrounds them with a new context" (208), but I cite only a few poems in support of that thesis. I hope the following examination of the last twenty poems of *Ultramarine,* roughly a fourth of the collection, will offer more substantial proof of my assertion. These poems[1] are "The Debate" (206), "Its Course" (206), "September" (208), "The White Field" (209), "Shoot- ing" (210), "The Window" (211), "Heels" (211), "The Phone Booth" (213), "Cadillacs and Poetry" (214), "Simple" (215), "The Scratch" (216), "Mother" (216), "The Child" (217), "The Fields" (218), "After Reading *Two Towns in Provence*" (219), "Evening" (220), "The Rest" (220), "Slippers" (221), "Asia" (222), and "The Gift" (223). However, instead of going from first to last, I would like to begin in medias res with "The Phone Booth," a remarkably com- plex poem whose doubling structure is emblematic of the way the poems dou- ble each other. From there I will move backward in the direction of "The Debate" and then return to "The Phone Booth" to pursue the interweaving and doubling structure of the sequence from there to "The Gift."

In "The Phone Booth" the narrator is too poor to afford a telephone and so must have recourse to a public one. He drives to one but finds it occupied. A woman and an older man are in the booth, evidently—from what the narrator can tell—hearing news of a death. First the woman is on the phone, weeping; then it's the man's turn to speak and shed tears. For a brief time they are together in the booth, which is too small for two people to occupy for long. Then the woman goes out to lean against their car, while the man discusses the "arrangements" to be made for the body of the loved one who has died. The narrator watches and overhears this from his car. Eventually the man in the booth hangs up and returns to his car, where he and the woman comfort each other while the narrator takes his turn on the phone. He leaves the door open to air out the booth. The phone is warm from is recent use, and the narrator is uncomfortably aware that it had conveyed news of a death. He has no choice but to use it, though, as any other public phone is miles away. While he puts his money in and dials, the man in the car starts his engine to drive away but turns it off again. The couple remain, spectators to the narrator's conversation as he had been to theirs. The woman whom the narrator has called begins shouting into the phone that their relationship is finished and that he can go to hell. He drops the phone and wipes his brow. The couple in the car roll down their window and watch; he has distracted them from their grief. The narrator returns to his car. Both he and the couple are in their vehicles for a time, and eventually each car drives off. This poem depicts a moment of human contact reminiscent of that in Carver's story "A Small, Good Thing," in which the baker offers the bereaved family fresh baked bread and comfort for the loss of their son, except that in this poem the narrator and the couple never speak.

The narrator and the couple are each other's doubles in several ways. He is aware of some of them: "I don't have a phone at home, either." He listens to the man in the booth "talk about arrangements," evidently for the funeral of the person who has died, and tells us that he is "waiting to make / my own arrangements" and "I put in coins and wait. / Those people in the car wait too." They are waiting to see what his phone conversation will be about. Each is spectator to the other's phone call. Each hears bad news on the phone, though perhaps for the narrator it is old news. Because he speaks of his own need to make "arrangements," it seems that he sees the burden of the phone call he has to make as comparable to theirs—the death of a relationship, perhaps of a marriage.

There is at least one parallel of which the narrator may not be aware. Early in the poem, after the man hangs up, he emerges from the booth and "wipes his face"; later, when the narrator is stunned by the hostility of the voice on the other end, "I . . . pass my hand / across my face." Clearly both the narrator and the couple are spectators to the other's grief. Another parallel emerges from the way the narrator tells us:

> I close and open the door.
> The couple in the sedan roll
> their windows down and
> watch. . . .
> . . . .
> Then they roll their windows up
> and sit behind the glass.

However, it is not clear whether he is aware of this parallel between opening and shutting the windows and opening and shutting the door. One more parallel emerges—not between the couple and the narrator but between the couple and the telephone, for the latter becomes a spectator too when the narrator expresses the hope that it "might / listen without taking sides."

By the end of the poem the narrator and the couple have become "we." Having returned to their cars after their visits to the phone booth, "We / don't go anywhere for a while. / And then we go." Actually, the first-person plural began earlier, at the moment the narrator puts his coins in and they watch, having decided not to drive off just yet after all: "Where to? None of us able / to figure it. Not knowing / where the next blow might fall, / or why." Both the narrator and the couple are defenseless before the blows that fate deals.

Some of the echoes that resonate within "The Phone Booth" can also be heard in "Cadillacs and Poetry," which follows it in *Ultramarine*. That is, the doubling effect that takes place in one poem also occurs between that poem and the next. The gesture of wiping one's face, which both the older man (who "Comes out and wipes his face") and the narrator ("I drop the phone and pass my hand / across my face") perform, is also enacted by the driver of the Cadillac, who had been going too fast on an icy street. The driver was hurtling sideways toward an intersection but came out of it safely; when it was over, he took off his woolen cap "and wiped his forehead." Car engines die in both: in "The Phone Booth" the older man "starts the engine then kills it"; after the Cadillac spun around 180 degrees, "The engine was dead." The couple in the car, watching the narrator in the phone booth, perhaps overhearing the voice shouting at him on the phone and certainly seeing him drop the phone and wipe his face, had "their tears stilled / for a moment in the face of this distraction." The driver of the car in the other poem, helpless on the ice and heading toward a possible fatal collision, finds himself distracted from death—his own, in this instance—by other thoughts: cats and a monkey he'd seen on the television news; the memory of taking a picture of a buffalo; his new fishing rod; "the polyps the doctor'd found on his bowel"; a line from a poem by Charles Bukowski about riding in a yet-to-be-built Cadillac. His mind was "a hive of arcane activity. / Even during the time it took his car" to make its 180-degree turn and point back in the direction from which it came.

It is almost as if "Cadillacs and Poetry" were an answer to the question asked in "The Phone Booth": "Where to?" Where do "we" (the narrator and the couple, and perhaps also the reader) go next? To the next poem, where we will have a brush with death. Like the Cadillac, the poem nearly turns around and points back to where we have just been. This kind of self-referentiality is, as I intend to show, widespread in *Ultramarine*. It grows out of subtle hints detectable in the poems that appear to point to the way each contains elements from the poems on either side in the sequence. How did Carver arrange his poetic collections? He said of *Fires*, published in 1983:

> The poems have not been put in chronological order. Instead, they have been
> more or less arranged into broad groups having to do with a particular way

of thinking and feeling about things—a constellation of feelings and attitudes—that I found at work when I began looking at the poems with an
eye toward collecting them for this book. Some of the poems seemed to
fall naturally into certain areas, or obsessions. There were, for instance, a
number of them that had to do in one way or another with alcohol; some
with foreign travel and personages; others strictly concerned with things
domestic and familiar. So this became the ordering principle when I went
to arrange the book. ("On Rewriting," 181)

Yet, this ordering principle, the commonality of ostensible subject, does not
well account for what is at work when we read "The Phone Booth" together
with "Cadillacs and Poetry." The connections we see there are not the obvious
ones of alcohol, foreign travel, and personages but smaller and more subtle ones
such as wiping one's face, killing the engine, or being distracted from sorrow or
dread.

Nor does it account for the way his poems sometimes speak of their situation of being neighbors to poems in which some of the same elements appear.
"Cadillacs and Poetry," for example, begins with the words "New snow onto old
ice" (repeated in reverse near the poem's conclusion as "Old ice, new snow") by
way of accounting for how slick the street was. It also has a way of telling us
how this poem fits in with its neighbors: something old, something new, something from the past beneath the surface of the present. Before "The Phone
Booth," where the narrator is naked in his anguish before the witnesses watching him make his aborted phone call, the narrator in "Heels" is quite literally
naked, outside his house, looking utterly ridiculous: "You raise your arms and
gesture. / A man with socks over his hands / under the night sky. It's like, but
not like, a dream." Fortunately, there are no spectators.

It is like the universal dream of being naked in public; it is also like a dream
in having the peculiar logic of what Freud called the "dream-work," in which
the recalled events of the day preceding the dream provide raw material for the
unconscious to work on: "the psychically significant impression and the indif-
ferent experiences from the previous day are brought together in the dream-
material, provided always that it is possible to set up communicating ideas
between them" (Freud, *The Interpretation of Dreams*, 261). Although the protagonist is awake and not dreaming in "Cadillacs and Poetry," he muses on this sort
of leftover residue as his car slides toward potential disaster in a way that parallels the way the unconscious muses over what Freud calls the day residue:
"The things that were passing through his mind? / The news film on TV of three
alley cats / and a rhesus monkey with electrodes implanted / in their skulls," and
the buffalo, the fishing rod, the polyps, and the line from Bukowski. This motif
often appears in other poems by Carver. In "Ask Him" (92), in *Where Water
Comes Together with Other Water*, the guard at the Montparnasse cemetery,
when asked if he would like to be buried there, "stops. / It's clear his thoughts

have been elsewhere. / Underwater warfare. The music hall, the cinema. / Something to eat and a glass of wine." "Woolworth's, 1954" (53), in the same collection, begins: "Where this floated up from, or why, / I don't know." In "Heels" he writes: "You're heading for the door / when a draft of air hits your ankles / and you're reminded of those wild swans / at Coole." The narrator in Carver's poems is constantly being reminded of one thing or another, and usually he can offer no reason why. When the reader encounters the recollection of Bukowski's line *We'd all like to pass by in a 1995 Cadillac* (italics in the poem), he or she will (or at least should) remember this allusion two poems back to Yeats's wild swans.

The poems follow each other as dreams follow the events of the immediately preceding day, each poem offering raw material for the next. That, at least, is one way of interpreting how the gesture of wiping one's face and the incident of a killed car engine reappear in "Cadillacs and Poetry" so soon after their appearance in "The Phone Booth." It is as if the unconscious were at work in these poems. It is a way of explaining how the phone booth itself is a new version, a redreamed version (since "Heels" is, like each of these poems, both a dream and raw material for the dream the next poem in the sequence will make), of the socks in "Heels" that were "worn yesterday and maybe / the day before, etc." and that, while they may have fit well on his feet, are now a bit cramping:

> You draw them on over your fingers
> and work them up to the elbow.
> You close and open your fists. Then
> close them again, and keep them that way.

The "tiny" phone booth was too cramped to hold both the woman and the man for long: "For a minute they are together / in the tiny booth. . . . Then / she goes to lean against the fender / of their sedan." Like the recently worn socks, the booth is redolent with the odor of its recent occupants when the narrator enters: "I . . . step inside. / But leaving the door open, it's / so close in there. The phone still warm to the touch." The couple's car, once they return to it and its closed windows grow "steamy" with their presence, likewise becomes a "cramped . . . place." The narrator opens the phone booth door in search of fresh air; in "Heels" he finds fresh air on his way to opening the door of the house: "You're heading for the door / when a draft of air hits your ankles."

Once he does get the door open in "Heels," he is surprised that it is still night. He had thought it would be morning, having awakened from a fitful sleep before looking for his socks. The experiment with the socks, wearing them in this unaccustomed and not quite proper way, took place in a time outside of time, in a morning that was not. The notion of doing that with the socks presents itself as an inclination he allows himself to indulge, a temptation accepted:

"You feel you could put your arm into one / and it wouldn't make a particle / of difference. So why not do this / one thing you're inclined to do?" This moment freed from normal restraint recalls a moment unrestrained in another way in the preceding poem, "The Window." The moment then had likewise been out of kilter with normality, with the landscape and with time. There had been a strange "vast calm" outside, in which the trees were "translucent" with ice, from a storm that had cut off the power in the house:

> at that moment
> I felt I'd never in my life made any
> false promises, nor committed
> so much as one indecent act. My thoughts
> were virtuous.

This "*one* indecent act" anticipates the "*one* thing you're inclined to do" in "Heels" (italics added).

This "moment" outside of the bounds of normality and responsibility ends when the sun comes out and melts the frost on the trees, "And things stood as they had before." In "Shooting," the poem before "The Window," another important "moment" occurs:

> The moon pales. Then loses face completely
> as the sun spears up over the mountains.
> . . . .
> Why do I pick this moment
> to remember my aunt taking me aside that time
> and saying, *What I am going to tell you now*
> *you will remember every day of your life?*
> But that's all I can remember.

This "moment," if we were to set the two side by side, coincides in its relation to the sky to what happens *after* the "moment" in "The Window," when the sun comes out "from behind the clouds" and establishes its dominance, melting the hoarfrost on the trees, as it made the moon turn pale and lose face in "Shooting." Yet, both moments are connected to memory and forgetting. In "The Window," he forgets things he should remember, his broken promises and his indecent acts; what he remembers in "Shooting" is that he has forgotten—that he can remember nothing of what his aunt told him except her assurance that he would remember it. He then goes on to say, "I've never been able to trust memory. My own / or anyone else's."

In "The White Field," immediately preceding "Shooting" in the sequence, memory and forgetting are just as thematic: "I felt as if I had lost my will, and my memory. / And I had." If someone had asked what he had done "even two days ago," he would be hard-pressed to say—at least at first; but then he does remember what happened two days before: he was tramping across a field of snow on his way with a friend to go fishing, only to find that some Indians had gotten there first. The Indians ignore the narrator and his friend and continue "working in *relentless* silence." At the end of the poem Carver returns to this adjective: "yesterday had its own *relentless* logic. / Just like today, and all the other days in my life" (emphasis added). In their relentlessness, both the Indians and yesterday pose an obstacle. The narrator can remember the day before yesterday (which is when he tried to go fishing), but "It's yesterday that got away, that slipped through / the net and back to sea."

The expression "all the other days in my life" is echoed in "Shooting" by the recollection of his aunt telling him that he will remember what she is about to say "every day of your life." In a way strangely parallel to his remembering only this of what his aunt told him, it is as if the expression itself were remembered from one poem to the next. Each of Carver's poems is a "day"; each has its own "relentless logic"; the narrator in one poem is sometimes able, sometimes not, to remember what happened the previous day, which is to say in the previous poem. Thus, almost as a joke, his fishing companion's expression of frustration at finding the Indians standing in the way of their fishing in that place—"'Christ almighty,' Morris said. / 'This is for the birds'"—is, so to speak, *remembered* in "Shooting," where it is precisely for the birds (to shoot them) that the narrator and a friend have ventured out before sunrise: "Suddenly, / the air explodes with birds."

That in "The White Field" he cannot remember what happened the day before but can remember what happened two days before is reflected in the fact that "The White Field" seems to bear a stronger connection to "Its Course," the poem that appears two before, than it does to "September," the one that appears immediately before. The motif of surprise at finding the place one thought was one's own occupied by someone else—the Indians at the fishing spot—is central to the argument of "Its Course," except that in the latter poem the surprise is retrospective, as the occupation had taken place long before. A neighbor informs the narrator that the spot the latter's house occupies used to be the site of a motorcycle run. Young men would come from all over to race up and down the slope, making a terrific noise: "I imagine / the roar of the engines as they surge / up this hill, the laughter and / shouting." It happened so long ago that the young men are old men now. Within the poem, this echoes something the neighbor had said earlier, about how the river there had radically changed its course over the years, how it used to run where houses stand now, and how the salmon would cross the shoal there, making "a noise like water boiling / in a cauldron, a noise like you were / scrubbing something on a washboard. / 'It could wake you up from a deep sleep.'" The "salmon run" corresponds to the "motorcycle run"; their noise, to the motorcycles' roar; the disappearance of their run, to the disappearance of the cyclists. We saw a similar doubling effect in "The

Phone Booth," between the narrator and the grieving couple. However, that doubling effect extends as well to "The White Field," where the Indians play the role of the motorcyclists and, in an interesting symmetry, of the steelhead salmon (in "Its Course") they are fishing for (in "The White Field").

How does the intervening "September" fit between "Its Course" and "The White Field"? The latter concludes with a meditation on the transience of all things: "Right outside my window is where / all this happened" (referring to the motorcycle run). "We vanish soon enough. / Soon enough, eaten up." The brief "September" is devoted to the question of what is left when things that had been there disappear. The

<blockquote>
last
of the sycamore leaves
have returned to earth.
Wind clears the sky of clouds.
What's left here?
</blockquote>

In both poems the narrator meditates on what has happened right by his house: "Right outside my window" in "Its Course"; in "September" he thinks of the pine struck by lightning "not far from the house."

Between "September" and "The White Field" there is this: In the former, the narrator asks, "What's *left* here?" (italics added). He meditates on the grouse, the silver salmon, and the blasted tree, for they are what is left. In "The White Field" he and his companion are "Every so often / turning around to look at the strange tracks / we'd *left*. Feeling glad enough to be *alive*" (emphasis added). What is *left* is proof that they are still alive. Proof of life emerges in "September" too: "A tree hit by lightning. But even now / beginning to *live* again. A few shoots / miraculously appearing." He tells the story of the failed fishing expedition in the context of his attempt to recall what happened two days before, and from that "day in all other respects unremarkable" he can recall nothing else "Except . . . the three-inch scar" his companion showed him, "across the back of his hand from the hot stove" he had fallen onto during a hunting trip. As a burn-induced scar, and as what is left (in Carver's memory of that day), it parallels the scar the lightning left on the pine (that too was part of the few things "left").

The title of "The Debate," which precedes "Its Course," refers to the debate going on for the narrator, who is torn between his responsibility to his publisher and the call of the river, where steelhead salmon are now coming in. Which course of action will he follow: stay home and work or go fishing? In the end, he claims it doesn't matter: "I'll live, and be happy, / whatever I decide." Recalling what Carver said in "On Rewriting" about the way he arranged his poems in *Fires* by subject, we can see that at work here, for both "The Debate" and "Its Course" are about steelhead salmon in the river. The neighbor who told him about the salmon run and the motorcycle run that used to exist "took 38 steelhead out /

of this little river"—obviously the same kind of salmon that used to cross the shoal where houses stand now. However, this kind of connection between poems is not nearly as interesting as the kind that Carver may not be acknowledging (unless such a connection is part of the "constellation of feelings and attitudes" to which he also alludes). I mean the symmetrical opposition between the narrator of "The Debate" having to choose between two courses of action, one of which is to succumb to "the pull / I feel toward the river," and the change of course the river is said to have undergone in "Its Course," running years ago where houses are now.

Like the river, I too will change course, moving forward now instead of backward, returning to "Cadillacs and Poetry" in order to follow where the remaining poems lead, to the end of *Ultramarine*. The next poem in the sequence, "Simple," quite brief (9 lines, 58 words), continues the theme of being distracted from thoughts of one's demise, as the narrator goes on "casually eating from the bowl / of raspberries. If I were dead, / I remind myself, I wouldn't / be eating them." In "Cadillacs and Poetry" the narrator was careening in an out-of-control car on an ice-covered street toward an intersection. He found that during that time his thoughts were elsewhere—on images from TV, his fishing rod, a line of poetry, among other things; and afterward as well he was "thinking all the while / along the same lines as before." This seeming irrelevance persists into "Simple," where despite being "filled with remorse" (for what, he doesn't say), "I go on casually eating" the raspberries. In other words, he defies remorse and, as the poem goes on to make clear, death by simply continuing to do what he had been doing. In "The Scratch," as brief as "Simple" (9 lines, 56 words), the narrator recalls waking up with a bloody forehead. Evidently he had cut himself during his sleep, making a scratch so deep it drew blood. This gives rise to the question "Why on earth would a man raise his hand / against himself, even in sleep?" The question is actually quite similar to the one suggested in "Simple": How can a man be eating raspberries if he's dead? That is, sleep and death are states that would seem to preclude such actions.

Self-directed violence persists as a theme into the next poem, "Mother," where the title character tells her son that "if this snow keeps on / she intends to kill herself." In "The Scratch" the narrator had awakened to see "a spot of blood / over my eye"; this gets transformed, in the way the unconscious transforms day residue into dream, into another instance of drops falling from above: "I tell her one of our skylights / has a leak. While I'm talking, the snow is / melting onto the couch." This is his reply to her declaration of suicidal intent. Snow is both dripping from the skylight (in the narrator's house) and (as it continues to fall outside her house) making her want to kill herself. Thus, in both poems the liquid (the blood, the snow) is directly connected to self-inflicted violence; in "The Scratch" it is the evidence of such violence, and in "Mother," the precipitating cause. Thus does Carver take what may at first seem a meaningless remark and weave it carefully into the fabric of his book, using it to tightly link one poem with the next, and his mother's state of mind to his own.

Despite this connection between mother and son, neither seems to understand the other. He insults her by saying that now that he's switched to a whole-grain cereal there's no danger of his getting cancer and therefore of her losing his financial support. She counters by saying that "The only time / she wants to *see* . . . me *again*, is from her coffin" (emphasis added). The first line of "The Child" repeats the motif of "seeing again" but places it in yet another parent-child context, that of the narrator and his son: "*Seeing* the child *again*" for the first time in a long absence, the father notices that his face is

> broader . . .
> Heavier . . .
> More like his father's now.
> Devoid of mirth. The eyes
> narrowed and without expression.

This is a child from whom one can expect neither gentleness nor pity, with a grasp in his little hand that is "rough, even cruel." It is hard to believe a father could talk about his son this way, but we know that Carver could. In "On an Old Photograph of My Son" (in *A New Path to the Waterfall*) he finds in his son a "Smirking" look, "the contemptuous expression of the wise guy, the petty tyrant. . . . / the look I never hoped to see again." He wants to "forget that boy. . . . / Oh, son, in those days I wanted you dead." In any event, what the mother says in "Mother" about not wanting "to see . . . me again" is eerily repeated in the first line of "The Child": "Seeing the child again." We see once more a parent seeing his or her child again, in yet another self-referential moment in the collection's sequential structure.

At the end of "The Child" the father, having held his son in his arms, lets him go, and the toddler goes running off, almost stumbling: "His shoes scuff against / each other as he makes for the door. / As it opens." As the narrator echoes his mother's words as "The Child" follows "Mother," as "The Fields" follows "The Child" he becomes a child again. Nearsighted, and evidently unsteady on his feet, he "was running once and fell / and came up with a mouthful" of dirt from a plowed-up field. After that, he always stayed away from fields "just after they'd been sliced open / to expose whatever lay teeming underneath." He never liked gardens either, with their "spuds lying just under the surface / with only part of their faces showing."

That is the way things used to be. Since then, however, "something's changed." Fields and their dirt are no longer a problem. "There's nothing I like better now than to walk into / a freshly turned field." If "I move / up close and look carefully, I can see all kinds of life / in the earth. . . . I'm gladdened, not concerned with the sight" of what can be found in the dirt: life in the form of ants, beetles, and worms. This change in attitude over time corresponds to the change over time, both physical and attitudinal, noted in "The Child." It is its opposite in a way: a change for the better in "The Fields"; a change for the worse in "The Child." What is really going on in these two poems, once we realize they are parts of the same poem, is that the field and its contents are a metaphor for the hitherto unexamined, or unexaminable—in particular for the son he was so uncomfortable looking at in "The Child" (and in "On an Old Photograph of My Son"). A clue to this is what he could not bear to gaze at in a garden, the faces he saw in the potatoes half-buried in the dirt, for these recall the first thing he noticed about his son: "His face." What seems to have happened, as recounted in "The Fields," is that the narrator has come to grips with his past, including even his son. He is no longer afraid to look in the dirt even if he finds faces there.

The faces may include his own, as if he were shying away from peering at his own grave, for "The Fields" is also redolent of death. Between the title and the poem, he quotes a "childhood ditty" (as he puts it): "The worms crawl in, / the worms crawl out. / The worms play pinochle / in your snout." He thinks of his own death, returning to the melting snow motif from "Mother," reinforcing the connection to death that it already had in that poem: "And what's it matter if the winter snow piles up / higher than fences, then melts and drains away / deep into the earth to water what's left of us? / It's okay." "The Fields" closes with the father doing what his son was doing in "The Child." The son's "shoes scuff against / each other as he makes for the door. / As it opens." The father focuses on his own shoes and, like his son, moves toward what is open: "I can push with my feet and feel the earth give / under my shoes. . . . And then / Amazing! to walk that opened field— / and keep walking."

Time passes in "The Child," the six months of the father's absence during which the child has changed: "There's something rough" in the child now, as he shows signs of becoming more like his father. Time passes in "The Fields" too, as over the years between childhood and now "something's changed" in the narrator's attitude toward opened fields. It likewise passes in "After Reading *Two Towns in Provence*": the time between the first time he picked up M. F. K. Fisher's book but was distracted from it when "Something came up" and the next morning, when he delved into it with great pleasure; and the time between 5:45 A.M. and noon that next day, during which he had no notion of the passage of time because he was so transported by the book. When he began reading the book that morning at dawn, "Men had already / gone into the fields to work." Those fields recall "The Fields," in which the narrator had spoken not just of fields but also, as here, of the men who work in them ("I've even made friends with some of the farmers. / The same men who used to strike me / as unfriendly and sinister"). In fact, in "The Fields" he counts himself fortunate "to live / close to the fields I'm talking about," and in "After Reading . . ." he alludes again to that proximity when he talks about the men having already gone, before dawn, to work in the fields.

Both "After Reading . . ." and "The Fields" are about seeing surprising value in something one had not paid proper attention to before. It was only late in life that he came to appreciate dirt and the life (and death) it contains; it was only after he picked up Fisher's book the second day, after having left it on the table the day before, that he really got into it, spending "the entire morning," he says to the author, "in your company," in Provence. "When I looked up," he recalls, six hours had passed. A similar delight can come to readers of *Ultramarine* who take the trouble to give it a second look. It will transport them, in the author's company it would seem (so strongly does the speaker of most of the poems appear to resemble what we know of Carver), and they will find all sorts of surprising things, as one could in the dirt of an open field. However, the field, and the poems, must be opened, "sliced open / to expose whatever [lies] teeming underneath." The second look of which I speak is also that of reading the poems twice, once by themselves and a second time in the context of the poems on either side.

The moment "When I looked up" in "After Reading" is an instance of this, for that moment, and even the words in which it is recounted, are repeated in a new context in "Evening" after the speaker recalls netting a silver salmon. "*When I looked*" into water below him "and *up*" (emphasis added) at the mountains above, he tells us, he did not anticipate the longing for that landscape that he would later feel. In both poems, after looking up, he begins to talk about the importance of place, and of himself in that place. In "After Reading . . .": "they all said I'd never find a place / for myself in this life!," a place where he could "be happy," but they were wrong. In "Evening": "nothing hinted" (when he netted the salmon) that "I would suffer so this longing / to be back once more, before I die" (back in the place where he had netted it).

In "Evening" he looked up at the "mountains / behind the town"; in "The Rest" he speaks of the "mountain range / behind my house." In the poem's earlier publication in *Poetry,* the line broke after "mountain": "over this mountain / range behind my house" (360); the change enhances the parallel between "behind the town" (in "Evening") and "behind my house" (in "The Rest"). Are these two poems (and the house, the town, and the mountains behind them) in the same place? In "Evening" he nets a salmon; in "The Rest" he cleans a salmon he has just caught. The fish he had netted in "Evening" was a "silver salmon"; the salmon he cleans in "The Rest" leaves his hands "silvery with scales." The title of the latter poem alludes to what remains of the fish after he cleans it and cuts off its head: "I bury what needs burying / and keep the rest." However, it would appear that "The Rest" is what it says it is in another sense, the rest of the story begun in "Evening," the story of netting a silver salmon at nightfall ("as darkness kept coming on" ["Evening"]; "the light / will go" ["The

Rest"]), cleaning it, and taking it home. It is unusual that two neighboring poems in *Ultramarine* should be about the same thing in the same context, for they are usually are about the same things in different contexts.

The same thing that connects "The Rest" and "Slippers" in different contexts is the act (voluntary in "The Rest," accidental in "Slippers") of burying. The nonedible parts of the fish get buried in "The Rest"; in "Slippers," slippers do. The speaker recalls picking up his wife's slippers and putting them beside the bed, where "a quilt fell and covered them / during the night." Not realizing he had put them there, and not seeing them because they were covered by the quilt, she "looked / everywhere" before finally locating them and uttering a cry a delight. The story of the lost and found slippers is presented as a possible sub-stitute for a dream. The speaker, his wife, and another couple were telling each other their dreams, but "All I could think to say, / but didn't" was the tale of the buried slippers. As Carver writes in "Heels," which also happens to be about footwear, "It's like, but not like, a dream"—though the speaker in "Slippers" does not say that it is *not like* a dream, just that he did not tell it in place of a dream, though he thought of doing so. In any case, "Slippers" is a beautiful example of the way poems in this sequence work like dream-work, and sometimes even seem to allude to their doing so. The story that might have substituted for a dream works like a dream in that it appears to take for its raw material what is left over (that is, *the rest*) from the immediately preceding "The Rest," namely burial.

The dream that is told in "Slippers" becomes, appropriately, the day residue (the raw material, *the rest*) to be recycled in the poem that follows it, "Asia." In that poem, horses on the beach "stand like statues of horses. / *Watching* the ship as it passes" (emphasis added). They are thinking about the same thing the sailors on the ship are thinking about: "in the mind / of the horses . . . / it is always Asia." Asia is the ship's destination, and the sailors "consider themselves / lucky" to be going there. The dreamer in "Slippers" awoke in the middle of the night to find herself barking like a dog and "her little dog, / Teddy, beside the bed, *watching.*" The watching dog becomes the watching horses.

The horses are thinking the same thing the sailors are, Asia, but not neces-sarily because they are reading their minds. On the other hand, knowing what the person one is watching is thinking does happen earlier in "Asia": "I know *what they're thinking*" (emphasis added), the narrator says about the sailors as he watches them from the balcony of his house. He knows they "look at him and consider themselves / lucky" to be heading for Asia. By contrast, in "The Gift" the narrator says that he and his wife cannot know what each other is thinking, though in their tenderness they act "as if sensing the other's rickety state of mind. / As if we knew *what the other was feeling.* We don't, / of course. We never do" (emphasis added). Dream-work that recycles day residue is of course not the only model the poems of *Ultramarine* suggest to account for what happens here; another way is that two side-by-side poems are like the speaker and his wife, side by side in bed, each behaving as if aware of the other's thoughts but not really knowing them. "Asia" and "The Gift" behave as if each knew the other's thoughts, in particular the thought of knowing the thoughts of the person right beside. Carver takes pains to point out that the men on the ship and the speaker on his balcony are in unusually close proximity:

> It's good to live near the water.
> Ships pass so close to land
> a man could *reach out*
> *and* break a branch from one of the willow trees.
>
> . . . .
>
> From my balcony I can read the faces
> of the men. . . . (emphasis added)

That reaching out is yet another image that is not only shared by these two poems but is at the same time a way of talking about that sharing, for that reaching out in "Asia" reaches out to another reaching out in "The Gift": the speaker remembers living, in straitened circumstances years before, in a house so small that the refrigerator was next to the bed. At least when he needed a drink of cold water in the middle of the night, all he had to do "was *reach out /* *and* open the door."

Ultramarine is full of moments when its poems refer to each other and to the fact that they are so doing. Each poem is "like, but not like, a dream," for something like dream-work as Freud describes it in *The Interpretation of Dreams* is at work in each, as each seems to find in its immediate predecessor remnants (as in what's "left" in "September" and "The White Field" and "the rest" in "The Rest") to put into a new context for its own dream. Each predecessor poem ceases to be a dream in order to become something more like lived experience, which it seems the narrator of the succeeding poem remembers, even as he complains about the bits and pieces of junk floating about in his memory (in "Cadillacs and Poetry" and elsewhere) and about his defective memory (in "The White Field" and "Shooting"); it is in that sense that each poem is "not like" a dream, at the same time that it *is* like one.

I began by placing this kind of reading in the context of my earlier reading of his stories, but in fact this approach, which is simple yet fruitful, should not be limited to Carver. The ordered collection is a genre with its own rich possibilities, yet to be fully explored by critics and commentators. I have argued elsewhere that *intra*textual doubling and self-reference are rampant in literary collections as diverse as Montaigne's *Essays*, La Fontaine's *Fables* and *Contes*, Montesquieu's *Persian Letters*, and the poetry of Robert Penn Warren. What happens in *Ultramarine* should be placed in that larger, and relatively uncharted, tradition—though "tradition" may not be the best term, for these phenomena are perhaps not so much handed down as rediscovered by writers as fresh and original as Raymond Carver.

Note

1. All references to Carver poems are from *All of Us: The Collected Poems*, ed. William L. Stull, introduction by Tess Gallagher (New York: Knopf, 1998), reprinted by permission of Tess Gallagher.

Works Cited

Carver, Raymond. *All of Us: The Collected Poems*, ed. William L. Stull, introduction by Tess Gallagher. New York: Knopf, 1998.

———. "On Rewriting." In *Call If You Need Me: The Uncollected Fiction and Other Prose*, ed. William L. Stull. New York: Vintage, 2001.

Freud, Sigmund. *The Interpretation of Dreams*, trans. and ed. James Strachey. New York: Avon Books, 1965.

Runyon, Randolph Paul. *The Art of the Persian Letters*. Newark: University of Delaware Press, 2005.

———. *The Braided Dream: Robert Penn Warren's Late Poetry*. Lexington: University Press of Kentucky, 1990.

———. *Ghostly Parallels: Robert Penn Warren and the Lyric Poetic Sequence*. Knoxville: University of Tennessee Press, 2006.

———. *In La Fontaine's Labyrinth: A Thread through the Fables*. Charlottesville, Va.: Rookwood Press / EMF Critiques, 2000.

———. *Reading Raymond Carver*. Syracuse, N.Y.: Syracuse University Press, 1992.

———. "La séquence et la symétrie comme principes d'organisation chez Montesquieu, La Fontaine et Montaigne." In *Le Recueil littéraire: Pratiques et théorie d'une forme*, 177–86, ed. Irène Langlet. Rennes: Presses Universitaires de Rennes, 2003.

William W. Wright

The Vocabulary of Affection

Attitudes toward Objects, Characters, and Other Writers in the Poetry of Raymond Carver

If we identify Raymond Carver as a love poet, it suggests that we find in his poetry not the emptiness, loss, or humiliation that is sometimes suggested in his fiction, but instead so much abundance, humanity, and hope. Turning our attention to the diction of love in Carver's poetry, we see how that love is manifest in attitudes toward objects, creatures, and people, and what effect that diction has on the readers and speakers of the poems. The overall claim is given away in the title. As a poet, Carver employs a vocabulary of affection to recognize, document, and often celebrate objects, the natural world, ordinary people, and writers. Those recognitions and celebrations offer a certain strategic humanity and dignity to objects, animals, and people, but they do not offer redemption. If anything, the fact that this vocabulary of love does not rescue or redeem the objects and people at whom it is directed makes the efforts on the part of the speakers of the poems all the more poignant and focused. There is, certainly, a persistent attitude of recognition in the poems, and if anyone or thing is redeemed by this affection, it is the speakers, as we will see in the conclusion of this consideration.

At the outset I make two borrowings from other commentators on Carver's poetry and fiction: the first is the presence and uses of silence, something many readers note in his work; the second is the tendency to negotiate, the inclination to use the poem to make contact across distance. In a discussion of the story "Feathers," Laurie Chapman suggests that "in Carver's fictional world, speech is therapeutic but silence is detrimental to characters" ("What's to Say," 194).[1] Kirk Nesset qualifies this notion in his readings of silence and sexual politics in early Carver. As he suggests, "silence is for such characters more than an outward expression of inner mayhem. . . . Like sex, silence can be medicinal, providing a respite in the ready-made flow of language that often confuses already confusing circumstances" ("This Word Love," 312). In Carver's poetry silence is more often not a limitation but an opportunity, a place for contemplation and recognition, even an act of love. The speakers of poems often stop what they are doing to observe the subjects and objects of their affection in these moments of silence. Negotiation across distance employs the poem as a transitional object, as a means of negotiating contact across distance. J. P. Steed, in a commentary on Sharon Dolin's readings of D. W. Winnicott, defines transitional objects "as those special objects, such as the first soft animal or doll, that a child uses to negotiate her or his separation from the mother, investing these objects with a magical significance" (Steed, "Raymond Carver and the Poem," 312). What we do is displace love and distance onto objects. Steed goes on to suggest that many of Carver's poems "become a means of negotiating loss or separation" (312). For Steed and Dolin, poems as transitional objects occupy "the space between self and the other" (311) and provide a means for bridging the gap between subject and object and between speaker and loss. This sort of approach lends itself to Carver's stories and poems, with their exploration of loss and separation, but for our purposes the poem as transitional object is the means by which the speakers make a space and time not for overcoming loss but for expressing love.

Evidence to support the general claim that Carver employs a vocabulary of affection abounds in the collected poems. In "For Semra, with Martial Vigor" (11),[2] the speaker tells us that "All poems are love poems." This is true in Carver, not simply for spouses and ashtrays and strangers but for other objects, fish, geese, the stars, people, writers, and the actions that make up our fragile and impermanent selves. There are plenty of love notes to former and current friends and lovers, for example, "Memory [1]" (113) and "My Boat" (82); plenty of celebrations of the love that strangers exhibit as the speaker watches, as in "My Work" (135); and plenty of celebrations for the world as it is, as in "The Best Time of Day" (191). In his parody of Bukowski, Carver has the speaker of "You Don't Know What Love Is" (19) say, "You have to have been in love to write poetry." In "Photograph of My Father in His Twenty-Second Year" (7), Carver in the voice of the speaker says, "Father, I love you, / yet how can I say thank you, I who can't hold my liquor either, / and don't even know the places to fish?" The poem "Tomorrow" (106) ends with "My bowl is empty. But it's my bowl, you see, / and I love it."

Other celebrations of the love of objects and people show up in poems to friends, rivers, historical figures, writers, and so on. We should not get the idea, though, that Carver is simply documenting his big heart or celebrating the grateful attitude he takes up in his eleven final, lucky, and extra years of love and sobriety. There are plenty of poems on the bleak and forlorn. "Distress Sale" (5) and "Morning, Thinking of Empire" (21), both from the collection *Fires*, explore how we are reduced by circumstances and how we diminish each other in our despair and disappointment. The collection *Ultramarine* offers a harsh contrast in its documentaries of loss and despair, particularly regarding family. There and elsewhere Carver visits themes we find in his fiction. Still, his poetry encourages what Tess Gallagher sees as "The insistent nature of Ray's belief in his own capacity to recover from reversals" (311) and what Carver himself identified as his interest in "survival, what people can do to raise themselves up when they've been laid low" (Boddy, quoted in Nesset, "This Word Love," 312). His poetry does indeed celebrate belief in our human dignity, in our capacity to recover for reversals, and it offers comfort in the struggle rather than redemption or amelioration. The love Carver celebrates in this vocabulary of affection does not save the pen in "The Pen" (198), Karl Wallenda in "Poem for Karl Wallenda, Aerialist Supreme" (46), or the baker, Balzac, Louise, or Carver himself in some of his poems, for death, disappointment, and dissolution still come. What we do in the face of their coming and how we celebrate presence in the struggles to recover are Carver's great lessons.

What we find in poems about objects is a loving respect for the work that objects do. Carver wanders happily into personification in some of his poems, but what he offers are objects as seen in the light of the speaker's affection for them. In "Locking Yourself Out, Then Trying to Get Back In" (73), the speaker's heart goes out to the "coffee cup and ashtray," though he still "bashed that beautiful window. / And stepped back in." In "Where Water Comes Together with Other Water" (63), the speaker begins, "I love creeks and the music they make," and ends, "Loving everything that increases me." In "Near Klamath" (32), the salmon fishermen "stamp our feet / on the snow and rocks and move upstream, / slowly, full of love, toward the still pools." In "Soda Crackers" (310), "You're even getting remarked / on in print! Every soda cracker / should be so lucky."

This attitude is illustrated as well in "The Pen" (198), in which the pen "that told the truth / went into the washing machine / for its trouble." Like many of Carver's objects and characters, the pen is celebrated because it rallies to its work, which it does twice in this poem—first in the lines about moonlight after "thinking it was finished" and then again, after being whacked "on the desk," in the lines about wind and "the golden morning air." Its reward is the fire and replacement by another pen, this one as yet "undistinguished." This poem demonstrates silence and the idea of negotiation. We are presented with a writer not writing. Hours pass between the few lines of poetry that the first and then the second pens can produce. The writer, like the pen, spends unproductive days beside the window, seems without conviction or will, and is ready to give up, or nearly ready. The writer "[tries] to write some more / but that was all." The last lines suggest the return of inactivity, fear, and psychological block, much the same as we find in the first stanza. The writer cannot give up writing, so the pen does that work for him, "quit[s] working forever." In this way the pen becomes something of a transitional object, taking on magical significance in its efforts to work and allowing both the writer in the poem and the writer of the poem to work across the gap between silence and work, between the page and the words. "The Pen" works something like William Carlos Williams's poem

"The Cure" (67), producing a poem of treatment in the act of lamenting the difficulties of production. In addition, there is respect. Yes, there is Carver's humor here but also a wry respect for the efforts to work until the end.

A similar respect, this time for animals, shows up in "My Crow" (103). Here, Carver observes a common crow that

> was not Ted Hughes's crow, or Galway's crow.
> Or Frost's, Pasternak's, or Lorca's crow.
> Or one of Homer's crows, stuffed with gore,
> after the battle. This was just a crow.

Here again Carver celebrates the humble, the undistinguished, or the undistinguished distinguished from all these other writers, the regular crow on a branch for a few minutes and gone. Once more we have a writer doing something besides writing, in this case looking out the window, and again there is loss, silence, and negotiation. The crow flies beautifully off and does not call out. It is a misfit, though we might wonder how the speaker knows that, and if like the pen it is a kind of muse, it does not stay. Yet, in being other than Hughes's or Homer's crow, the crow and the poem connect the speaker and Carver to those other writers. The speaker has recognized this crow as his and recognizes, even sets out, these other writers and their crows. This is not a negotiation of loss but of contact. Carver puts himself in their company in claiming this crow for himself. In both "My Crow" and "The Pen," the reward for effort is a common one in poetry, absence coupled with the promise of immortality in verse, a life in the poem itself.

A similar vocabulary is employed in poems about people, some well known and some not. Carver sets out his affection for them in sympathy for their various plights and in celebration of their humble heroism. When he writes about people who are or have been close—clinging mothers, alcoholic daughters, abusive sons, demanding ex-wives, destructive friends—the affection ebbs and flows. It is easier to offer love to the seventy-six-year old aerialist than to the mother in the poems "Son" (181) and "Mother" (216); more hopeful to wish a distant daughter success in a poem about her black eye, as in "My Daughter and Apple Pie" (86); more available to wish an ex-wife well with the recovery of an isolated memory of young hope. Even the past self comes in for critique and affection. Still, Carver loves people for their efforts. The speaker in "What the Doctor Said" (289) is told he is going to die and shakes "hands with this man who'd just given me / something no one else on earth had ever given me." The dead speaker in "Poem for Dr. Pratt, a Lady Pathologist" (36) is "in love with these hands." Both of these poems incline to silence. In "Poem for Karl Wallenda, Aerialist Supreme" (47), the wind "comes in from the Caribbean to throw itself / once and for all into your arms, like a young lover!" Wallenda dies offstage and without a word. Affection in these poems is often tinged with sympathy. The poem "Louise" (46), about a woman and her daughter who live in the trailer next to the speaker, offers another good example. This becomes evident when Louise pulls

> the line down, holds the line
> with her neck
> as she slings a shirt
> over the line and lets go—
> the shirt filling out, flapping
> over her head.

The speaker of the poem has been paying attention, knows that the woman sings Louise's faults "from morning to night," and recognizes that it is not a cat that has silenced Louise but this persistent verbal abuse and a mouth full of clothespins. Here and in other of his poems about people Carver recognizes that the subjects are at work, which they often do in silence. He also seems to love them for their perceptiveness. Louise, who can see that we are sometimes only less than we should be, ducks when startled by "this near human shape" of the shirt. If there is negotiation here, it is in the reaching across the noise of Louise's mother, who is never identified as a mother, and into and across the silence of a family drama that Louise and the speaker both observe, and to Louise herself. Such respect for perceptiveness and affection for effort show up more clearly in "The Baker" (9), where Carver points us to another silent hero: we see the anonymous husband, a baker who served Pancho Villa "barefooted, humiliated, trying to save his life." Like Louise, the baker is perceptive. Like Louise, he is doing what work he can in limited circumstances and in silence. He can see the handwriting on the wall and is marshaling his meager resources and bare feet for an attempt at escape. The speaker of the poem, observing from the safer perch of the future, respects our anonymous baker for his efforts and calls him hero, even as he encourages us to laugh at his loss and tiptoe escape. As with "Louise," Carver contrasts the silent baker with the talkers, Pancho Villa and Tolstoy's Count Vronsky, the latter of whom, at least, is anything but expert on women and horses. Carver uses the poem as a transitional object, a means of making space to recognize the writer's connection to another writer and the speaker's and readers' connection to the pathetic and heroic baker.

For writers who turn up in the poems, the respect is as deep and the embrace perhaps even tighter. In many of these poems there is silence, the writer contemplated in silence and/or the speaker contemplating in silence, and in that silence the creation of space and time for recognition. In "Radio Waves" (56), Carver celebrates Antonio Machado's poetry and recognizes his own love for the poems: "It was a little like a middle-aged man falling / in love again. A remarkable thing to witness, / and embarrassing, too." He finds in Machado the kind of encouragement he offers in his own poems. "'Pay Attention . . .' when anyone asked you what to do with their lives." He takes Machado's book to bed with him and on walks, and even looks for it when he wakes in the night. Also, he expresses a desire to transcend constraints of space and time so that he might speak to the dead writer, "tell you these things myself." The poem "Blue Stones" (21) is a valentine to Gustave Flaubert, to the importance of precision in writing, and to sex. Flaubert is addressed directly in the poem as we read about his determined and masturbatory reworking of a sex scene. In both the speaker's and Flaubert's voices we hear the phrase "Love has nothing to do with it" enough times perhaps to wonder whether it does. In "Work" (84), an elegy for John Gardner, Carver negotiates loss and reminds us of Gardner's hard and persistent work, as the last lines read: "And work. Yes, work. The going / to what lasts." Here and elsewhere Carver offers work as the action that makes us admirable.

In "Balzac" (28), Carver's speaker recognizes the impossible efforts that writers make and the very physical world that they inhabit. The poem begins in recognition, the speaker conjuring Balzac in his mind and then creating a silent tableau of Balzac at work "in his nightcap after / thirty hours at his writing desk." We see the writer there at the end of work and then again about to return to it:

> Wait! One last scene
> before sleep. His brain sizzles as
> he goes back to his desk—the pen,
> the pot of ink, the strewn pages.

Carver does Rodin one better here: his Balzac is not only in his bathrobe but also scratching himself, pissing in a chamber pot, lumbering and snorting like a work horse, and yet thinking, "Wait!" when of course he cannot wait and must return to the work and workings of art. Like Louise, the Balzac in this poem lives in a world he cannot completely control. Creditors prowl; lovers promenade; carriages rattle. Near human shapes loom. Like the crow and the baker, Carver's Balzac is silent, at work. Like the pen, he reaches across the space between the bodily world and the sizzling world of the brain. Like Gardner, for Balzac there is the work, the going to what lasts even after thirty hours at it away from that rest of the world. In this poem there is the gesture to legitimate action, the rallying for yet one more attempt. This rallying from a full bladder and hairy thighs, this turning away toward art are what the speaker celebrates in "Balzac." In a closely related poem, "This Room" (29), Carver offers a parallel image of his own work as a writer. The writer turns away from "the empty coach," "parasols," "an esplanade," until "There is noise in the street / growing fainter and fainter." Silence becomes a burden but also a place to make the love that is art, and the silence of contemplation becomes a transitional object or gesture that allows or demands that the speaker reach across the noise in the street to the writing at work on the page.

This affection, of course, spreads. In Carver's poems on objects, we find affection for the writer and the writing life. In poems on people, such as "Poem for Karl Wallenda, Aerialist Supreme," the celebration of the life of the aerialist leaks into a recognition of the value of work, even the work of the unnamed people who have to clean up after the accident. In poems on writers, we find affection toward their and our efforts, toward others whose struggles are less public or artful, and toward the self which can see some worth in speaking this affection. In many poems the speaker contemplates the self with the same patient affection that he shows objects and writers.

Such silence can be seen in "Switzerland" (99), Carver's encomium to James Joyce. We read of the couple who "Made love with each other. / Reaching into each other's clothes for it." These lovers do not speak and are ready instead for happy sleep. Nor does the speaker break silence at Joyce's grave. The memory of that grave "that came to [him] / in the midst of the show, / under the muted, pink stage lights" is connected not so much to loss as to sex, to congress, to connection, to a reaching into and toward each other. The negotiation here is a recognition, first of a fellow writer and then of a self working to raise himself up, then to "all of us." We look again at the end, where Carver makes the lions roar for all of us, however earnest or half-hearted our efforts, and notice how this poem and others celebrate the self of the poem's speaker. In the middle, Carver turns to a recognition of that self, not in control of its world, but accepting of it, even desirous in it, a kind of Louise in love, the baker with better luck, the pen given another chance. The affection in Carver is not for any revelations we might get but for the hope we practice, the insistent belief in our "own capacity to recover from reversals," however round-about and mysterious.

If there is any redemption, any remediation, or rescue in the affection Carver offers in poems, it is for the self represented in the speaker and the work that gets done. Some commentators have looked at the discourse of recovery in Carver's poetry and prose.[3] Recovery, perhaps, but I think a better word is "recognition." Again and again in his poems Carver recognizes difficult circumstances and celebrates, even loves, the everyday heroic effort, even his own. Two poems illustrate this recognition, "The Current" (44) and "Afterglow" (293).

"The Current" is a fishing poem in which Carver respects the efforts of creatures in a world that is both utterly familiar to them and beyond their control. In this poem Carver's focus is on one particular fish, which is

> heavy, scarred, silent like the rest,
> that simply holds against the current,
> closing its dark mouth against
> the current, closing and opening
> as it holds to the current.

Again, the subject is silent, doing its simple work, and again the poem acts as a bridge where respect for the fish reaches out toward self-respect for the speaker. The love that is here is for the unremarked persistence, the return of effort, the work that fish do, that children, cuckolds, and writers do outside of recognition, away from any certain hope of success or increase.

The second poem that illustrates recognition is "Afterglow," a self-portrait in which the speaker contemplates himself in much the same manner as he does objects and the natural world. Here the speaker describes how one can

> open a drawer and find inside
> the man's photograph, knowing he has only two years
> to live. He doesn't know this, of course,
> that's why he can mug for the camera.

The photograph is both silent and a transitional object, a bridge between the speaker and his best or luckier self, a recognition of the two of them. The "you" in this poem becomes the "I" of the speaker, the man both someone else as yet unmarked by disease and the speaker now marked. What is he doing, this man, but returning, coming back into the picture, squandering his good fortune, going on with his mugging, his hopeful posture, his jaunty cigarette? What is the speaker, who says, "I can't help myself, I glance once more / at the picture," doing but coming back, glancing once more at the picture, remarking and recognizing again the work before us?

In his vocabulary of affection, this is what Carver wishes for us; this is the advice he gives, to come back, to marshal ourselves for another effort, to put ourselves and our circumstances to work. "Make use of the things around you," as he says in "Sunday Night" (257); recognize, as he says in "Proposal" (291), that "any holding back had to be stupid, had to be / insane and meager." In late poems and in poems throughout his career, Carver turns to the idea of use and of transformation. To become like an object, an animal, or another writer is to recognize the capacity to love them. In two late poems, the speakers look to become something else, to love the selves that would change. In "On the Pampas Tonight" (298), the speaker says he wants to blend with seasonal change,

> to become like a pine tree
> or a reindeer,
> observe the slow grind and creep of glaciers
> into northern fjords,
> stand against this nemesis,
> this dry weather.

In the poem that follows this one, "Those Days" (299), the speaker says,

> Oh how I wish
> I could be like those Chinook salmon,
> Thrusting, leaping the falls,
> Returning!

This returning is not a compensation for loss or a resignation into silence. It is love. These poems and their celebrations of silence and work and contact make it possible for us to call Carver a love poet, make it possible for us to believe the drunken speaker of "For Semra, with Martial Vigor" when he says, "All poems are love poems." That, of course, is what we find poets and readers doing, returning to this idea of becoming, to work, to recognition, to change.

In conclusion, consider the first four lines from the late poem "The White Field" (209):

> Woke up feeling anxious and bone-lonely.
> Unable to give my attention to anything
> beyond coffee and cigarettes. Of course,
> the best antidote for this is work.

The works of a poet present us most directly with a sensibility, an attitude toward the world and the people, creatures, objects, and actions that make up that world. Carver's work presents us with speakers contemplating objects, the natural world, people, and writers. It presents us an affection that is both remarkable and embarrassing, a middle-aged poet engaged in the work of falling in love with pens, crows, bakers, water, writers, and himself. Yes, Carver is a poet of recovery, of nuance, miracle, medicine, of documentaries, of love. What that love does, what that sensibility exhibits is recognition. In a commentary on Plato's *Symposium*, Aryeh Kosman connects love and recognition: "Love on this view is *recognition*; it is seeing another as what that other might be, not in the sense of what he might be other than himself, but how he might be what he is. It is, in other words, coming to recognize the *beauty* of another" ("Platonic Love," 169).[4] With poetry we negotiate and look across the distance of separation, recognition, and hope, not simply as a response to loss but as an act of love. This is the love and recognition that Carver offers in his poems. In our postmodern and now posthumanist age, we should realize that such recognition is a strategic act, a rhetorical effort to build a case, that in no way diminishes us. It is useful to see connections between Carver's poetry and his life, between the poetry and the fiction, useful to trace the struggles with loss and language. We should not, though, forget the vocabulary of affection. This affectionate recognition of the work and dignity of objects, the natural world, people, and writers runs throughout Carver's poetry.

Notes

1. Graham Clarke discusses silence as a version of America in "Investing in the Glimpse: Raymond Carver and the Syntax of Silence," in *The New American Writing: Essays on American Literature since 1970*, ed. Graham Clarke (London: Vision, 1990), 99–122. William Magrino discusses reading silence in the fiction in this volume.

2. All references to Carver poems are from *All of Us: The Collected Poems*, ed. William L. Stull, introduction by Tess Gallagher (New York: Knopf, 1998), reprinted by permission of Tess Gallagher.

3. For a discussion of Carver and the discourse of recovery, see Hamilton E. Cochrane, "'Taking the Cure': Alcoholism and Recovery in the Fiction of Raymond Carver," *University of Dayton Review* 20, no. 1 (Summer 1989): 79–88; Jim Harbaugh, "Literature (and Other Arts): What We Talk about When We Talk about Spirituality and Recovery," *Dionysos: Literature and Addiction TriQuarterly* 11, no. 1 (2001): 53–59; and Robert Coles, "Teaching Raymond Carver," *American Poetry Review* 22, no. 1 (1993): 1–4.

4. Aryeh Kosman, "Platonic Love," in *Facets of Plato's Philosophy*, ed. W. H. Werkmeister (Assen: Van Gorcum, 1976), 53, quoted in G. R. F. Ferrari, *Listening to the Cicadas: A Study of Plato's* Phaedrus (Cambridge: Cambridge University Press, 1987), 169.

Works Cited

Boddy, Kasia. "A Conversation." *London Review of Books*, September 15, 1988, 16.

Carver, Raymond. *All of Us: The Collected Poems*, ed. William L. Stull, introduction by Tess Gallagher. New York: Knopf, 1998.

Chapman, Laurie. "'What's to Say': Silence in Raymond Carver's 'Feathers.'" *Studies in Short Fiction* 34 (1997): 193–201.

Clarke, Graham. "Investing in the Glimpse: Raymond Carver and the Syntax of Silence." In *The New American Writing: Essays on American Literature since 1970*, 99–122, ed. Graham Clarke. London: Vision, 1990.

Cochrane, Hamilton E. "'Taking the Cure': Alcoholism and Recovery in the Fiction of Raymond Carver." *University of Dayton Review* 20, no. 1 (Summer 1989): 79–88.

Coles, Robert. "Teaching Raymond Carver." *American Poetry Review* 22, no. 1 (1993): 1–4.

Dolin, Sharon. "'Bitter and Delicious Relations': The Transitional Object in Williams's Poetry." *William Carlos Williams Review* 22, no. 2 (1996): 19–26.

Ferrari, G. R. F. *Listening to the Cicadas: A Study of Plato's* Phaedrus. Cambridge: Cambridge University Press, 1987.

Gallagher, Tess. "Introduction to *A New Path to the Waterfall*." In Raymond Carver, *All of Us: The Collected Poems*, ed. William L. Stull. New York: Knopf, 1998.

Harbaugh, Jim. "Literature (and Other Arts): What We Talk about When We Talk about Spirituality and Recovery." *Dionysos: Literature and Addiction TriQuarterly*, 11, no. 1 (2001): 35–46.

Kosman, Aryeh. "Platonic Love." In *Facets of Plato's Philosophy*, ed. W. H. Werkmeister, 53–69. Assen: Van Gorcum, 1976.

Nesset, Kirk. "'This Word Love': Sexual Politics and Silence in Early Raymond Carver." *American Literature* 63, no. 2 (1991): 292–313.

Steed, J. P. "Raymond Carver and the Poem as Transitional Object." *Midwest Quarterly* 44, no. 3 (2003): 309–22.

Williams, William Carlos. *The Collected Poems of William Carlos Williams, Volume 2: 1939–1962*. New York: New Directions, 1991.

Robert Miltner

In a Mature Light

The "Second Life" Poems in *Where Water Comes Together with Other Water* and *Ultramarine*

In November 1984 Raymond Carver received a letter from a friend, the poet Hayden Carruth, who had written to praise the poems Carver had read at his home the night before when Carruth visited. Those poems, Carruth wrote, "are not like anything I have ever written or could write, but they are very acute, clear, moving, and, when intended, funny, and they remind me of how I felt when I was at the peak of my form in my late 40s or so. I envy you, and I can't help it. That spontaneous, pure originality—it's a wonderful thing to experience, one's self in total artistic selfhood" ("Letter to Raymond Carver"). The poems were from *Where Water Comes Together with Other Water*, Raymond Carver's first new collection of poems in eight years. What Carruth recognized in Carver's poems was the way a man in his forties is capable of producing his best work; what Carruth called "total artistic selfhood" was Carver's "second life" poetry, which celebrates sobriety, new relationships, memory, identity, creativity, and an acceptance of his full adult maturity.

The poems in *Where Water Comes Together with Other Water* (1985) and again in *Ultramarine* (1986)[1] were written when Raymond Carver was in his mid-forties, at a time when men examine the dreams and actions of their younger days by reconsidering them in a middle-aged light. Developmental psychologist Daniel J. Levinson, in *The Seasons of a Man's Life* (1978), recalls how Carl Jung first observed that men experience an "opportunity for fundamental change [which] starts at about 40, 'the noon of life'" (4); further, Levinson sees a man's life as divided into two distinct developmental stages: the first half being the years up to age forty, and the second half of life as the years a man ages after forty (33). This "Midlife Transition," as Jung called it, can bring men into a realization of their fullest individual growth.

Yet, Raymond Carver seemed not to have seen himself as part of "what might seem all-too-familiar territory: a change in life for a man in his early forties," as he observed in "Rousing Tales" (171), for the midlife transition is more characteristic of men who live ordinary lives, and his was not ordinary; instead, Carver saw himself as having had two lives, an alcoholic one and a sober one. As Carver's widow, Tess Gallagher, observed, "I don't believe Ray felt involved with the traditional understanding of midlife crisis. His life had really been in strong chaos for about ten years before I met him. Ray used the alcoholism as his marker. I came fully into his life when he was about 40 years old—meaning the time in 1979 we moved together to El Paso to begin our life with one another" (Miltner, interview with Gallagher, 1998). Certainly the conditions of mid-life transition are evident in Carver's life, for "Some of the things that go along with midlife transition in American life—adultery and depressions, bankruptcy, job failures—those things happened to Ray," Gallagher noted, adding, "His marriage failed. But Ray tended to see that as a result of the fact that he and his wife were alcoholic" (Miltner). Regardless of quick labels or stereotypical situations, Carver seemed fully aware at the time he was writing his mature poems that they reflected significant changes from his early work. In a 1986 interview with Nicholas O'Connell (published in 1987), Carver identified two clearly distinct phases in his life:

> There was a period in my life when I was writing and had children and so forth; it was hard, but it was a life, it was my life, and even though it was hard, I was, I'm sure, happy. And then there was a dark period for several years of emotional assaults on each other before the marriage ended. There's no question that I'm better off now, but the comparisons are difficult to make, and I'd rather just say that I've had two lives: one life that ended when my drinking ended, and another life, a new life that started after I quit drinking and met Tess. This *second life* has been very full, very rewarding, and for that I'm eternally grateful.
> (O'Connell, "Raymond Carver," 150; emphasis added)

Carver identified a culminating event that opened up the possibility of new growth as having occurred when he was thirty-nine and had gained sobriety; a new writing—or rather, a return to an earlier writing, poetry—was fueled by the fire of renewed enthusiasm.

The alcoholic past and the sober present—the past in which he was primarily seen as a writer of fiction and the present in which he returned to writing poetry—these are the strands that fused to form Carver's "second life." They operate like creeks that come together to form rivers, the metaphor central to Carver's mature poetry, as evident in "Where Water Comes Together with Other Water" (63),[2] the title poem of his 1986 collection, as he celebrates

> the places streams flow into rivers.
> The open mouths of rivers where they join the sea.
> The places where water comes together
> with other water.

Beyond the extended central metaphor, the content establishes that he "had done something" around age forty—sobriety, his new relationship with Tess

Gallagher—which clearly marked a transition, and this lyric-narrative poem clearly expresses his awareness of having passed through a transition to a new stage in his life:

> I'm 45 years old today.
> Would anyone believe it if I said
> I was once 35?
> My heart empty and sere at 35!
> Five more years had to pass
> before it began to flow again.

Considering the events that transpired in Raymond Carver's life between ages thirty-five and forty-five, this occasional poem on his forty-fifth birthday shows how he had learned to be open and loving again by accepting what his aging would bring him by "Loving everything that increases me," and what "increased" his life became the subjects of many of the new poems in both *Where Water Comes Together with Other Water* and *Ultramarine*. Consequently, if the water that came together with other water has been listened to and learned from, then the poet's task is to look hard at that water, to describe what he sees, and to explain that world with words, for, "it is seeing which establishes our place in the surrounding world" (Berger, *Ways of Seeing*, 50). Carver sees the water, noting it has a distinct color, not just a blue but a vivid ultramarine blue. Moreover, there are numerous things the speaker loves, and which increase him, including "creeks and the music they make," "[coastal rivers] the way some men love horses or glamorous women," and "[rivers] all the way back to their source."

Loving everything "back to their source" also has a geographic meaning for Carver, for after he received the Strauss Award in 1983, he left Syracuse, New York, and returned to the Pacific Northwest, where he was born and raised, settling in Tess Gallagher's hometown of Port Angeles on the north coast of the Olympic peninsula. In Port Angeles, Carver walked "the banks of Morse Creek, the river which became the central metaphor" of the poems in *Where Water Comes Together with Other Water* (Gallagher, introduction, in Carver, *All of Us*, xxix), especially its title poem. Moreover, in commenting as well on the poems in *Ultramarine*, Tess Gallagher notes the continued influence of Morse Creek in that collection, observing how "whenever Ray stands near a river in his poems there seems to be a communion with forces which are mysterious and beyond our daylight understanding" ("False Sky," 9). At age forty-five, Carver must have found things to be mysteriously changed: sobriety, a new relationship, a writing grant, and a return to the Pacific Northwest. No doubt, Morse Creek in Port Angeles must have felt like a holy and healing place. Ironically, while Carver's central metaphor for the past merging with the present is water, his metaphor for his new burst of poetic creativity is fire.

In considering the role of creativity in adult males, Daniel J. Levinson notes Elliot Jaques's observation that "great artists who continue their creative endeavors after forty tend to produce more profound, more 'sculpted' works than before" (quoted in Levinson, 26), works that exhibit "a decisive change in the quality and content of creativeness" of the artist's work (39). Jaques, whose idea of "sculpted creativity" developed from his study of Baudelaire, Goethe, Ibsen, and Rimbaud, noted, "If the artist is to endure, a change from the fevered pattern (of the spontaneous intense, hot-from-the-fire creativity that uses every experience as kindling, that combusts unselfconsciously and spews out work in whole ingots as if ready-made) generally emerges" (quoted in Sheehy, *Passages,* 256).

The poems that Raymond Carver wrote for *Where Water Comes Together with Other Water* and *Ultramarine* can be seen as representing Jaques's concept of sculpted creativity. Following the burst of poetic energy Carver felt in Port Angeles, his poems take on a lyric emotionalism that becomes enhanced as it intertwines with his anecdotal narratives. In describing this creative impulse, Carver employs the same imagery he uses in his essay "Fires" (1983), commenting that his fiction-writing teacher John Gardner had taught him that "what it took to be real writers" was "the necessary *fire*" (28). When describing what it felt like to write in Port Angeles, Carver evokes the same image, and one which echoes Jaques as well, stating, "I've never had a period in my life that remotely resembles that time. I mean, I felt like it would have been all right, you know, simply to have died after those sixty-five days. I felt *on fire*" (quoted in Schumacher, "After the Fire," 218).

Carver's humorous self-awareness of the fire that was fueling the creation of his new poems plays out in "The Pipe" (98), a metapoem parody of the experience, which opens:

> The next poem I write will have firewood
> right in the middle of it, firewood so thick
> with pitch my friend will leave behind
> his gloves and tell me, "Wear these when you
> handle that stuff."

Working like a list or catalog poem, as Carver used in "Fear" (60) and "The Car" (151), where repeated phrases on the left margins create form, in "The Pipe" the repetitions are embedded within the structure of the piece. Carver repeats the phrase "The next poem" a total of five times, grammatically, occurring at the beginnings and ends of lines in a left, right, left, right, left pattern. Stephen Dobyns recalls that for Carver, "the story or poem [Carver] liked best was always the next one. He was constantly pushing away the confines of the present and into the future" ("Interview," 112). Carver seems to be making that point near the end of "The Pipe" as he envisions how "the next poem will throw sparks!" In his new poems he let the fire burn so that his "sculpted" creative energy could shape his mature poetry: perhaps Raymond Carver, who began his writing career as a poet—his first three books were collections of poems—began to wonder if his dream of being a poet was neglected, and that his "body of work" required it.

Such new direction after a culminating event is typical of men who have completed a mid-life transition into the second life. According to Levinson, a man's transition is often triggered by a turning point or culminating event that "symbolizes the outcome of his youthful strivings" (31); in Carver's case, his "youthful strivings" generated three books of poetry between the ages of thirty and thirty-eight, [3] and yet during his early adult years Carver's successes were achieved as a result of his four books of fiction, [4] all in a brief seven-year period. If, in his middle adult years, his forties, the "neglected parts of the self [would] urgently seek expression" (Levinson, 200), then the "fire" in the forge of his creative impulse was his return to poetry. Was this why the poems burned a "fire" in him? Certainly, receiving the Strauss Living Award was an affirmation of his work as a fiction writer, the work he had so successfully carved out in his thirties; but what of his early aspirations as a poet, of those early books of poems he had published? His return to the Pacific Northwest acted as an unintended impetus for him to redirect his writing: "They gave me an award on the basis of my fiction," Carver told William Stull in 1986, "and the first thing I did was write two books of poetry" ("Matters of Life," 178). On reflection, he must have realized that time, place, age, and circumstance contributed to the blaze that fired his poetry, as he revealed in a 1987 interview with O'Connell: "I can't imagine I would have written those poems had I stayed in Syracuse or had I gone someplace else. So it's changed my writing in that regard, yes, and also my life" (148–49).

What was also emerging from Carver's burst of poetry when he moved to Port Angeles was new, richer material. Fictionally this is paralleled in the fuller stories that appear in the British collection *Elephant and Other Stories* (1988) and which are the "New Stories" in *Where I'm Calling From* (1988). Carver's writing did change, most noticeably in his poetry: while his earlier poems deal with menace, aimlessness, alcoholic bravado, places, and things, the new, second-life poems in the "two books of poetry"—*Where Water Comes Together with Other Water* and *Ultramarine*—take on new, more mature topics involving what Levinson would identify as the reintegration of fundamental polarities in the character of living (209). Consequently the second-life poems explore *memory and identity*, the time machine that allows Carver to explore how his childhood and his difficult alcoholic years shaped his second life, and *destruction and creativity*, the dichotomous relationship that contrasts how we lose the things we value, mismanage our inner resources, and become ravaged by addictions with how we survive to make art.

While much has been written on Carver's early alcoholism and working-class characters, less has been written concerning his memories of childhood in regard to what shaped his own adult years; and while much also has been written regarding the destructive nature of alcoholism, less has been written on the counterbalancing exploration of creativity in his late poetry. In *A Concert of Tenses: Essays on Poetry*, Tess Gallagher discusses the relationship between poetry and time: the poem is "like a magnet which draws into it events and beings from all possible past, present, and future contexts of the speaker," creating a "poem-time" in which "the present *accompanies* memory" ("The Poem as Time Machine," 96). Raymond Carver used poetry to bridge the two stages of his life, connecting the past with the present in order to reconsider his own childhood and his adult experiences during and after alcohol. Carver's poems thus "feature several themes that were not of major importance in the stories," observes Adam Meyer in his 1995 study *Raymond Carver*, noting that some of them "focus on the workings of memory" (167).

Interestingly, a childhood memory prompts the first poem in *Where Water Comes Together with Other Water*, "Woolworth's, 1954" (53), a semiautobiographical anecdote about first jobs. Just as Raymond Carver would have been sixteen in 1954, so too the speaker of the poem tells the reader that "I was sixteen, working / for six bits an hour." The reminiscence begins small and grows, as the narrator has done. Sol, the boy's mentor, taught him "what he knew," as the world opened up for a boy who is moving beyond the influence of the family into the influence of the larger world, the world of work and of adult experiences. By telling us, "How on my first job I worked / under a man named Sol"—whose name means "the sun" in the summer of the boy's summer, his youth—the speaker shows that he does find something new under the sun, an obvious pun on Ecclesiastes, one easily made by Carver, who grew up "in a house where the Bible was the only book his alcoholic father owned" (Tromp, "Any Good Writer," 79). As time begins to change, the poem takes on movement, arriving at the event which is the poem; there are flashbacks (to Sol and to Woolworth's) and forward narratives to being older, to a time when he experiences, firsthand, girls' undergarments. Yet, the source of his "most important memory / of that whole time" is clearly evident: his "opening / the cartons of women's lingerie." Just as the lingerie was "sweet and mysterious" to the boy then, so too is the nature of memory to the speaker now, as when memories, taken out "by the handful," are sweet and mysterious, emphasizing the dualism and balances of youth and age in this poem.

Time is therefore of primary importance in this poem, showing how recollection comes back from time and of how long it lingers. Consider the contrasting images of taking lingerie out of cartons "by the handful" with digging up clams with "the shovels full" of sand, a sands-of-time reference, as the time that has passed between the first job at sixteen and that as speaker at the time of writing the poem. Yet, as the boy grew, his hands removed the lingerie from young women as he gained sexual initiation and experience, learning what is revealed as the "linger-ey . . . underpants" would slip "down / off the belly, clinging lightly / to the hot, white skin." Like memory, the lingerie lingers, fading into the large pool of reminiscences, where it settles to the bottom; once the underpants are off the young women, they are "kicked free / onto the floor of the car and / forgotten about." Thus, one can seek to recall or one can wonder "Where this [memory] floated up from, or why," as Carver does in the opening line of the poem; regardless, the poem suggests that memory functions as a manifestation of the muse. "Woolworth's, 1954," a young man's coming-of-age poem, presents the speaker of the poem growing and maturing at sixteen, old enough to work, drive, and "park" with girls. Adam Meyer believes the poem to be more than merely "the memories of his first job and of 'those early days in Yakima'"; he sees it as an attempt to "detail the strange workings of memory and the role memory plays in the products of the creative artist" (167). Clearly an anecdote about a surfaced memory, about "Where this floated up from, and why," the poem's use of the verb "floated up" to describe a reminiscence is characteristic of much of the watery language of this book as a whole, a book about where one kind of water, the past, will merge with another kind of water, the present.

"Harley's Swans" (107), from *Where Water Comes Together with Other Water*, recalls other childhood events. Instead of memory surfacing, the speaker "looked down / the street for my boyhood," suggesting that it can be recalled. Capturing the speaker in a transitional point in his life, the poem moves from "boyhood" through adolescence (and into early adult life), another transitional phase in a man's life. This is largely a poem about the speaker's coming into manhood, and Carver considers the ways in which the societal stereotypes and the cultural icons shape this transition. He recalls getting haircuts with his dad at a barbershop, a man's world where there was a "rack of antlers mounted on the wall / next to the calendar picture of a rainbow / trout leaping," offering images of hunting and fishing—representative of the world of men—that would be noticed by a young man coming of age. The dichotomous experience of a boy approaching manhood is offered, by contrast, with the image of the mother with the long apron strings who "went with me to pick out / school clothes" and his embarrassment over his desire to shop in the men's department "for man-sized pants and shirts." A bittersweet scene is evoked, displaying a mix of awkwardness and embarrassment, tenderness and love, as the speaker recalls the poor self-concept of his adolescence: "Nobody, then, who could love me / the fattest kid on the block, except my parents." Is the self-assessment of himself as "the fattest kid on the block" an adolescent projection of the confused developing sexuality of the boy whose self-awareness of his own body is a necessary aspect of puberty? Certainly, this reference recalls Carver's "Fat"; the fat man's fingers in that story are seen as phallic symbols by Randolph Paul

Runyon, who concludes that "To be fat, then, is to be sexually powerful, even virile" (*Reading Raymond Carver*, 12). Are the swans—long necked—landing in a "pond / in a farmer's field" also phallic symbols? There are, after all, twenty-one swans, symbolic of the age of manhood. In addition, the bus full of children stops to view the approach of adulthood as Harley stops the bus, after which he and they "looked at [the swans] for a while and felt good"; they are all "lingering" or "loitering" as they look at the swans (like old Sol in "Woolworth's, 1954"). Moreover, with a name that evokes motorcycles, Harley becomes a symbol of power and manhood much like the antlers in the barbershop.

Even more so, this poem considers what happens after a man gains sexual and personal knowledge, as the speaker recalls his thoughts on betrayal, about "How that part always came easy. / It was what came after that was hard." What comes after is identified later as "this feeling of shame and loss." Granted, the shame could be the "embarrassment" of having a mother shop for an adolescent, or the loss could be for the speaker's own childhood, but the linkage to betrayal seems evident in the final stanza as the poem shifts time and the speaker returns to the time frame in which the poem began, noting that the winds (of change) blew all day and then that it is "almost dark now" (aging). He finds "The house / quiet and empty. The way I always thought I wanted it to be," suggesting that he is alone and not certain this is what he wanted, as evident in the questionable way he "thought" he wanted it to be. Moreover, the twenty-one swans suggest as well that there are ten pairs and a loner, echoing the sense of isolation or dissociation that the speaker seems to be feeling. Yet, the speaker who says "I want to try again" implies that he either wants to try again with the person he betrayed or wants to be true and not betray someone in a new relationship. Based on this interpretation, this poem can also be read as one about self-betrayal, about giving in to those images of manhood (barbershop, antlers, a Harley, a sensual body) that could lead to the shame and loss that affect self-esteem. In the final stanza the speaker had a Coke (childhood drink, not the adult alcohol) in a soda fountain (not a bar), perhaps representative of the speaker's current sober state.

Clearly Raymond Carver used memory as a time machine that allowed him to transcend boundaries of events and to bring the past forward into the present to better grow both as a human and as a writer. Through his childhood revisiting him, he rediscovered lost innocence, taking from the experiences what he needed to develop, and thus, by examining the past, enriching the present. As a recovering alcoholic, Carver was rebuilding his life by sifting through the destruction and devastation and by identifying parts that could be restructured through the creative self-discovery and catharsis of writing. Sometimes he chose the events that he would explore in his poems, though often the memories would surface on their own. Authentic memories like these are the subjects of some of Carver's poems that relate to his life before his alcoholism, as in the poem "The Old Days" (66), from *Where Water Comes Together with Other Water*, in which, as Tess Gallagher believes, he is "very much able to give a portrait of what it's like to have someone from 'back there' in the drinking days who is really still 'back there' in the helplessness of the booze, and yet who has penetrated the life of the narrator in the present moment with a phone call" (Miltner). In discovering and incorporating the lyric-narrative tendencies in which Carver became the anecdotal hero of his own poems, Carver discovered a writer's stance that allowed him to draw from some of the events he experienced before he ceased his alcoholism.

Norman K. Denzin, in *The Recovering Alcoholic* (1987), defines alcoholism as "an uneasiness of self, time, emotionality, and social relationships with others" (12); recovery from alcoholism is achieved only through sobriety, which involves "a recovery of time without the use of alcohol" (20). Carver's preoccupation with time is evident in "A Letter to Mr. Hallstrom," in which Carver advises another recovering alcoholic writer to "Use this time [getting sober after quitting] of not writing to just get reacquainted with yourself again, and do lots of reading and re-reading, the things that mattered so long ago when you were young and innocent, read those things over again" (106). Such recovery of the past is evident in several of the previously discussed poems from *Where Water Comes Together with Other Water* that touch on this, especially in childhood memory pieces such as "Woolworth's, 1945" and "Harley's Swans," in which there is a recovery of time, childhood, and self-esteem.

While Carver wrote numerous poems about the damaging nature of alcohol on his life, his family, and his art, he also clearly shows how his life as a recovered alcoholic, coupled with exploring his childhood reminiscences, contributed to the sense of self-worth and self-acceptance, of tenderness and love, that is evident in his late poems. Even in Raymond Carver's earliest poems, despite the creative act that is the making of poetry, a potential for destruction seems often lurking like a rock or log that lies submerged below the surface of a lake. As a recovering alcoholic, Carver knew how he had acted recklessly toward his family and toward himself; unable to undo the destructiveness of the past, as a writer, Carver could count the past with the present, tapping into his own artistic talent. Awareness of the one pole of destructiveness also implies awareness of the opposite pole of creativity, for even while a man realizes that he has acted in a damaging way, at the same time he has a strong desire to become more creative; in Carver's case, this would have meant writing stories and poems. Such counterbalancing forces—which seem more a menacing presence, or the potential for ruin—are amplified in Carver's later poems, showing how his destructive years as an alcoholic were redeemed by his creative years as a sober artist. This occurs in sobriety as a recovering alcoholic "learns new modes of self-presentation, self-feeling, and interacting" (Denzin, 20); moreover, there is a "relearning of emotional feeling" that involves "relinquishing the negative emotions of the previously divided self" by putting "emotional repair . . . at the heart of recovery" (20–21).

Emotional repair is certainly at the heart of the poem "This Morning" (141), which opens and sets the direction for *Ultramarine*. Separated from friends, family, and lover, the speaker walks the beach and notes the color of what he sees: "blue sky. The sea was blue, and blue-green." If the sense of hearing is important in *Where Water Comes Together with Other Water*, then *Ultramarine* is about the importance of the sense of sight. Still, the sight of "the sea, the sky," and "the white beach" are prompts for the writer whose instinct is to ruminate, and his need is to "will / myself to see what I was seeing / and nothing else." What he encounters in his thoughts are many of the themes that thread through both *Where Water Comes Together with Other Water* and *Ultramarine*: "tender memories (memory as time machine), thoughts of death"; "how I should treat / with my former wife"; and "What / I've trampled on in order to stay alive" (the creativity and destruction theme), so that at the end the speaker is going, like the birds, those images of freedom, "in the direction I needed to be going," which, in this case, is in the direction of emotional recovery.

Immediately following "This Morning" in *Ultramarine* is the poem "What You Need for Painting." Taken from a letter by Renoir, it can be read as a metapoem about the creative impulse, the connection between artists, whether visual or verbal. Unlike Carver's stories, which are "mostly . . . set indoors" (Simpson and Buzbee, "Raymond Carver," in *Conversations*, 51), in "This Morning" the speaker is going out "for a walk" to see "what Nature had to offer" as material for his poetry. Seemingly the poet is seeking the kind of plein-air (open-air) approach used by the late nineteenth-century Impressionists called *pleinairistes*, a group that included Renoir; this approach found artists "working directly in the ambience of light and atmosphere" instead of in the studio, seeing new realist effects in their art (Meyer, 318). While walking, Carver "took in what Nature had to offer"; his artist's eye notes how the landscape is "bathed in a pure / cold light" (light and atmosphere), leading him to confront the real ("The stuff I live with every day"). So it is, then, that "What You Need for Painting" begins with "a list of some eighteen different colors for the palette, among which is hidden—as the titles of Carver's stories were so often hidden—the title of the collection itself: '*Ultramarine* blue'" (Runyon, 208). These two poems are linked as well by the artist forcing his concentration to be as sharply in focus as is possible; Renoir advises that the artist have "Indifference to everything except your canvas," while the speaker in "This Morning," who lacks this indifference, recognizes that his "thoughts / began to wander." In both cases this requires commitment, or will, as Runyon has noted: "In other words, the need 'to will'—and for Renoir too it was a question of will, since among the prerequisites the poem goes on to list is 'an iron will'—'to will / myself to see what I was seeing / and nothing else'" (209–10).

Michael Schumacher has noted the connection between the visual artist's work and the poet's work in "What You Need for Painting." The final lines, he feels, were great instructions for a young writer: "Indifference to everything except your canvas. / The ability to work like a locomotive. / An iron will." Moreover, the poem seems to offer "advice on the ingredients needed to write a good poem or short story" (227). Carver agreed that this seemed to be his "philosophy of writing, if I have one" (227) and then confirmed the necessary connection between the visual and verbal arts: "When you're writing fiction or poetry—it really comes down to this: indifference to everything except what you're doing. Your canvas, as it were. Which, translated to fiction or poetry, meaning indifference to everything except that piece of paper in the type-writer" (227). Carver's description of artistic production as work, consistent in his writing, occurs here, where writing, producing art, depends on working "like a locomotive." The idea of creative endeavor as time on task at hard work, metaphorically represented by the image of a locomotive, is certainly consistent with Carver's working-class background, even when relating to Renoir. He carried the idea further, explaining to Tromp, in a 1984 interview, the difference between having talent and working that talent, relative to his consistent reference to his own writing as work: "Look, being gifted isn't enough. Everyone is gifted. Some writers, for example, have the gift of being able to write a story in one sitting. I wasn't born with that one. That's why I'm so conscientiously involved with my writing: I compensate for the talent I don't have through hard work" (81). Clearly creativity, from Carver's viewpoint, is not a gift but rather is developed through time devoted to task, which in his case involved emotional repair and redirected energy.

Closely related both to "This Morning" and to "What You Need for Painting" is "What I Can Do" (63), in which imaginative escape and freedom, as suggested by the birds, seek to counterbalance the negative power of familial guilt. Having unplugged the phone, a symbol of communication, so that the speaker's "loved ones can't reach out and put the arm / on me," all the speaker wants to do is "keep an eye on these birds / outside my window," an obvious delaying tactic from dealing with needy relatives. The birds, images of freedom, "don't ask for a thing / except sunny weather," unlike the speaker's family, who asks for money. Further, the birds present a peaceful scene he witnesses "outside his window"; inside the window, where the poet sits, is a different reality where he lives with his problems. When it comes time for the speaker to "plug in the phone and try to separate what's right from wrong," however, the speaker tries to set boundaries ("I've told them the well has run dry"), which his family members will not accept ("They won't hear of it"). The actions of the birds outside the speaker's window mirror his own emotional response and desired action: "Suddenly [the birds] stop singing and turn their heads. / It's clear they've felt something. / They dive into flight." In this scene there is a familiarity that echoes the final lines of "This Morning," the poem in which the speaker is also able to "forget / myself and everything else," and in which the speaker turns back just as the birds "turn" their heads. While the birds in "This Morning" "rose up / from the gnarled trees" and "flew / in the direction I needed to be going," the birds in "What I Can Do" "dive" down from where they "perch in the branches" into "flight." The differences are noteworthy: in "This Morning" the speaker, separated from others, has an uplifting (rose "up") insight, symbolized by the birds, that takes him in a positive direction, the direction in which he "needs to be going"; while in "What I Can Do" the speaker has a negative experience of having been reattached to others from his past, shown as the birds symbolically "dive' (down) and take "flight."

While some of the poems that explore the relationship between creation and destruction lean more decidedly toward one pole than the other, in *Ultramarine* some show a balance between the two. Moreover, given the distance between Carver's creative second life and his destructive first life, humor colors some of the second-life poems. "The Car" (151), for example, is a list poem that turns damaged goods into a creative work. This poem operates similarly to New York artist Joseph Cornell's "assemblages" of "found art," in which, at first glance, one sees "objects with no particular relevance to each other" and yet, on further consideration, one notices how "a sense of order and precision pervades" ("Joseph Cornell," 107). Similar to the humorous list or catalog poem "Fear" in *Where Water Comes Together with Other Water*, "The Car" in *Ultramarine* offers an inventory of all the broken-down cars a person could own:

> The car with a cracked windshield.
> The car that threw a rod.
> The car without brakes.
> The car with a faulty U-joint.
> The car with a hole in its radiator.

By offering a list, the poem sounds like a litany of troubles. Individually, of course, each problem is stressful, difficult, troublesome ("Car of my sleepless nights"), and yet listed collectively, the sheer mass becomes absurdly comical in effect. Part of the humor also derives from the personification of the car, making *it* responsible for things for which the driver ought to feel responsible, for it was the driver who "left the restaurant without paying" and who "hit the dog and kept going." Regardless, this is the car he has been given, and he makes the best—and most creative use—of the car of his "dreams." Carver was turning his awful, real-life car experiences into an imaginative work in this poem, for he owned numerous cars that broke down constantly. Dobyns, for example, recalled Carver owning a terrible car in 1978 when they were at Goddard College teaching together: "He bought an old Oldsmobile. I think it was a '63 or '64. He called it his Okie car. It was February and about fifteen below and after the first night the car wouldn't start" (109). Carver apparently "never had a car that worked," according to Tess Gallagher; yet, "when, in 1982, we had finished the rewrite of a script on the life of Dostoevsky for Carlo Ponti, Ray took his share of the money and went down to the Mercedes-Benz dealership in Syracuse, N.Y." ("Carver Country," 10), where he bought his first new car. Presumably, though he employed humor in "The Car" as a way to laugh at difficulty, one imagines that Carver had the last laugh driving off in his fully warranted Mercedes-Benz.

Carver's humor is also evident in another *Ultramarine* poem, "The Pen" (198). The image of the pen was introduced in "An Afternoon" (143), the poem immediately following "What You Need for Painting" (142); "An Afternoon" makes it clear that the narrator is not a visual artist but is instead a writer: "As he writes, without looking at the sea, / he feels the tip of his pen begin to tremble." Pages later "The Pen" appears, and the pen that "told the truth" and was then drowned in the washing machine comes back to life, writing, as if the pen itself is the poet, such lines as "The damp fields asleep in the moonlight" and "A light wind, and beyond the window / trees swimming in the golden morning air." Clearly, the speaker's lines sound vaguely like lines Carver himself would write, for they use Carveresque images such as moonlight (hope), wind (change), the window (seeing the real), and morning (new starts). Since the pen, a metaphor for writing, has been washed and dried, it seems to have been "laundered" to tell a particular "clean" version of the real; its role as a truth-giver or reality-identifier diminished as "it lay quietly on the desk / under the window. Lay there / thinking it was finished." Interestingly the relationship between Carver's writing desk, where the pen lay, and the window near it echoes the scene in "Locking Yourself Out, Then Trying to Get Back In" (73), from *Where Water Comes Together with Other Water,* as the narrator looks in through the window "at my desk, some papers, and my chair"; presumably, this self-parody is a kind of doubling, both for the poet and for the desk, each on opposite sides of the window. Conversely potential destruction is represented in "The Pen" by the arrival of "an undistinguished pen / that hadn't proven itself / yet," one which warned: "Darkness gathers in the branches. / Stay inside. Keep still." Yet, the inside is where stories are often set, and it is the outdoors where adventures and opportunities for creativity exist.

Such an adventure is the impetus for "Eagles" (131), a lyric-narrative from *Where Water Comes Together with Other Water.* The poem employs a carefully selected personal anecdote, one of the traits of the lyric-narrative, to demonstrate how it is human nature to create from accidents and from accidental discoveries. At the edge of "the green woods," seemingly symbolic of fertile nature, the eagle, a powerful symbol in and of itself, "shares" its bounty by dropping its catch, a just-caught fish, at the poet's feet. Nature's destructive elements are presented in graphic images of "puncture marks in the sides of the fish / where the bird gripped with [the eagle's] talons! / That and a piece torn out of the fish's back." Still, the speaker picks up "a miraculous ling cod" that an eagle dropped, only to take the fish home and eat it, talking over dinner about "an older, fiercer order of things" when people were closer to nature and presumably better able to use a gift creatively when it was given. Yet, the source of this poem is autobiographical, for Carver's friend Tobias Wolff relates the following story concerning the poem "Eagles":

> The writer Jim Heyen once told Ray a story about something strange that had happened to him. As Jim was coming out of a bank, a bald eagle dropped a salmon bang on the hood of his car, which salmon Jim took home and ate. Not long after Jim told Ray this story he read a poem of Ray's in which the eagle drops a salmon ("ling cod") at the poet's feet while he's out taking a walk. The poet cooks it up. Later Jim asked Ray about it, asked if by chance Ray had made use of the story. "Well, Jim," he said, "I guess I must have, because I don't take walks." ("Appetite," 244–45)

Seemingly the dinner was an innovative appropriation of the fish much like the subject of the poem was a novel appropriation of a gift of a story; besides, any narrative (prose or poetry) is a kind of "fish" story anyway.

The stories of childhood memories and creativity that are at the core of Raymond Carver's second-life poems clearly demonstrate how Carver's return to his geographic source in the Pacific Northwest, during his mature, sober years, prompted a "fire" of creativity to return, producing the two books of poetry that are filled with what he felt "increased" him. The mature poetry from his second life displays the profound and sculpted quality typical of men who have passed through midlife into mature adult life. Carver's early death less than two years after the publication of *Ultramarine* denied readers of what he might have achieved had he lived into his late adult life. Instead, the late, mature work offers perhaps the best from the body of Carver's poetry, for his second-life poems are precisely as Hayden Carruth saw them: acute, clear, moving, and when intended, funny.

Notes

1. The poems in *Where Water Comes Together with Other Water* and *Ultramarine* were closely linked and relatively interchangeable. Eight of the poems from *Where Water Comes Together with Other Water* were published as *This Water*, a limited edition of 136 copies, by William Ewert in 1985, the same year of publication, and ten poems from *Ultramarine* were published as *Early for the Dance*, again in an edition limited to 136 copies, by William Ewert in the same year of publication. Moreover, in 1987 *In a Marine Light: Selected Poems* was published by Collins Harvill in England, with no corresponding American edition. *In a Marine Light* "presents 112 poems from [*Where Water Comes Together with Other Water* and *Ultramarine*] arranged in a unique six-part sequence," notes William Stull in "Appendix 4: A Note on *In a Marine Light*," from *All of Us: The Collected Poems*. The title, taken

from the poem "In a Marine Light near Sequim, Washington," in *Where Water Comes Together with Other Water,* further suggests Carver's view of his late poetry, as represented by *Where Water Comes Together with Other Water* and *Ultramarine*as a body of work that can be presented in varied combinations. Given Randolph Paul Runyon's discussions of intratextual doubling and self-referentiality as they apply to Carver's fiction and poetry—*Ultramarine,* in particular—it would be interesting to investigate how offering different orderings of the same poems, folding together poems from different collections, or culling selected poems would create optional readings of Carver's poems.

2. All references to Carver poems are from *All of Us: The Collected Poems,* ed. William L. Stull, introduction by Tess Gallagher (New York: Knopf, 1998), reprinted by permission of Tess Gallagher.

3. *Near Klamath* (1968), *Winter Insomnia* (1970), and *At Night the Salmon Move* (1976).

4. *Will You Please Be Quiet, Please?* (1976), *Furious Seasons and Other Stories* (1977), *What We Talk about When We Talk about Love* (1981), and *Cathedral* (1983).

Works Cited

Berger, John. *Ways of Seeing.* London: BBC/Penguin, 1977.

Carruth, Hayden. "Letter to Raymond Carver, November 19, 1984." Carver papers and manuscripts. William Charvat Collection of American Fiction. Ohio State University Library Special Collections, Columbus.

Carver, Raymond. *All of Us: The Collected Poems,* ed. William L. Stull, introduction by Tess Gallagher. New York: Knopf, 1998.

———. *Carver Country: The World of Raymond Carver.* Introduction by Tess Gallagher. Photography by Bob Adelman. New York: Charles Scribner's Sons, 1990.

———. *Elephant and Other Stories.* London: Harvill, 1988.

———. "Fires." In Raymond Carver, *Fires: Essays, Poems, Stories,* 19–30. Santa Barbara, Calif.: Capra Books, 1983.

———. "Letter to Mr. Hallstrom." In Carver, *Carver Country,* 105–7.

———. "Rousing Tales." Rev. of *Legends of the Fall,* by Jim Harrison. In Raymond Carver, *No Heroics, Please: Uncollected Writings,* 71–75. New York: Vintage, 1990.

———. *Where I'm Calling From: New and Selected Stories.* New York: Vintage, 1989.

Denzin, Norman K. *The Recovering Alcoholic.* Newbury Park, Calif.: Sage, 1987.

Dobyns, Stephen. "Interview." In *Raymond Carver: An Oral Biography,* ed. Sam Halpert, 109–17. Iowa City: University of Iowa Press, 1995.

Gallagher, Tess. "Carver Country." Introduction to Carver, *Carver Country,* 8–19.

———. "False Sky." Introduction to Raymond Carver, *Ultramarine* (Japanese Edition), 1–13, trans. Emiko Kurodo. Tokyo: Chukoron-Sha, 1990. Reprinted, this volume, 1–7.

———. Introduction. In Raymond Carver, *All of Us: The Collected Poems,* xxiii–xxx, ed. William L. Stull. New York: Knopf, 1998.

———. "The Poem as Time Machine." In Tess Gallagher, *A Concert of Tenses: Essays on Poetry,* 90–102. Ann Arbor: University of Michigan Press, 1986.

Gentry, Marshall Bruce, and William L. Stull, eds. *Conversations with Raymond Carver.* Jackson: University Press of Mississippi, 1990.

Jaques, Elliot. In Levinson, *Seasons of a Man's Life*, 26, 39. Also in Sheehy, *Passages*, 256.

"Joseph Cornell." In *The Art Book*. London: Phaidon, 1990.

Jung, Carl. In Levinson, *Seasons of a Man's Life*, 4.

Levinson, Daniel J. *The Seasons of a Man's Life*. New York: Knopf, 1978.

Meyer, Adam. *Raymond Carver*. New York: Twayne, 1995.

Miltner, Robert. Interview with Tess Gallagher. By mail, February/March 1998, Bucknell University, Lewisburg, Pa.

O'Connell, Nicholas. "Raymond Carver." In *At the Field's End: Interviews with Twenty Pacific Northwest Writers*, ed. Nicholas O'Connell, 133–50. Seattle: Madrona, 1987.

Runyon, Randolph Paul. *Reading Raymond Carver*. Syracuse, N.Y.: Syracuse University Press, 1992.

Schumacher, Michael. "After the Fire, into the Fire: An Interview with Raymond Carver." In *Reasons to Believe: New Voices in American Fiction*, ed. Michael Schumacher, 1–27. New York: St. Martin's, 1988. Also in *Conversations*, ed. Gentry and Stull, 214–37.

Sheehy, Gail. *Passages: Predictable Crises of Adult Life*. New York: Dutton, 1976.

Simpson, Mona, and Lewis Buzbee. "Raymond Carver." In *Writers at Work: The Paris Review Interviews*, 7th series, ed. George Plimpton, 299–327. New York: Viking, 1986. Also in *Conversations*, ed. Gentry and Stull, 31–52.

Stull, William L. "Matters of Life and Death." *Bloomsbury Review* 8 (January/February 1988):14–17. Also in *Conversations*, ed. Gentry and Stull, 177–91.

Stull, William L., and Maureen P. Carroll, eds. *Remembering Ray: A Composite Biography of Raymond Carver*. Santa Barbara, Calif.: Capra, 1993.

Tromp, Hansmaarten. "Any Good Writer Uses His Imagination to Convince the Reader." *Haagse Post* (Amsterdam), August 4, 1984, 40–43, trans. Stephen T. Moskey. Also in *Conversations*, ed. Gentry and Stull, 72–83.

Wolff, Tobias. "Appetite." In *Remembering Ray*, ed. Stull and Carroll, 241–50.

Sandra Lee Kleppe

Raymond Carver's Poet-Voyeur
as Involved Spectator

In Carver's poems and stories, characters spend much of their time looking, watching, and spying when they are not busy listening, overhearing, and eavesdropping. The themes of sight/blindness, voyeurism/exhibitionism, hearing/deafness, and even vision/clairvoyance crowd the lines and pages of Carver's works. An example can be taken from Carver's poem "A Tall Order" (169), in which a family's maid observes the strange doings of her employer: "she'd *seen* and *heard* the most amazing things. / *Sights* like plates and bottles flying. / An ashtray traveling like a missile / that hit the dog in the head" (italics added).[1] The emphasis on perceptory verbs and nouns in this poem ultimately moves sight into the realm of apparition. The concluding lines of "A Tall Order" read: "If she kept *watching*, she was sure to *see* / the elephant step out of the trees and trumpet / as it did every Monday at this house, at this hour" (italics added). Carver's subtle gliding between poles—here between the real and the surreal—is a characteristic feature of his verse, as is his tendency to create a persona who is simultaneously close and distant, present and absent, active and passive. The maid in this poem provides one example of how Carver positions a viewer as someone who is an insider but also peripheral to the scene. This essay will examine voyeurs in Carver's verse who function as *involved spectators,*[2] as people who both spy on and participate in intimate acts.

Though many scholars have remarked on the presence of voyeurism in Carver's works, the persistence of this aspect of involvement has not been explored. Boxer and Phillips's seminal essay from 1979, "*Will You Please Be Quiet, Please?:* Voyeurism, Dissociation and the Art of Raymond Carver," established voyeurism as a central feature informing Carver's short stories. They note the long precedent in literary history of the use of voyeurism as "emblematic of an ultimate form of identification and empathy" and yet point out that "in our century a strong bond has been forged between voyeurism and alienation, disconnectedness rather than connectedness" (78) and illustrate how the latter is present in Carver. This essay will consider Carver's voyeurism in light of premodern (pre-Enlightenment) literature in order to make the case for a continuity that can contextualize a parallel but understudied side of Carver's hallmark dissociative fiction: namely that many of his poet-voyeurs also function as mediators offering a reassociative bond between readers and characters.

Carver scholarship took a new turn in the wake of his more expansive stories of the 1980s as well as the appearance of three substantial collections of poetry during the last five years of his life. It is clear from our vantage point in the twenty-first century that his accomplishment as a writer was not limited to minimalist fiction and that his preoccupation with dissociation and despair was complemented by strong strains of humor and empathy. Several critics have discussed Carver's more generous late phase in light of a new-felt spirituality,[3] but more relevant in this context is Arthur A. Brown's remark that Carver's later works "leave behind the themes of dissociation and alienation, which post-modern writers inherited from modernists, and show that reassociation is possible" ("Raymond Carver," 125–26). Carver's persistent use of the figure of the voyeur suggests an ongoing creative experiment that ultimately could not reach full expression within the aesthetic paradigms of his time, and it is therefore not far-fetched to seek comparisons with other literary periods.

Preliminary Remarks on Voyeurism in Literature

The French loan word "voyeur" (one who sees) did not become current in English until 1900 and is a specifically twentieth-century concept linked to gratification obtained from concealed viewing of undressing or of sexual acts. The term "Peeping Tom" is a much older one that originated in the Anglo-Saxon legend of Lady Godiva, who in the twelfth century presumably rode naked through the marketplace, observed only by a tailor named Tom. The term was recorded as familiar in written English in the eighteenth century with the meaning "a nick name for a curious prying fellow."[4] However, among critics it is the term "voyeur" rather than "Peeping Tom" that has become yoked to narrators in both modern and premodern literature who spy on intimate acts and record them for readers. This is perhaps unfortunate in Carver's case since it shrouds the fact that his voyeurs are like the Peeping Toms of premodern literature who possess a passionate curiosity that draws them not just toward the secrets of physical and sexual intimacies but toward the mysteries of the human condition in general.

Some of the most frequently cited references to the poet-voyeur tradition in Western literature point to this element of curiosity and are found in classical works. Boxer and Phillips cite Odysseus's spying on Penelope as a case in point (78), and another well-known example is in book 1 of Ovid's *Amores*, when the poet undresses and seduces Corinna, positioning the reader as voyeur. In an essay on voyeurism in Renaissance poetry, Mark Taylor argues that this Ovidian passage was a key influence on the sonnet tradition and that "Ovid is both narrator of and participant in this story, and it appears as if the two roles are in conflict: his physical involvement with Corinna . . . prevents his continuing with her description, which is designed, as it becomes progressively more intimate in detail, to engage fully the reader's curiosity" ("Voyeurism and Aposopesis," 271). This yoking of curiosity and intimacy to conflict (passive/active, moral/immoral) became a constant of voyeurism in literary production through the ages and is also a salient feature of Carver's reuse of the tradition.

In an essay on the philosophical implications of voyeurism in literature, Joel Rudinow has examined a related recurring constant of voyeurism. The conflictual nature of what he terms the "voyeuristic project" involves an asymmetry in "the wish to be in two places at once, both in and out of the presence of the object of interest" ("Representation," 177). In order for the project to be successful, this asymmetry must be upheld and the voyeur must remain hidden, even as he or she desires to take part in the private acts under view. There is a parallel to the act of reading that Rudinow draws attention to and that is a sort of commonplace in the history of literature. Readers can be present during intimate scenes without being discovered by the characters; readers are granted the privileged position of being invisible and thus do not run the risk of being discovered or of violating the privacy of others. Metaphorically, then, the reader is the epitome of the voyeur, safe yet imaginatively involved, a spy with immunity.

In contrast to the notion that the voyeur must retain a distance from the scene in order to fulfill the voyeuristic project, Carver involves the writer, the reader, and the characters in a mutual pact of intimacy. The wish, as expressed in "Locking Yourself Out, Then Trying to Get Back In" (73), discussed below, "to be there, inside, and not be there" is repeatedly explored in his creation of personas who are involved spectators. The two sections below present close readings of poems that have specific links to the literary history of curiosity, intimacy, and asymmetry in voyeurism. Carver's preoccupation with secret life in general inspired him to write both with and against traditional allusions by transgressing the limits of sight and bringing in the sense of touch. In doing this, Carver attempts to rewrite the voyeuristic project by working to establish involvement as a metaphor for mediation rather than intrusion and by transforming passive dissociative voyeurs into active empathic ones.

The long tradition of voyeurism in premodern literature can thus provide a surprisingly relevant background for reading Carver's employment of the phenomenon. The figure of poet-voyeur in Western literature had its roots in the classical period and continued to exert a significant influence on both medieval and Renaissance poetry. By the time of the Renaissance (roughly 1350–1600 in Europe), voyeurs had come to occupy a privileged if precarious[5] position as mediators between audiences and characters. In Alastair Fowler's book *Renaissance Realism* he dedicates a whole chapter to what he terms "Involved Spectators," pointing out that the expected response to art in that period "took for granted viewers' empathy with the things and people pictured. This may seem contradictory, on modern assumptions of the disengaged spectator. But in Renaissance painting, people and objects on opposite sides of the picture frame commingle more freely" (75). The same goes for the literature of the period; Fowler notes that "spectating was anything but passive" and that Renaissance writers and artists regarded "active empathy as normative" (77). Fowler's terms are helpful in describing the literary project of Carver. The problem for a poet writing in the postmodern age, however, is that there exists no such empathic contract between readers and characters.

In virtually all of Carver's uses of voyeurism, there is an aspect of participation, and it is this element of active involvement that works towards reestablishing connections between the audience and the characters. Most readers are familiar with Carver's tiny voyeuristic story "The Idea" from *Will You Please Be Quiet, Please?*, which exemplifies his preoccupation with the motif of involved spectatorship. In the course of the five pages of "The Idea" there are six instances of the verb "watch," twelve of the verb "see," and fifteen of "look." The narrator relates how she and her husband Vern spy on the strange behavior of their neighbor, who almost every evening play-acts the Peeping Tom while his wife undresses for bed: "We were hunkered on the floor with just our heads showing over the windowsill and were looking at a man who was standing and looking into his own bedroom window" (1976, 18). The man then enters the house, turns off the lights, and apparently engages in sex with his wife. The story thus presents several levels of involved spectatorship: the Peeping Tom and his wife both participate in the voyeuristic ritual and are also observed by the narrator and her husband. As readers with privileged access to a view of both homes, we are pulled into the story as we watch the protagonists watching their neighbors engage in an odd nightly performance.

One of the poems to be examined in greater detail below, "The Man Outside" (304), is a similar experimentation with multiple roles, with an overlapping of the position of the voyeur and the exhibitionists, and with contact in the midst of concealment. "The Man Outside" contains the most explicit treatment of voyeurism in Carver's poetry, and in it the couple having sex become aware of the voyeur's presence:

> Lights on, nude, we sit
> at the vanity table and stare frantically
> into the glass. Behind us, two lips,
> the reflection of a glowing cigarette.

The Peeping Tom outside the window becomes an involved spectator in several senses in this poem, one of which is Carver's transference of the cliché of the postcoital cigarette to his mouth. Likewise, the couple who are active participants become passive spectators as they sit and *stare* in their mirror, gazing at the face of the voyeur outside their window. This commingling of passive and active roles is characteristic of Carver's peculiar brand of voyeurism and has both aesthetic and ethical implications that have historical echoes.

From Looking and Listening to Touching and Telling

Carver apparently possessed an incurable curiosity about the intimate lives of others. A description by Carver's friend the writer Tobias Wolff underlines his appetite for details about others' secrets: "[Ray] was a great listener. His curiosity was almost predatory. He listened with his head cocked and a slight squint in one eye, like a man taking aim" ("Appetite," 244). Another of Carver's writer friends, Tom Jenks, described him in this way: "Ray's generosity, his willing suspension of disbelief (even to the point of gullibility) made him a good listener. The other side of it was that he couldn't keep a secret . . . I discovered this the hard way" ("Shameless," 142). Both Jenks and Wolff go on to tell accounts of how Carver would use intimate anecdotes he had witnessed, or heard under confidence, and shamelessly display them in poems or stories, often to the embarrassment of his friends and family. The use of the poet's eye and ear—"he *listened* with a squint in one *eye*, like a man taking aim"—is inextricably linked to the coupling of intimacy and betrayal in literature that employs poet-voyeurs.

The concepts of looking and spying go hand in hand with listening and eavesdropping. A. C. Spearing's book *The Medieval Poet as Voyeur* is subtitled *Looking and Listening in Medieval Love-Narratives,* and his study illustrates how poets remain concealed to look and listen, then expose confidential information in poems. It is this medieval role of the voyeur as tattletale that Spearing claims is the forerunner of the poet-voyeur in the Petrarchan sonnet tradition as it flourished in the Renaissance. A common denominator in voyeuristic poetry that employs intimacy to arouse curiosity is betrayal or disclosure of secret life displayed in the words of a poem. In the medieval and Renaissance traditions, betrayal almost always begins with the *eye.* The eye is a dangerous organ likened to Cupid's arrow; when a poet's or lover's glance enters another's eye, it can penetrate to the heart, putting in jeopardy the deepest personal secrets.[6] By the Renaissance, the idea of making profit from illicit literature had become so common that poets were aware of the risks of criminalization involved in their vocation.

Carver's shortest poem, entitled "Betrayal" (305), is a remarkable rewriting of the convention of the eye's power to steal and sell secret information: "like bad credit," betrayal "begins with the fingers" as they tell "lies." The first line about credit thus links illicit behavior to market economy as in the tradition of the voyeuristic text; yet, the absence of sight imagery is conspicuous since Carver's poems and stories almost always include some form of watching. The use of the fingers rather than the eyes as the infidel culprit in this poem is one way that Carver expresses an active rather than passive writer's role. The fingers may indicate the act of writing (a poem) or of touching (a body). On the one hand, Carver contextualizes betrayal as a metareflection on art as the process of stealing and revealing the secrets of others, while on the other hand, the fingers represent an expansion of the poet's role from spying and telling to touching and telling.

Carver's early poem from 1967, "The Sunbather, to Herself" (299), also employs the faculty of touch rather than sight to imply active transgression of intimacy. The woman in the poem basks in the sun, feeling that it makes her entire body "glow" under the "touch" of its rays. She addresses the sun as "you" and "husband," imploring it/him, in a sexually charged language—"pour into me" —to strengthen her against an unidentified "bastard." This is a striking Carver poem, for several reasons. Not only does it contain an indirect reference to a key Ovidian voyeuristic text—the bathing Diana and Actaeon myth—but it also presents an inside female perspective in a poem that is not technically a sonnet but mimics certain features of the form. The two stanzas present two separate movements in octaves. The verb "glow" in the first stanza combines with adjectives and nouns ("airy dullness" of the "head," "heart," and "fingers" in the sun) to enhance the lyrical. Three imperatives in the second stanza move beyond the description of the woman's body parts and into a command to be possessed: "pour into," "be rough with," and "strengthen," all followed by "me," turn rhyme into rage, passivity into imagined action.

There is no possessive male gaze in "The Sunbather" as there is in much of the sonnet tradition that is preoccupied with detailing the charms of the female body. Indeed, the voyeuristic gaze is only implied in this poem; the woman is the subject, and the readers, male or female, are the voyeurs. Here penetration is invited rather than feared, and intimacy is offered rather than stolen. The persona's incantation to the sun is a plea for empowerment, and Carver's tone is one that clearly empathizes with the woman. Her intimate inner life is disclosed; yet, in allowing the woman rather than a poet-voyeur to control the flow of information, Carver transfers power from the viewer to the viewed.

The goddess Diana is also a powerful woman, but one who acts out rather than thinks about revenge. In Ovid's *Metamorphoses*, book 3, Actaeon accidentally becomes a voyeur when he stumbles upon the naked goddess. She punishes him by splashing him with water, which turns him into a deer to be torn apart by his own hunting dogs. In Carver's poem the woman is not bathing but sunbathing, an interesting shift since the sun god in classic mythology is Diana's brother, Apollo. In "The Sunbather, to Herself" the reader is invited to spy on a woman who fantasizes about gaining strength through intercourse with the sun, which would make this an oddly incestuous rewriting of the myth. However, in both the Ovid and Carver texts, it is the faculty of touch that is associated with the woman's power. Diana's hands touch the water that touches and transforms Actaeon. The sunbather's skin is outwardly touched by the sun's rays in the first stanza of Carver's poem, and in the second stanza her consciousness is moved by the idea of those rays transforming her on the inside.

There is also a link between the Diana myth and the legend of Lady Godiva and Peeping Tom. Tom, like Actaeon, unwittingly became the voyeur of a naked lady and was blinded for his crime. The motifs of punishment, guilt, and shame for the transgression of viewing nakedness or intimate acts are strong ones in Western literature. In "The Sunbather, to Herself," however, the focus is on the woman's fantasy of espousing the sun, whom she addresses as "husband." Whether she avenges herself and punishes whatever "bastard" has offended her is a less prominent motif than her invocation for strength. In this poem Carver explores the problem of disclosing secret life without trespassing on privacy. He does this by enabling the perspective of a sunbather who is outwardly passive as she lies on the beach and inwardly active in her desire for empowerment. In "The Sunbather," the poet remains a would-be voyeur; as such, he can slyly spy on a woman's body and secret thoughts, yet escape punishment at the same time.

Outside and Inside Space

In "The Sunbather" the perspective shifts from outside to inside as the woman presents her own body and thoughts. In both of the poems discussed below, Carver brings in a spatial, architectural dimension to examine a persona-voyeur's changing position in relation to the events being viewed. In Rudinow's discussion of the status of voyeurism in literary representation, he expresses the asymmetrical project of the voyeur in spatial terms, that is, the wish to be in two places at once. Yet, this paradoxical project, as he points out, is "concerned not with location but with intimacy, i.e. mutual presence" (Rudinow, 177). Examining Carver poems with a concentration of images of outside and inside spaces will put in focus his experiments with the possibilities for mutual presence in the same location.

The first half of "The Man Outside," which appeared in Carver's first book, *Near Klamath*, in 1968, outlines a threat to the persona's domestic tranquillity in terms of space: "Inside" there is "my wife, / my son and daughters," who represent "gentleness / and affection"; and "outside / my bedroom window" is a Peeping Tom who lurks every night. Told from the perspective of the spied-on man, the first three stanzas relate what it feels like to be the object of such a voyeur. The experience is communicated in terms of safety (the inside of the house) and danger (the outside). At this point in the poem, the man outside is a feared and unseen intruder whose space is limited to the physical area outside the window, and yet his psychological impact has already penetrated into the intimate life of the persona.

In the second half of the poem the voyeur does not physically cross the threshold separating outside and inside; rather, he is discovered by the couple who are inside, and this event transforms the voyeuristic project. Instead of calling the police, the couple begin to interact with the onlooker in a curious ménage à trois: "The next night and the next," he explains, "I rouse my wife," and "she comforts me and / rubs my legs" under the gaze of the man outside. This man is cast in the role of Peeping Tom, but he does not attempt to remain concealed and discreetly spy on the couple's bedroom activities; his presence has the power of transforming them into exhibitionists, as they start undressing and performing—"parading up and down the bedroom floor"—while he watches. He has a curiously active *and* passive role; everyone commingles here. The persona is the spied-on lover, an active participant; yet, he becomes this through the gradual and repeated awareness of the voyeur. By the end of the poem the persona and his wife become voyeurs in a double sense: by looking in the mirror they can watch both themselves and the Peeping Tom: "Lights on, nude, we sit / at the vanity table and stare frantically / into the glass. Behind us, two lips, / the reflection of a glowing cigarette." The onlooker is thus acknowledged and in turn becomes the object of the couple's interest, the instigator of their sexual excitement that leads to their strange parading around the room.

In this poem the intimate life of the couple becomes a shared arena that links the inside and the outside through the motifs of mirror and window. In postmodern literature there is a profusion of the use of mirrors and windows in connection with contemporary ideas of the shiftiness of identity, and the threatening tone of the poem indeed underlines a process of dissociation in which the "gentleness and / affection" that characterized the inside space of the first stanza are replaced by a vocabulary of threat as the poem progresses: "terrified," "shudder," "trampled," "tense," "fright," "shame," "anxious," and "frantically." Yet, Carver has some additional errands here in his use of spatial imagery to convey the couple's loss of safety and privacy.

Windows and mirrors represent different types of viewing, and Carver fuses here the reflection of the naked self in the mirror with the face of the outsider looking in at the scene through the window. The naked persona is thus subject to the transgression of his most private place, the bedroom, and his most intimate relationship, marriage. The three participants (voyeur, husband, wife) are initiated into a secret nightly ritual that changes all of their roles and transforms their shared space from semipublic to semiprivate. In Renaissance poetry the prevailing convention was to express secrecy in terms of architecture. As Wendy Wall, among others, has pointed out, "architectural metaphors were essential for delineating a private sphere since the Renaissance did not have another vocabulary available . . . for depicting the inner self" ("Disclosures in Print," 39).[7] Twentieth-century writers need not respect such conventions, as they have access to a wide variety of aesthetic techniques for exploring the secrets of the self. In "The Sunbather," as we have seen, Carver gives a woman's consciousness free rein, and her thoughts wander from her body to her inner world. However, in the two poems in this section, Carver makes an effort to underline space as a metaphor for intimacy in which interior and exterior are initially juxtaposed but ultimately intersect.

In "The Man Outside" it is the point of contact between the three participants that gives the poem end weight. In the final stanza there is a mutual awareness that includes both sight, as the couple stares in the mirror at the voyeur, and voice, suggested by the image of his lips rather than eyes. The age-old theme of the spy who tattles is thus implicit in this poem, but more interestingly, the voyeuristic project has become a joint effort in which the roles of the passive viewer and the active viewed overlap. The fusing of the images of the "glass" in front of the vanity table and the window becomes the focal point and physical location of the characters' intersecting contact. What, then, is the reader's position in this bizarre spectacle?

What I initially termed a pact of secrecy between the writer, the reader, and the characters is in an early phase of expression in "The Man Outside" (published in 1968 when Carver was thirty). In this poem the persona and the voyeur are separate characters, but they interact through the architectonics of mirror and window, and it is up to the reader to decide whether the players in this voyeuristic performance deserve our pity, curiosity, sympathy, disdain, or other. Whatever the choice, readers have been given access to highly intimate details of these lives; the home of the couple has literally been opened to our view through the space of the poem. Like so many other of Carver's characters who are drawn into a voyeuristic situation—consider the house sitters in the story "Neighbors," who try on their neighbors' clothes, medicine, alcohol, and identity, or the couples in "The Idea" discussed above—Carver shows the readers their secrets without passing judgment on their actions.

In the final poem to be examined, "Locking Yourself Out, Then Trying to Get Back In" (73), Carver seems to have reached a resolution of the ethical and aesthetic problems involved in the disclosure of the details of secret life by merging the roles of the narrator and the participant. In the first stanza the persona describes how he has literally become a man outside by leaving his house without a key: "You simply go out and shut the door." In this 1985 poem from the collection *Where Water Comes Together with Other Water,* Carver weaves in some interests that were present throughout his career, and the double level of realism and metaphor introduced in the opening lines—the absurdity of the situation described "sounds / like the story of a life"—sets the tone for the stanzas that will follow. The poem constructs a spatial inside/outside dynamics in which to meditate on both thematic and metapoetic concerns. The predicament of the persona—being locked out—can be likened to the predicament of the author, who must find ways of obtaining and disclosing inside information. The line "look back / at what you've done" suggests not only a glance back at the shut door of the immediate situation but also a backward glance at a whole life of mistakes and/or a career of recording the private lives of others.

The verb "look" is repeated in the second stanza, which also employs "stare" twice; in the first instance the persona is staring *in* "at the sofa, plants, the table / and chairs," and in the second he recollects how, when inside, he would "stare out when I sat at my desk." The shift in pronoun from "You" in the opening stanza to "I" in the second one is significant: the first stanza suggests either a distance from the self ("you" as singular) or a duplicity ("you" as plural). By the end of the second stanza Carver has managed to fuse the man locked outside, the narrator, and the man who usually sits inside, the writer: they are the same person. The persona has thus become the Peeping Tom of his own experience; he spies on himself for the rest of the poem, which consistently employs "I." In this stanza there is an active empathy toward a double life: he observes his downstairs life as an everyman, embracing the interior objects through his italicized apostrophe "*Hello, friends,*" and then turns his attention and curiosity to his upstairs life as a writer. The moment of contact between the interior and exterior man comes when the persona reflects, "I'd raise my eyes / and stare out," exactly at the spot where he is now standing.

This moment offers the persona a quiet epiphany that he comments on in stanza 3, which will repeat the verb "look" twice. The hallmark colloquial diction of Carver's late verse conveys the eloquence of his seemingly inarticulate characters, whose language is in fact sufficient to address even extraordinary experiences: "it was something to look in like that, unseen" and "to be there, inside, and not be there" at the same time. By the end of this stanza the empathy toward objects has been extended to the "people I loved then" and implicitly to the self who writes about those people. The persona had stared in through the "windows" in the previous stanza, but now the choice of the word "glass" ("I brought my face close to the glass") bolsters the event of fusion between outside and inside selves. In "The Man Outside" the word "glass" is used in connection with the mirror at the vanity table at the point in the poem when mirror and window allow the three characters joint contact: they "stare frantically / into the glass" at the lips of the man outside the window. In "Locking Yourself Out" it is the joining of the voyeur outside and the writer inside that is highlighted in a moment of association rather than dissociation. The window has become a mirror for the double self: the persona is the author of and main character in his own life.

In the final stanza the fusing that occurred in words (you/I, window/glass, man outside / man inside) becomes a literal reconnection as the persona penetrates into the interior of the writer's work space: "I bashed that beautiful window. / And stepped back in." That he experiences a "wave of grief" and feels "violently ashamed" in this stanza just after his identification with the self as writer underlines how Carver is working through the dilemmas of the poet-voyeur as thief and the text as a betrayal of stolen information displayed in the marketplace of readership.[8] In his development from the 1968 "The Man Outside" to the 1985 "Locking Yourself Out," Carver strives to find a stance that enables him to steal and yet be redeemed in the process. It is a negotiating position to occupy, walking a fine line between trespassing on privacy and expressing empathy with the human participants in the scenes described. Carver's experiments with voyeurs who are involved spectators include moments of connectedness and identification, such as those between the Peeping Tom and the couple in "The Man Outside" and the outside and inside selves in "Locking Yourself Out."

In these poems it is the active involvement of all the characters that fills the fissure of distance between the viewer and the spied-on, between the subject and the object. During much of his career Carver was preoccupied with the paradox of viewing *and* participating and moreover with the writer's task of communicating secrets to the reader without violating the intimacy of the people portrayed. How can this be approached in an age when, to use Fowler's terms, "participation is no longer in the reader's or viewer's contract" (79)? For Carver, this challenge was approached by portraying *being there* and *not being there* at the same time. By casting the writer as the person spying and being spied on, Carver betrays no one but himself and harms nothing, with the exception of that beautiful window. By bashing the window, Carver not only steps back into his vocation as poet but also adds his own idiomatic twist to a long history of voyeurism in literature by fusing the Peeping Tom with the person inside.

Many Carver poems embrace a premodern pact of complicity between viewer and the viewed at the same time as they are marked by a postmodern skepticism of any such trust. By the twentieth century, identification between the writer, the reader, and the characters in the form of active, empathic involvement had been replaced by ideas of authorship as suspect, identity as fragmented, and character as estranged from the self.[9] The insertion of involved spectators in Carver's works can be seen as an aesthetic experiment that moves toward breaching the gap between a world in which characters experience a profound disconnectedness and one in which communion is possible through gestures of eye contact, touch, and invitations to identification with humans and the objects that fill their lived space. Carver's use of the poet-voyeur as someone who is a mediator in such acts of reassociation paradoxically enabled him to move beyond a minimalist and dissociative poetics by incorporating elements of an older tradition of voyeurism in literature.

Notes

1. All references to Carver poems are from *All of Us: The Collected Poems*, ed. William L. Stull, introduction by Tess Gallagher (New York: Knopf, 1998), reprinted by permission of Tess Gallagher.

2. The term "Involved Spectators" is taken from the title of chapter 5 of Alastair Fowler's *Renaissance Realism: Narrative Images in Literature and Art* (Oxford: Oxford University Press, 2003). His use of it is discussed below.

3. One of the most substantial discussions of Carver's more generous work of the 1980s is William L. Stull's "Beyond Hopelessville: Another Side of Raymond Carver," *Philological Quarterly* 64, no. 1 (Winter 1985): 1–15. The essays in this volume reflect the

double critical reception of Carver as a dire minimalist as well as a more humoristic and spiritually expressive writer.

4. "Peeping Tom."

5. In her essay on the Renaissance voyeuristic text, Wendy Wall explores how the arrival of mass production went hand in hand with the conception of the publication of voyeuristic texts as a kind of theft for which a writer could be prosecuted; see "Disclosures in Print: 'Violent Enlargement' of the Renaissance Voyeuristic Text," *Studies in English Literature 1500–1900* 29 (1989): 35–59.

6. A. C. Spearing notes that the trope of the eye as Cupid's arrow "ultimately harden[ed] into a cliché of courtly literature" (*The Medieval Poet as Voyeur: Looking and Listening in Medieval Love-Narratives* [Cambridge: Cambridge University Press, 1993], 10).

7. See also Roy Eriksen's *The Building in the Text: Alberti to Shakespeare* (University Park: Pennsylvania State University Press, 2001), which documents a related phenomenon, i.e., the extent to which Renaissance art relied on architectural principles to construct literary texts.

8. Wendy Wall examines the topics of market economy and voyeurism as they developed during the Renaissance in "Disclosures in Print."

9. Walt Whitman is, of course, an important missing link in this discussion, and the appearance of the empathic voyeur in *Song of Myself* is an obvious forerunner to Carver's use of the figure. David Boxer and Cassandra Phillips discuss this in their informative article "*Will You Please Be Quiet, Please?:* Voyeurism, Dissociation and the Art of Raymond Carver," *Iowa Review* 10, no. 3 (1980): 78.

Works Cited

Boxer, David, and Cassandra Phillips. "*Will You Please Be Quiet, Please?:* Voyeurism, Dissociation and the Art of Raymond Carver." *Iowa Review* 10, no. 3 (Summer 1980): 75–90.

Brown, Arthur A. "Raymond Carver and Postmodern Humanism." *Critique: Studies in Contemporary Fiction* 31, no. 2 (Winter 1990): 125–36.

Carver, Raymond. *All of Us: The Collected Poems*, ed. William L. Stull, introduction by Tess Gallagher. New York: Knopf, 1998.

————. *Will You Please Be Quiet, Please.* New York: McGraw-Hill, 1976.

Fowler, Alastair. *Renaissance Realism: Narrative Images in Literature and Art.* Oxford: Oxford University Press, 2003.

Jenks, Tom. "Shameless." In *Remembering Ray*, ed. Stull and Carroll, 141–43.

Rudinow, Joel. "Representation, Voyeurism, and the Vacant Point of View." *Philosophy and Literature* 3, no. 2 (1979): 173–86.

Spearing, A. C. *The Medieval Poet as Voyeur: Looking and Listening in Medieval Love-Narratives.* Cambridge: Cambridge University Press, 1993.

Stull, William L., and Maureen P. Carroll, eds. *Remembering Ray: A Composite Biography.* Santa Barbara, Calif.: Capra, 1993.

Taylor, Mark. "Voyeurism and Aposopesis in Renaissance Poetry." *Exemplaria: A Journal of Theory in Medieval and Renaissance Studies* 4, no. 2 (1992): 267–94.

Wall, Wendy. "Disclosures in Print: 'Violent Enlargement' of the Renaissance Voyeuristic Text." *Studies in English Literature 1500–1900* 29 (1989): 35–59.

Wolff, Tobias. "Appetite." In *Remembering Ray*, ed. Stull and Carroll, 241–50.

William L. Magrino

American Voyeurism

Why Does Raymond Carver Want Us to Watch?

Speech is a mirror of the soul: as a man speaks, so is he. (Publilius Syrus, 42 B.C.)

I like to watch. (Chauncey Gardiner, 1970 A.D.)

In his short fiction Raymond Carver opens the lives of his characters to the eyes of a voyeur. Carver presents specific, private moments in the lives of ordinary Americans from a distinctly exterior point of view. Setting his stories in the working-class communities of contemporary "flyover" America, far from the spiritual distractions of coastlines and commerce, Raymond Carver chooses to "deal not with cosmic dilemmas but with the routine unhappiness of marriage and family life, in which subjects like alcoholism, casual infidelity, dull jobs, and unemployment have become trite" (Dickstein, "The Pursuit for the Ordinary," 507). Carver offers almost no interior motivations for the interactions among his characters. They live within a prefabricated world of institutions called "adolescence," "marriage," and "parenthood." "What's in Alaska?," "What We Talk about When We Talk about Love," and "Why Don't You Dance?" reflect the narrative presence, and subsequent instability, of the voyeur in Carver's fiction. As the reader watches these people exist at certain points in time within the confines of their respective afflictions, the varying perspectives that are offered to the voyeur illuminate the impact of the field of the gaze upon subjectivity. Shunning "physical description, narrative texture, atmospheric detail, and authorial commentary" (Dickstein, 508), Carver presents interrelated subjects in medias res for his readers to watch. Once the characters have been introduced, the author quickly removes himself from the scene to allow the action to progress, therefore causing the bonds between these characters to regress.

Carver's style of writing creates and maintains a deliberate distance among his subjects and, by extension, his readers. Frequently, in Carver's prose, "a typical sentence is blunt and uncomplicated, eschewing the ornaments of descriptive adverbs and parenthetical phrases" (Weber, "Raymond Carver," 48). Miriam

Marty Clark identifies the characteristics of this uniquely straightforward form of prose: "Carver's fiction is rarely playful; nor is it often marked by allusion, double meanings, reflexive or metafictional gambits" ("Raymond Carver's Mono-logic Imagination," 240). Reflecting the fractured subjectivity, and consequently the fragmented lives, of his characters through an assembly of sparse, stark, and frequently incongruous language, "Carver is generally acknowledged to be 'the chief practitioner of what's been called 'American minimalism'" (Meyer, "Now You See Him," 239).

In accord with the experiences of his characters, Carver's readers are provided information on a need-to-know basis. The more Carver withholds, the more everyone must look. In both subject and style, Carver's minimalist technique forces his reader to become a voyeur, peering in from the outside on intimate, and completely physical, events. However, what is inconspicuous on the exterior often becomes infinitely complex once the facade is removed and the primary image begins to be revealed. The richness of Carver's fiction remains concealed until the reader enters the field of the gaze to peel away the layers of subjectivity.

Analyzing the desires of the characters by looking in on them in the present moment, Carver's readers assume a voyeuristic position to reassemble these continuously fragmented lives. This attempt at unification of the subject requires the reader to revisit Jacques Lacan's *mirror stage* to discover the other-ness of the primary image. As linguistic representations, and representatives, of the Freudian ego, these characters are fragments of a greater whole. In "The Mirror Stage as Formative of the *I* Function," Lacan establishes the human subject as the victim of "a veritable *specific prematurity of birth*" (6) in its forced reliance on a reversed and disconnected image to gain entry into the symbolic order. The existence of the image in itself, and the process of subjectivity predicated upon this misrecognition in "a form that is more constitutive than constituted" (4), precludes the fruition of a *self*. The defenses adopted by Carver's characters, in attempts to evict the other from the self-image, merely emphasize this otherness to the voyeur. Inversely a realization of this repression of the subject necessitates the presence of the voyeur. Agency is produced not by the physical act of looking but from the *presence* of the voyeur within the field of the gaze, completing "the illusion of the consciousness of seeing oneself see one-self" (Lacan, "Of the Gaze," 83). Making his readers privy to private moments, requiring conscious assemblage, Carver initiates an exchange of signifiers in which *watching* precedes, and necessitates, *creating*.

Shoe Fetishes and Dimly Lit Gazes

In "What's in Alaska?," Carver articulates his title in the form of a question. This method, apparent in several of his stories, signifies the initiation of an exchange with the reader. As opposed to an invitation to join a conversation, however, these questions seem to reflect the dubious nature of language and how one signifier leads to another, equally bereft of inherent meaning. One learns quickly that any active participation by the reader leads to more questions. The open-endedness implied by the title reflects the instability of subject, and subsequent impossibility of the unity of image, made apparent by the action of the story. Carver's readers gain knowledge by deciphering action and reaction. The opening scene involves Jack's impulsive purchase of a new pair of shoes. The narrator describes Jack stopping at a store to buy the shoes before coming home after work but never explains the relevance of the purchase. Under closer scrutiny, however, the reader's line of sight within the interior of Jack's car reveals a symbolic relationship between subject and object. Knowledge is transmitted within the field of the gaze between Jack and "the soft beige-colored shoes that made his feet feel free and springy" (Carver, *Where I'm Calling From*, 70). The reader is directed to look only down at the shoes and up at Jack from the time he leaves the store until he arrives home. The subject is never complete in this scene—it is always Jack or the shoes.

As Lacan, assuming the role of the subject within the field of the gaze, observes, "The picture, certainly, is in my eye. But I am not in the picture" (Lacan, "Of the Gaze," 96). This opening scene is almost entirely an exterior description of Jack's errand. Carver's only hint at the interior thoughts of Jack is in the line "Driving home, he felt that his foot moved freely from pedal to pedal" (Carver, 70). Jack's feet no longer feel the sensation—it is now Jack. Even through this atypical moment of introspection, the reader is unable to determine Jack's motivation for buying the shoes. One can easily envision Jack observing his own reactions in the rearview mirror of his automobile, or even in the dual image produced by the shine of his new shoes.

Jack's feeling of *jouissance*, or fleeting, symptomatic release from repression, shared by the narrator is a result of Jack's desire to feel whole. The freedom now felt by Jack is not due to the technology in footwear but by the illusion of wholeness provided by the symmetry of the new shoes. As prosthetic devices, the shoes provide Jack with the unity of action and recognition denied by Lacan's mirror. The presence of the voyeur, providing agency to Jack's look, completes the gaze in its ability to attribute Jack's subjectivity to his object of desire.

Upon returning home, Jack's feeling of completeness is challenged by his partner's entry into the gaze. When Jack arrives and Mary sees his shoes, she simply comments, "You needed new shoes" (Carver, 70). The gaze is now mediated between the shoes and Mary. Her facial expressions reveal an apparent unhappiness with the shoes. We see Mary only look at the shoes. In her gaze the shoes are no longer part of Jack—they now represent his lack in her eyes. In this opening scene, the view of the voyeur is necessary to complete the image. The shoes do not reappear as objects of any importance until much later when Jack spills cream soda on them at their friends' house. In this scene Jack is clearly concerned about the accident, but apparently only because they are new shoes. The shoes are mentioned again only at the end of the story when Jack is in need of an item to throw at the unknown disturbance that has been keeping him awake.

Carver's choice of these shoes is ambiguous to the reader, but they are obviously meaningful to the character. For Jack, the space between his eyes and his shoes is informed by Lacan's *objet petit a*. They signify his desire to approach the Other of language and, simultaneously, represent his ineffectuality as a speaking subject. As a voyeur of the action, the reader is able only to watch Jack attempt to understand his motivations concerning his attachment to these shoes. As with all of Carver's characters, this means of narrative provides numerous possibilities for interpretations of Jack's actions. This purchase could be a response to a specific earlier criticism from Mary or, more likely, a symptom of internal lack, reflected by his general discomfort at home. It would be quite easy for Jack to blame the physical state of his shoes for the emotional condition of his life. What is clear, however, is the visual attempt of this subject to acquire and maintain a sense of *self* through an incorporation of *other.*

In "The Sexual Aberrations," Sigmund Freud identifies voyeurism as a perverse manifestation of scopophilia, or pleasure in looking. In his discussion of the symptomatic operations of perversions, Freud refers to scopophilia as one of the components of the sexual instinct, which is in constant tension "against certain mental forces which act as resistances, and of which shame and disgust are the most prominent" (28). Usually attributed to the viewing of sexual and/ or excretory acts, to repress a desire of the voyeur, this manifestation of the scopic drive places the subject and object in a Hegelian dialectic between the ego and the object.

For Freud the act of looking is Oedipal and reaffirms the lack of the female. This privileged *male gaze* objectifies the female and places her in the subordinate position of being watched. Freud's binary fetishism of the scopophilic drive produces a direct, but restricted, field of vision for the subject and object, as well as creates an immediate sexual satisfaction for the looker. In this visually and temporally limited manifestation of scopophilia offered by Freud, the object remains as Other and the function of desire produces, for the subject, a false sense of self granted by phallic possession. Tracing the prevalence of voyeurism in the French novel as a means of possession of the object, Dorothy Kelly offers the following:

Voyeurism in literature fulfills more than one simple role in the negotiation and attempted resolution of conflicts. One of the reasons for its prevalence is, perhaps, its link to another instinct that has an obvious importance in literature. In psychoanalytic writing, voyeurism and the scopophilic instinct go hand in hand with this other instinct and another malady: the instinct for knowledge, and the malady Freud labels, "epistemophilia." (*Telling Glances*, 8)

Through Lacan's post-Cartesian lens, the more these characters know, the less they see, and the more they want to know, the less they are. The distances produced by Carver—through a gradual transfer of knowledge about the characters—maintain a desire to possess the object. Fulfillment, however, is never attained for either the reader or the characters. Paradoxically subjectivity becomes increasingly disjointed as each character imparts additional information to the reader. Self-reflexivity, therefore, simply reveals the illusion of wholeness. Any fleeting illusion of privilege, male or otherwise, is quickly subverted by a shattering of the mirror of subjectivity. In fact, there is an identifiable strain of androgyny pervading the words and deeds of these characters. In the case of Jack and Mary in "What's in Alaska?," vaguely defined gender roles accentuate *the lack* experienced both individually and in tandem. As products of misrecognition, any knowledge that has been acquired by these subjects is actually misknowledge, or, to use Lacan's term, *me connaissance*. Jack's attempts at possession are usurped once Mary enters *the gaze*. As evidenced by the introduction of the shoes, Jack's subjectivity is jeopardized by the knowledge that his image is incomplete. Mary's presence within the gaze simply reaffirms Jack's repression.

Emphasizing a voyeuristic point of view, Carver frequently structures his stories in a distinctly dramatic fashion. As in a one-act play, Carver permits his characters to act and interact unimpeded, while requiring his readers to watch from a distance. In accord with his performative style of narration, Carver employs several dramatic conventions. Carver changes scenes in his stories through blackouts to indicate passage of time. Frequently dialogue about past events is spoken without any exposition from either the participants or an omniscient narrator. Bordering on David Mamet–like parataxis, the characters' desperation to communicate actually obscures meaning. Like an audience seated before a proscenium, Carver's readers are allowed to watch the characters' lives only through a linear progression of physical movements and spoken utterances within the present.

The narrative structure of "What's in Alaska?" parallels that of a one-act play. There are seven distinct scenes in the story, separated by sudden breaks in action, all indicating either a new location or a passage of time. The breaks in the action of this story allow the reader to witness the actions of the four characters through progressive states of marijuana influence. The changes in dialogue and confusion in the actions of the characters are the only means for the reader to analyze their altered psychological states. Carver does not pause from the action to evaluate the motivations of the characters. In keeping with the unique perspective in his fiction, "Carver's narrator, although omniscient, is neither intrusive nor judgmental" (Stull, "Beyond Hopelessville," 7). The actions and interactions are simply presented in a removed, third-person mode for the reader to observe.

Although Carver's stories primarily focus on the crisis of male subjectivity, there does not seem to be a privileged view for anyone within the field of the gaze. Laura Mulvey's seminal essay "Visual Pleasure and the Narrative Cinema" discusses the historically patriarchal voyeuristic implications of the cinematic arts. Examining the logistics of audience position within a screening room, she equates the illusory nature of the cinematic experience to the subject's initial act of misrecognition. Inspired by Lacan's mirror, in which "the position of the spectators in the cinema is blatantly one of repression of their exhibitionism and projection of their repressed desire onto the performer" (17), Mulvey illustrates how the phallic lack of the audience members contributes to the agency of the image. Marking the distinction between the scopophilic viewing of film and live theater, Christian Metz identifies a cinematic "extra reduplication, a supplementary and specific turn of the screw bolting desire to the lack" (*The Imaginary Signifier*, 61). Although the multiplicity of the experience of cinema does respond to the scopophilic drive in its perpetual removal of the object, the theater's focus on the inherent linguistic distance and resulting shifts of positioning between subject and object provides an appropriate venue for Carver's gaze.

In the live theater, the gaze is returned by subjects who are aware they are being watched. The seating of the audience, within an authentic three-dimensional environment, allows for a variety of vantage points and produces a completely original image for each subject. In terms of language, as well as action, the drama is always different from one performance to the next. Unlike at the cinema, the audience in a theater is actively involved in creating the text of the play. An actor's awareness of audience also influences the projection of image. Whether overt or not, audience reaction does not go unrequited in the theater. This component of the craft creates a full, unobstructed field of vision within the space of the theater.

Uta Hagen, who devoted over five decades of her life to the continuous exploration of the actor's impact on the world of the stage, acknowledges this symbiotic relationship to her students. In *A Challenge for the Actor* she states, "Ideal communication between actor and audience occurs when the actor is intensely alive, physically and psychologically involved in fulfilling his character's needs, in action—*within* the magic circle of his playing area" (154). The closer proximity of the object of desire in a live performance provokes the voyeur to actively peruse the object, through an acknowledgment of one's respective role in the discourse. Although there frequently are extraneous apparatuses at work in a theatrical production, they are not required to produce the image. As in Raymond Carver's work, in which language and space are primary, the theatrical image is constituted and projected by speaking subjects. As legendary experimental director Peter Brook admits, "until an audience is present the object is not complete" (*The Empty Space*, 127).

Indicating the immediate nature of a voyeuristic experience, all of the action in "What's in Alaska?" surrounds and unifies the experiences of four main characters. There is no extraneous reference to the world outside of the characters' lives, and all action provides immediate results. The only reference to the characters' lives outside of the immediate circumstance concerns Jack and Mary's plans to go to Alaska. This impending move to Alaska involves Mary's opportunity for a job, and they both seem excited to go at the beginning of the story. However, when questioned by their friends about their plans, neither Jack nor Mary can tell them what is in Alaska. The following exchange concerning Jack's announcement of the possible move to Alaska signifies the distant and unknowable nature of the outside world for these individuals:

> "We might go to Alaska," Jack said.
> "Alaska?" Carl said. "What's in Alaska? What would you do up there?"
> "What's wrong with here?" Carl said. "What would you guys do in Alaska? I'm serious. I'd like to know."
> Jack put a potato chip in his mouth and sipped his cream soda. "I don't know. What did you say?"
> After a while Carl said, "What's in Alaska?"
> "I don't know," Jack said. "Ask Mary. Mary knows. Mary, what am I going to do up there? Maybe I'll grow those giant cabbages you read about." (Carver, 76–77)

Through this dialogue the reader can conclude that these characters know neither what is in Alaska nor why they would like to go there. The only apparent collective motive is an intention to go somewhere. Alaska could be anywhere except where they are now. In the focus of their conversation, Carver is simply providing a point of reference onto which the characters may project their desires. According to Gary Krist, Carver's characters "more often than not, end up fixating on a seemingly random image or idea—moving to Alaska, say—that we readers recognize as an apt comment on their existential condition" ("Fiction Chronicle," 126). The dialogue concerning a longing for change among the characters appears to be casual and frivolous through most of the story. Freud, in "The Sexual Life of Human Beings," acknowledges that "alongside of those who seek their sexual satisfaction in reality are those who are content merely to *imagine* that satisfaction, who need no real object at all, but can replace it with their phantasies" (306). Similarly an infant need not approach an actual looking glass to enter Lacan's *mirror stage*. The mirror can be any other who represents a unity of being for the child.

Mary is the only character who outwardly suggests a mood of desperation. As she and Jack are walking back home, she longingly states, "'When we get home, Jack, I want to be fucked, talked to, diverted. Divert me, Jack. I need to be diverted tonight'" (Carver, 83–84). Typical of Carver's technique, moments of *jouissance*, replacing authentic communication, reveal this couple's repressed needs and desires. In this story the couple's source of dissatisfaction is not specifically identified by either the narrator or the characters. Carver merely provides his readers with the bits of language and motion with which his characters attempt to communicate. Analyzing this minimalist form of self-expression, Kirk Nesset states:

> They [Carver's characters] talk, however unsuccessfully; they have sex, or avoid it. They employ both their bodies and their tongues in efforts to find themselves again, struggling to reassemble the bits and pieces of their tattered identities—and they continue struggling, even as their bodies get them into trouble, as their tongues, taking them forever in circles, fall silent. ("This Word Love," 295)

Silence, whether shared or experienced alone, seems to be the medium in which Carver's characters attempt to express the inexpressible. In the futility of their words and deeds, these individuals are additionally burdened with their idle emotions and desires. Carl and Helen's cat, Cindy, is present during the party and is described in the following line as watching the participants: "'Look at her eyes.' Mary said. 'Look at the way she looks at us. She's high, all right'" (Carver, 82). The two couples then proceed to watch the cat eat a mouse that she had dragged in earlier. These moments of silence, and the corresponding actions that emphasize them, are the agencies of expression in which one may see what cannot be said. Instead of removing the object from discourse, silence serves to magnify its importance and accentuate its distance. Mary's acknowledgment of their existence within the gaze is both the source and reflection of Jack's anxiety.

Jack's subjectivity is threatened by Mary in that she is the physical representation of his unattainable object. Discussing the voyeuristic implications of alignment of subject and object, Regina Schwartz attempts to quantify the ability of an object to possess its subject. Schwartz insists that without a fixed, definitive positioning of subject and object, the resulting line of sight is suspect. This inability for the voyeur ever to receive an accurate depiction of the source of desire, in fact, produces the desired effect for the subject. If the effect is what is desired, and not the actual object, as Schwartz contends, "to observe *is* to imagine" ("Through the Optic Glass," 150).

Raymond Carver's characters are drenched in this pursuit of the unattainable. This instability of position is the source of the voyeuristic effect of Carver's fiction and why these stories and "Their constituent parts—characters, gestures, images, and turns of phrase—are sometimes so similar that we might wonder if they are not perhaps interchangeable" (Runyon, *Reading Raymond Carver*, 134). As these stories progress, a deeper realization of an inaccessibility to material as well as emotional fulfillment, although frequently remaining obscured to the characters, becomes incrementally more visible to the reader.

The final scene of the story most strongly reflects the characters' feelings of being watched. As Jack attempts to go to sleep after he and Mary arrive home, he has a disturbing experience. The narrator states, "Just as he started to turn off the lamp, he thought he saw something in the hall. He kept staring and thought he saw it again, a pair of small eyes" (Carver, 85). Jack proceeds to pick up one of his new shoes to throw at the apparition, but the story ends before he actually releases it. It is unclear whether the eyes are simply a hallucination or an actual animal, but Jack's reactions clearly reflect a feeling of uneasiness about being watched. Jack's anxiety in this scene could stem from his fear of watching himself. These "glowing animal eyes . . . embodying his paranoias about the future and his girlfriend's fidelity, stalk him in the darkened hallway" (Nesset, 301) and force Jack to look at his situation and both voyeur and exhibitionist in an uncanny fashion.

Speaking Others or Signifying Nothings

The dialogue of "What We Talk about When We Talk about Love" symbolically elucidates the fractured subjectivity explored in "What's in Alaska?" Once again Carver presents a series of scenes separated by blackouts to signify the passage of time in the shared experience of two couples. In this story, however, the reader is watching these characters become progressively inebriated from gin. Similar to the previous story, the dialogue and actions of these characters change to reflect their commonly altered states of consciousness. Once again four individuals are engaged in an extended conversation about a subject that they clearly do not know anything about. These people are unable to communicate their emotions in a meaningful manner, although they talk a great deal. In this case the characters are attempting to explore the meaning of love through the retelling of stories and anecdotes. The two couples trade stories and situational philosophies in an attempt to define true love.

In certain respects "What We Talk about When We Talk about Love" is a departure for Carver in terms of character and point of view. However, neither of these anomalistic features obscures this story's voyeuristic implications. This piece is told in the third person, but in a style that places the narrator on the fringe of the action. At first it seems as if this story is being told to a close friend. On closer examination it is not difficult to believe that the narrator is not telling this story but merely retelling it in his own mind. As the events unfold in the past tense, the narrator seems to be replaying these events, of which he was party, but removing himself enough to watch what really happened. As a flashback, indicating a *return of the repressed* of the narrator in the vein of Willy Loman or Tom Wingfield, the sobering effects of time seem to have given the narrator additional clarity.

As opposed to the more traditional first-person account, this story focuses on the narrator's friend Mel McGinnis. Mel is introduced to the reader as a cardiologist who, according to the narrator, uses his elevated position within his limited society to feel more confident about expressing his views. As a *heart* doctor, Mel possesses a clinical knowledge of the *fragmented subject* he embodies. The narrator, Nick, remains unnamed until Laura takes it upon herself to state that they know what love is. Instead of speaking, though, Laura and Nick provide affectionate gestures, to which Terri, Mel's partner, replies, "You're still on honeymoon, for God's sake" (Carver, 175).

The only account which seems to approach a conventional ideal of physical evidence of true love is Mel's recollection of the old couple he had treated as a result of a car accident. The reactions to Mel's anecdote show that neither he nor anyone else in the room would be able to recognize a display of love if they actually saw it. Mel's response to the husband's depression over not being able to see his wife was one of amazement and disgust. As Mel emphatically states at the conclusion of his story, "Can you imagine? I'm telling you, the man's heart was breaking because he couldn't turn his goddamn head and see his goddamn wife . . . I mean, it was killing the old fart just because he couldn't look at the fucking woman" (Carver, 183).

As Nelson Hathcock notes, "'What We Talk about When We Talk about Love' speaks less of love than of the inadequacy of language to convey those monumental abstractions that spring from 'unbridled emotions'" ("The Possibility of Resurrection," 32). Involving characters searching for an object that does not exist, as they plod along the axis of metonymy, this story is not about love any more than "What's in Alaska?" is about Alaska. Illustrating the idea that love is, by definition, the unattainable, the dialogue of the story represents the effects of desire on Lacan's signifying chain.

As a result of this breach in communication among these characters, the message to the reader is loud and clear. At times, especially when characters do not possess the language to express the most fundamental human emotions, the pauses impregnating conversation can speak louder than the spoken words. As Arthur F. Bethea observes, "Although the story omits a privileged definition of love, the text seems to determine Carver's skepticism of the L-word and his preference for the tactile expression of love instead of the verbal" (*Technique and Sensibility*, 95). It is left to the reader, therefore, to see the love among these characters, possibly made more visible in the absence of words. The absence of the definition of love, punctuated by the dialectical demand for it by the characters, becomes its most authentic definition. According to Lacan, in "The Subversion of the Subject and the Dialectic of Desire," "there is no metalanguage that can be spoken, or, more aphoristically, there is no Other of the Other" (298). As they continue to use language in attempts to approach the object, these characters are subsequently distancing themselves from it, and correspondingly from each other.

In this story, as in "What's in Alaska?," the characters express a desire to go somewhere. Although Carver's characters sometimes wish to leave their present situations, they are never emotionally strong enough to change things for themselves: "Visions, after all, are not escape routes, and just as Carver rarely affords his characters visions, he never affords them routes of escape" (Nesset, 300). In this case the characters repeatedly insist on going to "that new place" (Carver, 182) for dinner but never leave the table.

The final scene of "What We Talk about When We Talk about Love" reflects a collective consciousness of the characters being watched by each other in response to the futility of their use of language. Kirk Nesset indicates, "Carver's characters are not simply voyeurs, but 'voyeurs . . . of their own experience,' seekers in perilous games of peek-a-boo which, if carried far enough, yield 'sudden, astonishing glimpses behind the curtain which separates their empty lives from chaos'" (296). The narrator of the story closes with the following image: "I could hear my heart beating. I could hear everyone's heart. I could hear the human noise we sat there making, not one of us moving, not even when the room went dark" (Carver, 185). In this scene Carver allows his readers to see and hear what his characters cannot talk about. This purely physical representation of emotion allows the reader to share in this collective experience. In the form of *hearts* speaking, Carver illustrates Julia Kristeva's distinction between the *semiotic* and the *symbolic*. The image of the human heartbeat, within a space occupied by several heartbeats, represents the primary maternal rhythm. Only when words exasperate, and further repress the emotion, do "preverbal *significances* allow complex and intraverbal experiences to be brought to the other; they help in forgiving, in transferring" (Kristeva, *Intimate Revolt*, 19).

This image of love, and resulting frustration in its adequate expression, is evident in "that automatic idle, in the form of a heartbeat, presiding over being even after the collapse of language, after dissociation is ruinously complete" (Nesset, 304). Once again Carver leaves his characters in stillness as the scene fades to black. As Hathcock queries, "What more apt rendition of a scene in which 'nothing will be achieved' than the stasis and darkness that blot out this story at its end, leaving literally nothing for the 'eye' to rest upon?" (33). The eternal repression of meaning at the hands of the symbolic order is most palpable by this *speaking* of hearts.

Reassembly from the Inside Out

"Why Don't You Dance?" presents the inevitable surrender of awareness of a subject to the voyeur. The story opens to an enigmatic scene in which a man is in the process of moving his furnishings from his house into his driveway. Although he inhabits his kitchen as he mentally matches the current appearance of his belongings to their former logistical state within the house, the man's gaze never leaves the driveway. As Michael Trussler interprets the opening scene, "From the outset of the story, the inherent difficulty involved in the interpretation of events is suggested" ("The Narrowed Voice," 30). Carver offers no explanation as to why this nameless man is moving the furniture and appliances outside. The man's only thought on the subject, while arranging the items and supplying the appropriate power through an extension cord, is that "Things worked, no different from how it was when they were inside" (Carver, 156). Apparently, in the view of the man, the reassembly of these household items outside of the walls of the home has not affected their utility. The man is comforted in his recognition of the *mirror image* that he constructs from the components of his former domestic life. Once freed from the confines of his domicile, and assembled from the man's memory, the fragments only now seem to take form.

The reader's point of view in this story is much like that of the curious passersby who have slowed their cars from the street to attempt to make sense of the curious spectacle. The reader must accept the man's word that the items in the front yard and driveway accurately depict the former interior of his house. The only mention of the current state of the interior of the residence, besides the acknowledgment of the empty closets, is that "except for the three cartons in the living room, all the stuff was out of the house" (Carver, 156). The initial field of vision is limited to the man watching this mock-up of his living space from the kitchen until he later appears outside. Once the man returns to find two guests who have assumed there is a yard sale in progress, the reader's line of sight is confined to the exterior of the house for the remainder of the narrative.

This story progresses in a dramatic structure, similar to the previous two. There are three main characters sharing a simple, communal event in the man's driveway. Carver provides appropriate breaks in the narrative to indicate passage of time and to introduce characters arriving on the stationary set. The names of the characters in the story accentuate the anonymity of the people to the reader. They are simply known as the man, the boy, and the girl. These descriptions are in line with the frame of knowledge a random passerby would have of these people. From a casual, fleeting viewpoint, not much else could be known. In addition, classifying these three characters by only age and gender thus prejudices the reader with certain limitations regarding their possible relationships.

The young couple indicate their intention to purchase the items in the driveway, and the man agrees to a sale. The man's reactions to the young couple's offers suggest to the reader that he was not initially interested in holding a garage sale. However, for someone searching for a drastic change of lifestyle, it does not seem like a bad idea. The man's only apparent desire is for change. However, in this case, instead of talking about leaving his surroundings, he seems to be considering the results of his surroundings leaving him. As he announces to the young couple as they haggle over the price of his furniture, "everything goes" (Carver, 159).

The man's motivation for his bizarre behavior is never explicitly stated in the story. One may assume, however, that his action is the aftermath of a distressing domestic situation. The only clue the man gives the reader that something unusual had occurred is through the following exchange:

> "Those people over there, they're watching," she said.
> "It's okay," the man said. "It's my place," he said.
> "Let them watch," the girl said.
> "That's right," the man said. "They thought they'd seen everything over here. But they haven't seen this, have they?" he said. (Carver, 160–61)

The implications of voyeurism in this passage are fairly obvious. The neighbors watching the dancing and drinking in the man's driveway could easily be Carver's readers. Here the characters are the objects of a voyeur, as well as willing exhibitionists themselves.

For Freud the ego's defense mechanism uses the senses to combat the instincts. Aligning voyeurism with sadism and exhibitionism with masochism, Freud states in "Instincts and Their Vicissitudes" that "reversal of an instinct into its opposite resolves on closer examination into two different processes: a change from activity to passivity, and a reversal of its content" (127). Although, at first glance, the actions of the protagonist of this story seem to be an exercise in passive disintegration, it becomes apparent that his act of exhibitionism is, likely, his most active attempt at reassembly. The reader is not provided enough information to make clear-cut judgments about the circumstances of the characters. All one can see is the absence, in which "man's desire is the Other's desire" (Lacan, "The Subversion of the Subject," 300). As the girl dances with the man during the final scene, she reveals all one can ever know about them and all they need to know about themselves—"'You must be desperate or something,' she said" (Carver, 161).

The characters of "Why Don't You Dance?" have given up all previous attempts at hiding their desperation. They are, actively, putting it all on display. In his discussion of the knowledge gained through the act of voyeurism in the contemporary media, Clay Calvert gauges the frequency of America's attention to "unsuspecting people in a state of *distress* rather than a state of *undress*" (*Voyeur Nation*, 50). In the case of the lines of sight offered by Carver, the gaze, however pleasurable for the reader, does not exploit. It informs in the only way possible for these individuals—through the presentation of one fragment of subjectivity at a time. There is little doubt that these subjects are victims, but not of the voyeur. They are victims of a more pervasive and destructive entity—the disparity between their circumstances and their subjectivity.

The crisis of the speaking subject is at the heart of psychoanalysis. As opposed to merely projecting the image of subjectivity, the voyeuristic gaze contributes to its construction. As the characters acquire more knowledge about themselves and their circumstances, the trajectory of the voyeur's line of sight shifts in angle and scope. The reader's image changes because the characters do, in fact, change. Even when the change in view is beyond the character's field of vision, the voyeur is contributing to the assemblage of subjectivity.

In Raymond Carver's work, the knowledge acquired by the reader corresponds to what his characters, as subjects, learn about themselves. Although Carver's minimalist style appears to limit the development of his characters, much more is revealed in the continuous shifting of the voyeuristic gaze. In "The Transference and the Drive," Lacan contends, as a result of this constant flux in position of subject and object, "What the voyeur is looking for and finds is merely a shadow, a shadow behind the curtain" (182). Lacan's examination of the instability of subject and object, and the resulting fantasy which produces the voyeuristic effect, is reflected in Carver's juxtaposition of character to character and, by extension, character to reader. In light of the voyeur's limited access to the lives of Carver's subjects, it becomes the reader's responsibility to determine the interior motivations of these characters through an analysis of their emotional histories, within the framework of the author's choice to submit these lives to the reader.

As Arthur A. Brown has stated in his examination of the postmodern implications of Carver's fiction, "Seeing is intrinsically related to being. The writer's art is not separate from existence but is a part of it, not merely because it is the writer's task to see clearly and to show what he sees to others, but because seeing is a part of all of our lives" ("Raymond Carver," 127). As a conscious manifestation of unconscious desires, the fragmented state of Carver's fiction is, in fact, a mirror of his own subjectivity. If art is, according to Freud, "a path that leads back from phantasy to reality" ("The Paths to Symptom-Formation," 375), the artist then requires the presence of the voyeur to complete the bridge. As an image of misrecognition, and therefore absent from the picture, the Lacanian subject can find adequate illumination only within the gaze of the voyeur.

In Carver's fiction the reader takes on the role of a voyeur to gain knowledge as well as contemplate the source of that knowledge. Through a minimalist structure of narrative and a dramatic essence to the setting, Carver maintains a distinct distance among his characters, as well as between them and the reader. This proximity, within the field of the gaze, is what allows the reader to complete the image by reflecting the misrecognition of the subject. As Raymond Carver expressed in a 1986 interview, "It is the image, and the emotion that goes with that image—that's what's important" (Alton, "What We Talk About," 7). Throughout these works Carver provides "only spare, disjunctive details which we ourselves as readers must assemble" (Dickstein, 508). One may only watch these people live and interact from a comfortable distance in a series of moments to find one's own definition of truth. Raymond Carver provides an opportunity for his reader to return to Lacan's mirror. Only a realization of the image, as a representation and constitution of the ego, can lead a subject to awareness. Here, in Carver's world, the reader must perpetually watch the *other*, and, in turn, knowingly be watched, if there is any hope to recognize the *self.*

Works Cited

Alton, John. "What We Talk about When We Talk about Literature: An Interview with Raymond Carver." *Chicago Review* 36, no. 2 (1988): 4–21.

Bethea, Arthur F. *Technique and Sensibility in the Fiction and Poetry of Raymond Carver.* New York: Routledge, 2001.

Brook, Peter. *The Empty Space.* New York: Atheneum, 1981.

Brown, Arthur A. "Raymond Carver and Postmodern Humanism." *Critique* 31 (1990): 125–36.

Calvert, Clay. *Voyeur Nation.* Boulder, Colo.: Westview, 2000.

Carver, Raymond. *Where I'm Calling From: New and Selected Stories.* New York: Vintage, 1989.

Clark, Miriam Marty. "Raymond Carver's Monologic Imagination." *Modern Fiction Studies* 37 (1991): 240–46.

Dickstein, Morris. "The Pursuit for the Ordinary." *Partisan Review* 58 (1991): 506–13.

Freud, Sigmund. "Instincts and Their Vicissitudes." In Sigmund Freud, *The Standard Edition of the Complete Psychological Works*, 14:117–40.

———. "The Paths to Symptom-Formation." In Freud, *The Standard Edition of the Complete Psychological Works*, 16:358–77.

———. "The Sexual Aberrations." In *Three Essays on the Theory of Sexuality*, trans. and ed. James Strachey, 1–38. New York: Basic Books, 1962.

———. "The Sexual Life of Human Beings." In Freud, *The Complete Psychological Works*, 16:303–19.

———. *The Standard Edition of the Complete Psychological Works of Sigmund Freud*, trans. and ed. James Strachey. 24 vols. London: Hogarth, 1953–74.

Hagen, Uta. *A Challenge for the Actor.* New York: Macmillan, 1991.

Hathcock, Nelson. "'The Possibility of Resurrection': Re-Vision in Carver's 'Feathers' and 'Cathedral.'" *Studies in Short Fiction* 28 (1991): 31–39.

Kelly, Dorothy. *Telling Glances: Voyeurism in the French Novel.* New Brunswick, N.J.: Rutgers University Press, 1992.

Krist, Gary. "Fiction Chronicle." *Hudson Review* 42 (1989): 125–32.

Kristeva, Julia. *Intimate Revolt: The Powers and Limits of Psychoanalysis*, trans. Jeanine Herman. Vol. 2. New York: Columbia University Press, 2002.

Lacan, Jacques. *Ecrits: A Selection*, trans. Bruce Fink. New York: Norton, 2004.

———. *The Four Fundamental Concepts of Psychoanalysis*, trans. Alan Sheridan, ed. Jacques-Alain Miller. New York: Norton, 1998.

———. "The Mirror Stage as Formative of the *I* Function." In Lacan, *Ecrits*, 3–9.

———. "Of the Gaze as *Objet Petit a*." In Lacan, *Four Fundamental Concepts*, 67–119.

———. "The Subversion of the Subject and the Dialectic of Desire in the Freudian Unconscious." In Lacan, *Ecrits*, 281–312.

———. "The Transference and the Drive." In Lacan, *Four Fundamental Concepts*, 123–200.

Metz, Christian. *The Imaginary Signifier: Psychoanalysis and the Cinema*, trans. Celia Britton et al. Bloomington: Indiana University Press, 1982.

Meyer, Adam. "Now You See Him, Now You Don't, Now You Do Again: The Evolution of Raymond Carver's Minimalism." *Critique* 30 (1989): 239–50.

Mulvey, Laura. "Visual Pleasure and the Narrative Cinema." In Laura Mulvey, *Visual and Other Pleasures*, 14–26. Bloomington: Indiana University Press, 1989.

Nesset, Kirk. "'This Word Love': Sexual Politics and Silence in Early Raymond Carver." *American Literature* 63 (1991): 292–313.

Runyon, Randolph Paul. *Reading Raymond Carver.* Syracuse, N.Y.: Syracuse University Press, 1992.

Schwartz, Regina. "Through the Optic Glass: Voyeurism and *Paradise Lost*." In *Desire in the Renaissance: Psychoanalysis and Literature*, ed. Valeria Finucci and Regina Schwartz, 146–66. Princeton, N.J.: Princeton University Press, 1994.

Stull, William L. "Beyond Hopelessville: Another Side of Raymond Carver." *Philological Quarterly* 64, no. 1 (Winter 1985): 1–13.

Trussler, Michael. "The Narrowed Voice: Minimalism and Raymond Carver." *Studies in Short Fiction* 31 (1994): 23–36.

Weber, Bruce. "Raymond Carver: A Chronicler of Blue-Collar Despair." *New York Times Magazine*, June 24, 1984, 36–50.

Abigail L. Bowers

Seeing Ourselves from the Outside

Voyeuristic Empathy in Raymond Carver's
Will You Please Be Quiet, Please?

Raymond Carver's fiction charts a real world where people struggle daily for dignity and self-respect. In 1976 Carver published the collection of short stories *Will You Please Be Quiet, Please?* In this collection Carver's world appears as a place where the capacity for need, violence, and obsession overtakes the lives of those he writes about, the working class of America. Carver's short fiction suggests that our lives are reflected by the world in which we live, as well as the notion that human beings tend to measure their own lives through the accomplishments of others. The comparison of our lives to others' lives presents a voyeuristic sensibility; as a result, the experience of seeing ourselves from outside ourselves can have a peculiarly transforming impact. Raymond Carver presents us with characters we not only feel sympathy for but can empathize with as well. This uncomfortable empathy that Carver creates makes his voice unique in the world of literature and also proves him to be a driving force in the world of American fiction emerging in the 1970s.

A distinct failure of communication acts as Carver's theme. Arthur M. Saltzman states that these stories may have unremarkable phrasings, but that "their urgency cannot be underestimated. Most telling in this regard may be the title that heads the volume and connotes both the ineffectuality and the threat of communication. Intimacy is either impossible to achieve or too terrible to bear . . . Carver's characters are victims of anguishes they can neither brave nor name, only suffer" (Saltzman, *Understanding Raymond Carver*, 21). Carver places his characters in moments they are aware of but refuse to question. For them, these situations develop into a form of communication that is unbearable. Silence becomes the best syntax of all, and this absence of communication implies stagnation on the part of Carver's characters. Carver suggests through his articulations of this working-class world a growing need for understanding of these characters.

Simply stated, these blue-collar-class characters make the plots of his stories thick with meaning. Robert Towers notes that the characters in *Will You Please Be Quiet, Please?* are "displayed before us [as] a series of delicately mounted specimens taken from a population—a vast population—that most often eludes or falls through the net of our fiction. Carver's people are not grotesque or notably eccentric, nor rascally or amusingly loquacious. . . . Their ordinariness is unredeemed" ("Low Rent Tragedies," 37). Carver's characters have the distinction of being people we know: economically depressed human beings who cannot, through circumstance or lack of trying, pull themselves out of their current situation. David Boxer and Cassandra Phillips note that Carver's characters are "the unemployed and the unhappily employed, laconic members of the non-upwardly mobile working and middle classes . . . [their] lives are in suspended animation, verging on disarray" (*Will You Please*," 76). This places them in an almost unreal world, as the suspended animation suggested by Boxer and Phillips illustrates a place where people are between jobs, stories, or even sleep.

Carver's characters seem to be detached from humanity, because they seem to lack the ability to truly transform their lives. Dean Flower points out that the security of Carver's characters is often threatened, and usually contains the terror at the deadly entrapments of life and their unconscious attempts to erase this threat ("Fiction Chronicle," 282). Surrounding these stories is a discomfiture that Gary L. Fisketjon refers to as "the terrifying implications of Normal Life, apparently serene but filled with a desperate and hopeless sense of something-gone-wrong. . . . The circumstances vary from story to story, but common to all is a soured domesticity" ("Normal Nightmares," 132). Carver's characters may never do anything; however, readers can closely identify with them, and this makes his stories terrifying. Morton Marcus notes

> What was astonishing, even unique about Ray's stories . . . was not that they engaged everyday American life and went behind the doors of suburban middle-class and blue-collar homes, but that they were scenarios of our worst dreams about the reality of our neighbors' existences, scenarios about the spiritual barrenness at the heart of American life which the majority of us were living, whether we admitted it or not. ("All-American Nightmares," 57)

As Marcus says, readers would rather not admit that they can sense something of themselves in these narratives, because what Fisketjon calls "the terrifying implications of Normal Life" can seem, at times, extremely close to the surface.

Of course, some feel that Carver's characters are written in ways that allow them to understand the situation they are in. Ann Beattie, in a review of *Will You Please Be Quiet, Please?*, notes, "Whatever Carver's characters are 'willing to be,' it never happens: what they don't will . . . is sure to undo them. Moreover, the characters are detached from themselves; their minds are separated from what actions they will (or can) take"; Beattie further states that they are "still at the mercy of the wind, or whatever is going to overcome them" ("Carver's *Furious Seasons*," 179). However, Carver does not present his characters in a way that evokes pity from the reader; rather, as Thomas R. Edwards notes, "Other writers might invite us to pity the[m]—how little they need to arouse their diminished selves, but Carver does not pity them. His tight, laconic stories illuminated a kind of life that sophisticated fiction seldom deals with without condescension or sentimentality" ("The Short View," 36). No pity exists in these stories, as Carver's style allows for a realistic view to be taken. Instead of evoking sympathy, though, empathy arises from the impression of appearing "mundane" in an "ordinary" world.

The empathy felt by the reader is often expressed by the writer as well. Readers experience a certain level of discomfiture when perusing *Will You Please Be Quiet, Please?* because Raymond Carver highlights desperate circumstances of the working- and lower-middle-class members of society, who largely make up the United States. These characters are always people we know, and instead of curling up with a tale of fantasy, Carver delivers a realistic blow impossible to overlook, as well as impossible not to feel. As Carver notes, "I've known people like this all my life. Essentially, I *am* one of those confused, befuddled people, I come from people like that, those are the people I've worked with and earned my living beside for years" (McCaffery and Gregory, "An Interview with Raymond Carver," 112). Indeed, Carver's characters are realistic, uncomfortably so, and he manages to carefully express both the underside of the plebeian world and an abiding humanism for the circumstances of their lives. He carefully and tactfully deals with their confusion and befuddlement as they travel down a road laced with alcohol, drugs, sex, infidelity, and unemployment in order to find some sort of significance to their seemingly meaningless lives. Carver delicately captures the voice of what seems to be an inferior class, and his style becomes indicative of a writer sympathetic, as well as empathetic, to the lives he portrays on paper. This becomes especially evident in "Fat," "They're Not Your Husband," and "Neighbors."

"Fat" details the story of a waitress relating a story to her friend Rita. She tells Rita of a particular customer, a fat man, who came into the restaurant while she was working. She explains, "This fat man is the fattest person I have ever seen, though he is neat-appearing and well dressed enough. Everything about him is big. But it is the fingers I remember best. . . . They look three times the size of a normal person's fingers—long, thick, creamy fingers" (3). The narrator's attitude alters, however, throughout her telling of the story. She begins to sympathize with the fat man for reasons that she cannot comprehend, not recognizing that her sympathy actually develops into empathy. Like the fat man, she lives a life that she feels somewhat trapped in, and although she is cognizant of the need for change, the actual ability to do so will evade her.

Carver's genius lies in simple statements; in fact, it is through the paring down of sentences that the true meaning comes out. For example, when the narrator serves the fat man his dessert, he attempts to explain himself:

Thank you, he says.

You are very welcome, I say—and a feeling comes over me.

Believe it or not, he says, we have not always eaten like this.

Me, I eat and I eat and I can't gain, I say. I'd like to gain, I say.

No, he says. If we had our choice, no. But there is no choice. (7)

This encounter leaves an impression on the waitress, as she tells Rita, "I know now I was after something. But I don't know what" (6), and what she does not realize is that she now sees others around her differently. When the fat man comments on the lack of choice, it becomes clear that life, at times, is entirely out of our hands; that is, "we can not grab the 'nature' lying at the center of us" (Bracken, "Review," 170). The waitress, who knows only that she is after something, does not grasp that her very nature transforms when she waits on the fat man. Furthermore, the differences between her and him become based on the walks of life—the socioeconomic situations—from which they come.

This encounter with the fat man affects the waitress profoundly, and she now finds herself identifying with him, although she is unsure why. This identification is the crux of the story, because the waitress comes to an awareness that she no longer relates to those around her. Instead, she remarks that Rita seems to be waiting for something, but she is unsure what. In fact, the story ends with the narrator musing, "*Waiting for what?* I'd like to know. It is August. My life is going to change. I feel it" (8, emphasis Carver's). However, her life has already been transformed, although she does not appreciate it. Her wakefulness, displayed through her feeling that her life will alter in some way, represents a sort of awakening to the tenuousness of human connection (Boxer and Phillips, 85). Her encounter and subsequent empathy with the fat man have caused her dissatisfaction with her proletarian life, particularly her life as a waitress.

A definite pathos exists in this story, as well as in much of Carver's other fiction, through the hope that the narrator, in her brief encounter with the large man, manages to glimpse a world beyond the one in where she now feels emotionally suffocated. Carver conveys this theme through a variety of careful techniques, particularly that of oral communication. Carver notes in an interview with John Alton that "Fat" is based on "the idea of people looking on, or people looking *through* something at someone else—a real and a metaphorical frame for the story" ("What We Talk About," 155, emphasis Carver's). The narrator frames the story through her verbalization of her encounter to Rita, although she does not feel she explains it well. After all, Rita seems not to understand the point of the fat man, and truthfully, neither does the narrator. However, it is equally important to recognize that she waits tables at a busy diner, where oral communication constantly takes place in the giving and taking of orders, and the fat man is not her only customer. Adam Meyer comments that Carver "has the narrator note that, when the fat man sat down at her station, she also had [other customers]. Through his empathy, Carver demonstrates the value he places on the working class, people who would ordinarily not be deemed worthy of serious literary consideration" (*Raymond Carver*, 33). The concept of communication within this blue-collar class is seen as a stunted procedure.

The actual communication that does seem to take place, however, is the silent one between the waitress and her obese customer. The narrator remarks, "He has this way of speaking—strange, don't you know. And he makes a little puffing sound every so often" (3). The strange way of speaking to which the narrator refers is the fat man's use of "we" instead of "I." She starts to see him as more human when he tells her, "we don't eat like this all the time. . . . You'll have to excuse us," to which she replies, "Don't think a thing about it, please . . . I like to see a man eat and enjoy himself." The fat man replies, "I guess that's what you'd call it" (5). Although the two talk, the diction uttered separates them on more levels than his large body and her small one. He shows her kindness, and in turn, she does the same. The two truly correspond through some sort of understanding, particularly when this communication has the narrator believing that someday her life will change.

This indication of variation, of something different coming into the narrator's life, illustrates itself through her relationship, and subsequent identification, with the fat man. This random acquaintance provides her with a way to reflect on her own life and turns into a catalyst that sets in motion something larger and more elemental than she has ever encountered before (Edwards, 35). Nevertheless, the waitress is not necessarily overwhelmed by this, as Thomas R. Edwards suggests. Rather, this large, elemental "something" appears in the form of a large man, and as a result of this meeting—and the empathy sparked within her—she avoids becoming overwhelmed. They are both trapped in some way, he by his large body and she by her job and those around her. She grasps the significance of this meeting but is unsure of what to do with her newfound realization. Her epiphany is brought about due to the fat man's treatment of her: "Perhaps it is the surprising dignity and pleasantness of the fat man that is so remarkable—one can easily surmise what sort of coarse treatment she is accustomed to—and that causes her to defend him . . . [however] she still characterizes herself as passive, waiting for transformation" (Saltzman, 24). The narrator glimpses kindness and compassion, even tests it out herself, but remains locked in her inability to communicate these actions, so she waits for something else to happen. Though she is locked in the syntax of silence as to how to do so, the fact that she knows life will transform, or needs to, gives hope that the revolution she seemingly waits for will occur.

Carver's story "They're Not Your Husband" also relates an account of people for whom a random encounter at a diner propels them to reevaluate their relationship. The man in this story experiences the transformation, but it is not one that bodes well emotionally for him. The story chronicles a waitress, Doreen, and her out-of-work salesman husband, Earl. Although Earl goes on several job interviews, the story actually details his displeasure at Doreen's physical appearance after he overhears a conversation between two men about her. In other words, and not unlike the narrator in "Fat," Earl sees himself and his wife differently once he catches an indication of how others view her. As a result of this random exchange, Earl implores her to lose weight. The story centers around her weight loss and his subsequent obsession with having men make comments about Doreen's shrinking figure.

Although the image of Earl and Doreen's diminished lives would give the impression of being a pathetic tale, Carver manages to have the story come off as anything but that. The tight prose allows for action to take place: although Doreen's actual weight loss is not documented in numbers, Carver comments on it through his description of her as she loses pounds. Doreen's overall tiredness from not eating, her need to buy a uniform that fits her shrinking body, and the fact that people at the diner are saying she is "too pale" and that she "do[esn't] look like herself" (27) allow for documentation to take place without overwhelming detail. Robert Towers remarks that Carver's style is "sternly denotative, allowing no scope for metaphor or linguistic exuberance. A certain price is paid, of course, for this asceticism: one misses the sudden bursts of vivid or lurid imagery that light up some of the greatest stories in our literature" (36). These simple descriptions may be void, as Towers suggests, but to say that Carver's style leaves no room for metaphor is inaccurate. He does not need to go into graphic, detailed description about Doreen's weight loss; rather, he simply uses the statements others make to her in order to get the picture across. Carver's minuscule metaphor is more powerful than any description that could actually be given, and it evokes a reaction in the reader without being overly demonstrative.

In Carver's dismal blue-collar world, being out of work is synonymous with being out of control. Consequently, when people are unemployed, they feel the need to have power over something. Earl feels inadequate in his own life, so Carver paints this inadequacy through Earl's need to dominate Doreen in some way. This authority identifies itself when Earl buys a scale and records Doreen's progress weekly. When he catches her eating scrambled eggs and bacon one day, he erupts:

> "What are you doing?" Earl said.
> She continued to chew the food, cheeks puffed. But then she spit everything into a napkin.
> "I couldn't help myself."
> "Slob," Earl said. "*Go ahead, eat! Go on!*" He went to the bedroom, closed the door, and lay on the covers. He could still hear the television. He put his hands behind his head and stared at the ceiling.

She opened the door.

"I'm going to try again," Doreen said.

"Okay," he said. (26, emphasis Carver's)

Earl's need for power, and his inability to communicate the real issue with himself, clearly is not constructive for his relationship with his wife. This erupts into a verbal violence, and although he does not strike her, his name-calling forces Doreen to feel guilty and return to her diet. At the end of the story, however, no one takes note of Doreen. This causes Earl to find himself a failure once again, as he can manage Doreen but not the reactions to her slimmer figure. He finds, at the end of the story, that he cannot even sell his wife to other men. Our empathy is evoked through the desperation he feels, and the conviction that we have all, at one point or another in our lives, failed at something so seemingly insignificant. This portrait is a more disheartening view of the human condition than that in "Fat," but again, Carver manages to create an empathy with both Earl and Doreen that prevents us from feeling superior. These are wounded human beings caught in circumstances that are out of their control (in spite of Earl's attempts at such with his wife), and Carver seems to say to his audience, "Patronize them at your own risk."

The voice of the common resounds throughout Carver's fiction, and his characters are stuck in a world where mobility is stagnant. Much like the epiphany of the waitress in "Fat," the knowledge that something needs to transform exists, but the inability to actually do so thematizes these characters in "They're Not Your Husband." Doreen loses weight, but the situation presented at the beginning—the two men mocking her large butt—never resolves itself. Earl's satisfaction becomes short-lived as he comprehends that no one else seems to think that he has "something special." The waitress in "Fat" grasps that her life will, someday, change; however, she is unaware that it already has. Earl, Doreen, and the waitress in "Fat" are all in the same place—the stagnant world of a depressed working class, where upward mobility in any way, shape, or form is thought about briefly and quickly dismissed.

The question then arises: What would happen if variation actually were to occur in Carver's stories? One of Carver's best-known tales from *Will You Please Be Quiet, Please?* is "Neighbors," a story about an ordinary couple, Bill and Arlene Miller, who agree to cat-sit for their neighbors, Harriet and Jim Stone, while they are away on vacation. The Millers are an "ordinary" couple, with jobs as a bookkeeper and a secretary, whereas Jim Stone is a salesman for a machine-parts firm and often manages to combine his business trips with pleasure. On this particular trip, the Stones would be away for ten days, leaving the Millers to attend to their apartment, cat, and plants (9). However, obsessed with their neighbors' lives, the actions of the Millers can be cataloged under the weird, and the uncannily familiar, as Carver explores what people do—and feel—when no one is looking.

As the Millers take care of the Stones' apartment, Bill and Arlene experience a metamorphosis. Bill assumes "cat duty" the first night, and as he enters the apartment, he notices that the air is "already heavy and vaguely sweet" (10). This intrigues him, so he wanders throughout the house, eventually stealing small things such as a bottle of Harriet's medication, as well as drinking their liquor and trying on their clothes. Arlene is not immune to the draw of her neighbors' lives either and exhibits the same sort of voyeuristic behavior as Bill, telling him, "It's funny. You know—to go in someone's place like that." Bill agrees and figures out that Arlene too has been enjoying the Stones' apartment (15). This sparks the Millers' libido, and when Arlene realizes that she has forgotten to feed the cat one night, Carver notes: "'Oh damn,' she said. 'Damn, damn,' she sang, girlishly clapping her hands. 'I just remembered. I really and truly forgot to do what I went over there to do. I didn't feed Kitty or do any watering.' She looked at him. 'Isn't that stupid?' 'I don't think so,' he said. 'Just a minute. I'll get my cigarettes and go back with you'" (15). Obviously Bill and Arlene delight in her absentmindedness, and they look forward to the notion of "becoming" someone else in their neighbors' apartment, even if only for a little while.

The communication between Bill and Arlene shatters on the revelation that they are locked out of the place they most want to be in. With the key to the apartment locked inside, Carver ends the story with the couple clinging together in the hall. Arlene's "lips were parted, and her breathing was hard, expectant. He opened his arms and she moved into them. 'Don't worry,' he said into her ear. 'For God's sake, don't worry.' They stayed there. They held each other. They leaned into the door as if against a wind, and braced themselves" (16). The Millers brace themselves for more than just an explanation to their neighbors about why the cat has gone unfed: thanks to their own carelessness and excitement, they are preparing themselves for a future that converts into one just as previously bleak as it had looked. Adam Meyer notes that their relationship "had indeed been strengthened by their voyeurism and playacting, but whether this new excitement can be maintained remains very much in doubt; as the final image suggests, permanently reinvigorating their lives will be quite a struggle" (38). Dependent on the alternate life they had created through the use of their neighbors' apartment, Bill and Arlene are once again locked into a life where connection and conversation languish. As Saltzman observes, "Shaken, they cling to one another, exposed and vulnerable as a postlapsarian Adam and Eve cast out of Paradise" (26). The Millers can never return to the lives they once inhabited, because their communication changed in such a way that prevents any of their old life to creep back in. They are no longer the people they once were, and as Saltzman notes, Bill and Arlene are cast out of Paradise through their own carelessness.

The disenfranchisement of the Millers evidences itself through their desperation at wanting to be in a paradise created through a voyeuristic means. Carver's reflective use of the common jobs of the Millers—a bookkeeper and a secretary —exacerbates the need for his characters to grasp at happiness through these voyeuristic means, and when this is taken away, the impression that the Millers were once perfectly content with their lives is forgotten. Carver points out, "Bill and Arlene Miller *were* a happy couple" (9, emphasis mine). Although they *were* a happy couple, the Millers are not satisfied with their thoroughly "average" life. As a result, they feel the need to steal from the Stones, adopting their life by lounging on their bed, eating their food, and taking their pills. They are not diminished, however. The suggestion that an escape from their ordinary lives through the adoption of their neighbors' presents itself, and when the possibility of this newfound knowledge is stripped from them, Bill and Arlene must prepare themselves. As Ann Beattie notes, the Millers "are on the brink of something. . . . No matter that they might get the superintendent to let them in—by this point in the story the reader, too, has forgotten the real and practical world; in their horror and surprise, they clutch each other in the hallway" (178). The violence of the world descends on them, and they are expelled from their own "Eden" because of the sins they gain awareness as having committed. The practical world ceases to exist, and the reader, along with the Millers, gets caught up in the horror and the realization of what has actually happened throughout the course of the story: voyeurism at its finest, and the punishment awarded for wanting to escape a dismal life.

Furthermore, we feel empathy for the Millers because they think their lives are the ones that are diminished. The intimacy forged by the couple evidences itself only when they can take off the cloak of their old lives and adopt that of their neighbors. The scene in the hall, with the two clinging to each other, shows another form of communication breakdown. The question remains as to whether or not the Millers will ever be able to get back their lives as they were, and if they do, everything will be different. The communication—physical, mental, and emotional—that had flowed between them thanks to the Stones' apartment has been halted by their own carelessness. We as readers know that they can easily get a key, as Beattie suggests; however, we also know the fear and shame associated with actually going to ask for the key. The plight of the Millers lies in the fact that they hoped for too much, and tried to enhance their lives by adopting that of the Stones.

The three stories echo several similar themes. The narrator in "Fat" is, after all, a waitress, and when shown kindness, she deciphers that something in her life needs to change, although she is unsure as to what this ought to be. Earl's inability and inadequacy in his own life mirror themselves in his desire to alter Doreen's appearance so he can hold onto "something special," only to come to terms with the fact that no one really cares, and that transformation has not effectively occurred. The Millers feel that the Stones' lives are much better than their own, which causes them to become erotically charged every time they enter their neighbors' apartment. The concept of wanting variation from a bleak and dismal life, and the inability for this to occur, reflects itself in each of the stories from *Will You Please Be Quiet, Please?* It is not through lack of trying, however. Rather, a lack of understanding that modification has transpired, in some way or another, and what to do with this, leaves Carver's characters clueless and lost.

Each story also explores interaction between various groups of people in a working and middle-class world, and what happens when that communication breakdown exposes itself. A feeling of hopelessness erupts, but there is also a feeling of a conversion poised to occur, although it probably will not. However, Carver's characters are never aware of what this is or how it can happen, so they remain stagnant in their lives. Dean Flower suggests, "As in a relentless close-up, we hear and see exactly what these people do, but why they do it—or whether anything intelligible goes through their minds as they do it—we cannot confidently explain. Carver's is an art of disconcerting" (282), and although Carver does not record his characters' thoughts, the actions he explores speak volumes. We do not really need to have the reasoning behind their actions spelled out for us; rather, we can guess at them, and the compulsion of renovation is often the result of something or someone coming along to disrupt their lives. This, in turn, forces a confrontation with a hidden or suppressed part of their characters (Boxer and Phillips, 84), and the reactions to these outside events are explanation enough as to why Carver's characters act the way they do.

Arthur Saltzman notes that the characters in Carver's *Will You Please Be Quiet, Please?* always attempt to fortify themselves, but this never happens. In fact, these attempts frequently turn into missions of appropriation. Despairing of meaningful engagements, the protagonists become obsessed with vicariousness. They stake their fates on the hope that prospects are not so desolate on the other side. Thus, they are more voyeuristic than visionary, for they barely hesitate to jeopardize their own identities in deference to petty intrigues or somewhat more exotic personalities (Saltzman, 22). This voyeurism is not necessarily of a sexual nature, however. Carver's characters are voyeuristic in the sense that they wish to have someone else's life, because they are unable to comprehend their own. It becomes the need and want of something distant and unnamed, an unattainable sense of self (Boxer and Phillips, 76). At the same time, the characters will latch onto a kindness—any kindness—on which to structure their lives around. These lives are measured in desperation that reflects itself in the bleak, gloomy, economically depressed world around them, although a hope endures that something, anything, will transform. However, Carver's characters lack the power to modify their lives themselves, because they lack the knowledge of what that alteration needs to be. To them, kindness is, at times, so foreign that they have no clue what to do with it when they happen to stumble across it.

Raymond Carver's collection *Will You Please Be Quiet, Please?* places readers in a discomfiting space. Instead of merely reading a story and being able to put it aside, readers find themselves in an uncomfortable position. Like the narrator of "Fat," they too might be waiting for their lives to change, and probably will not appreciate that through Carver's tight prose, they already have. There is an emphatic, and empathetic, response to Carver's characters, though, thanks to this tight prose and his keen eye for common small details that we imagine as unique to our own circumstances and personal histories. We often forget that we are reading fiction and instead suspect that we are dealing with echoes of our own words and lives (Koehne, "Echoes of Our Lives," 9). This uncomfortable empathy that Carver creates makes his voice unique in the world of fiction, and it also proves him to be a driving force in the world of American fiction emerging in the 1970s. We find ourselves seeing ourselves from outside. Instead of pitying people in hopeless situations, such as those of the waitress in "Fat," Earl and Doreen in "They're Not Your Husband," and the Millers in "Neighbors," we find ourselves identifying with them. This voyeurism, although uncomfortable, creates in us a sense of belonging, and as Carver notes, "God, the country is filled with these people. They're good people. People doing the best they could" (Weber, "Raymond Carver," 92). In Carver's world, we all do the best we can, and he develops into the champion for the often discarded blue-collar and middle-class world.

Works Cited

Alton, John. "What We Talk about When We Talk about Literature: An Interview with Raymond Carver." In *Conversations*, ed. Gentry and Stull, 151–68.

Beattie, Ann. "Carver's *Furious Seasons*." *Canto* 2 (1978): 178–82.

Boxer, David, and Cassandra Phillips. "*Will You Please Be Quiet, Please?*: Voyeurism, Dissociation and the Art of Raymond Carver." *Iowa Review* 10, no. 3 (Summer 1979): 75–90.

Bracken, Tom. "Review of *Will You Please Be Quiet, Please?*" *Fiction International* 6/7 (1976): 169–70.

Carver, Raymond. *Will You Please Be Quiet, Please?* 1976. New York: Vintage Contemporaries, 1992.

Edwards, Thomas R. "The Short View." *New York Review of Books*, April 1, 1976, 34–36.

Fisketjon, Gary L. "Normal Nightmares." *Village Voice*, September 18, 1978, 132, 134.

Flower, Dean. "Fiction Chronicle." *Hudson Review* (Autumn 1977): 270–82.

Gentry, Marshall Bruce, and William L. Stull, eds. *Conversations with Raymond Carver.* Jackson: University Press of Mississippi, 1990.

Koehne, David. "Echoes of Our Lives." In *Conversations*, ed. Gentry and Stull, 8–10.

Marcus, Morton. "All-American Nightmares." In *Remembering Ray: A Composite Biography*, ed. William L. Stull and Maureen P. Carroll, 53–67. Santa Barbara, Calif.: Capra, 1993.

McCaffery, Larry, and Sinda Gregory. "An Interview with Raymond Carver." In *Alive and Writing: Interviews with American Authors of the 1980s*, ed. Larry McCaffery and Sinda Gregory, 66–82. Urbana: University of Illinois Press, 1987. Also in *Conversations*, ed. Gentry and Stull, 98–116.

Meyer, Adam. *Raymond Carver*. New York: Twayne, 1995.

Saltzman, Arthur M. *Understanding Raymond Carver*. Columbia: University of South Carolina Press, 1988.

Towers, Robert. "Low Rent Tragedies." *New York Review of Books*, May 14, 1981, 37–40.

Weber, Bruce. "Raymond Carver: A Chronicler of Blue-Collar Despair." In *Conversations*, ed. Gentry and Stull, 84–97.

Marc Oxoby

The Voluminous Impact of Television
in the Fiction of Raymond Carver

Raymond Carver's short story "After the Denim" opens on a scene of Edith Packer sitting in front of a television with its sound turned off. The image is a deceptive one, for the TV, by its very presence, speaks volumes, as it does in many of Carver's other stories. Carver's work rarely, if ever, seems directly about television, but by virtue of its attention to life in modern America, it does engage this medium that seems so ever-present in many Americans' lives. Indeed, although the lives of Carver's characters may not revolve around the TV, it is striking just how often it makes its presence felt. None would claim that Carver writes "about" television, but as an object it appears in Carver's short stories with a frequency at least equal to that of alcohol and cigarettes. Garnet Henderson's cover of one edition of Carver's collection seems telling. While the proverbial judging of a book by its cover carries some risks, the painting nevertheless reflects the presence of television in Carver's work quite well. It depicts a man seated at a table, cross-legged, cigarette in one hand, drink in the other, glancing backward at a television screen glowing with a picture of a cathedral. Clearly it is a depiction of the collection's title story, but Henderson's television is emphasized in a way that the medium is rarely discussed in Carver criticism. The TV, shining with blue light, which bathes the entire scene, glows from a black background. It is unclear what kind of surface the TV sits on; instead, it seems to float in the darkness. There is something almost mystical about the television in this depiction, and while very little comes across as mystical or otherworldly in Carver's work, TV does, nevertheless, seem to be an almost constant presence, casting its light on the figures who occupy his short stories. The characters are often only passingly aware of its presence, but their sometimes brief interactions with the medium resonate with the common themes that appear repeatedly in Carver's work.

It is by no means the intention of this essay to suggest that television is the driving force of all, or even any, of Carver's fiction. Rather, my argument is that television serves as a more significant character in his work than most critics have noted. Indeed Carver's fiction takes great pains to consider human relations in the modern age, and by that logic television, a defining object of modern living, likewise plays a defining role in Carver's work. I am not the first to explore this aspect of Carver's work, and this essay should be seen as an attempt to build on the opening salvo fired by Bill Mullen, in a study of

Carver's fiction which has unfortunately gone largely unanswered. Mullen, in "A Subtle Spectacle: Televisual Culture in the Short Stories of Raymond Carver," suggests that, while television does not provide a "key" to understanding Carver's fiction, it "may be read as a polyvalent sign in Carver's fiction that is important to its being readable as both formal minimalism and a variety of social realism in the tradition of working-class or proletariat writing" (101). He also suggests that "Carver's fiction, particularly in its structure and tone, may be read in part as a critique of televisual culture, yet one grounded primarily in television's capacity to dull or eliminate awareness of both class consciousness and class inequities in contemporary American culture" (101).

Mullen's essay provides an excellent starting point for the examination of TV in Carver's fiction, but, as good as the essay is, it is merely a starting point. As such, it is an essay with at least two limitations. The first one is that in its focus on *What We Talk about When We Talk about Love*, it fails to take into account Carver's later fiction and, by extension, fails to fully consider the evolution of television's presentation in his work. While this volume features many of Carver's best-known stories, and by its spareness represents what many see as the archetypal Carver style, a full understanding of the author's treatment of television's cultural impact must also take into account the evolved style of Carver's later work. Second, it is my contention that television does, despite Mullen's claim, provide a "key" to understanding Carver's fiction. It is by no means *the* key, to the exclusion of all other approaches to this body of work. Nor should it be thought of as providing all the answers to all of Carver's fictions; it is not, typically, a central focus of his stories. However, its presence does dovetail very well with significant themes and preoccupations that repeatedly appear in his work.

Mullen offers close readings of several stories, including "After the Denim," "Mr. Coffee and Mr. Fixit," and "Why Don't You Dance?," in the latter of which the focal characters find themselves sitting in the unnamed protagonist's front yard watching TV. This story, the first in *What We Talk about When We Talk about Love*, does indeed provide an excellent example of how TV manifests itself in Carver's fiction. The story's protagonist, we suspect, has recently seen his marriage collapse, and the movement of his bedroom furniture to his front yard is, it would appear, a response to this collapse. It is telling that the story opens with the protagonist looking at the furniture on the lawn from his kitchen, presumably through a window, evoking a frequent device in Carver's fiction. Indeed, "Why Don't You Dance?" bears considerable similarity to the story "Viewfinder," which features a narrator suffering in much the same way as the former story's protagonist. Among the stories in *What We Talk about When We Talk about Love* that make no direct mention of television, "Viewfinder" nevertheless offers a fine example of some of Carver's preoccupations that mesh with concerns about the impact of TV on American life. While it is true that neither of the stories' characters are depicted watching the tube, the act of spectating, as the title suggests, is vital to how human relationships are treated in Carver's fiction. The story tells of the interaction between the narrator and a man who attempts to sell the narrator a photograph of his own house. The conversation between the two is casual, friendly, but not without elements of reservation. Within the first page, the photographer, who has chrome hooks in the place of hands, refuses to explain the loss of his extremities, and the narrator, who indirectly offers coffee (only implying an offer with his statement "I just made coffee"), holds off offering any of the Jell-O he's also made (11). The conversations that follow are laced with the same kind of reluctance seen in this early exchange. The narrator, trying to defuse the photographer's defensiveness, tells him, "I was trying to make a connection" (13), but making a connection is something with which the narrator, who we discover has been abandoned by his wife and kids, has considerable difficulty.

The problem of forging personal connections is not something that necessarily need be associated with the notion of mediated experience, but in "Viewfinder" it is difficult to see it otherwise, whether there is a TV onstage or not. Consider, for instance, how the characters first see each other. The photographer captures the narrator through the camera, while the narrator has been watching the photographer through the window. In each case one character is watching the other, and each is doing so through a device that frames the other, a camera's viewfinder or a window's frame. The mediation, in this case, can be seen as a limitation on how extensively the characters may "connect," in the words of the narrator, or "sympathize," in the words of the photographer. This is even more pronounced when the narrator examines the photo of the house and sees "my head, *my head*, in there inside the kitchen window" (12). More than simply being separated from the photographer by the window pane or the viewfinder, the narrator now finds himself double-framed, looking at himself from the outside. The mediation, therefore, disrupts not only interpersonal relationships but also *intra*personal ones, so that the narrator seems to feel an abject distanciation from the self, apropos of the radical alteration of his life brought on by the dissolution of his family. The protagonist of "Why Don't You Dance?" similarly looks from kitchen to front yard and sees his life from outside of it, just as he watches the young couple dance. Mullen makes note of this, writing that "plot, structure, and narrative strategy in Carver's stories suggest constantly that people are paralyzed by their personal dilemmas *as if they were seeing them happen to someone else*" (103).

Although it is presumptuous to claim that these devices of mediation are the same as television, it is worth noting that many television critics—Jerry Mander, Bill McKibben, Neil Postman, Marie Winn, and others—have written of the medium in much the same way as the window frame and viewfinder are depicted in the story. We might consider, for instance, Mander's claim that "by the process of removing images from immediate experience and passing them instead through a machine, human beings lose one of the attributes that differentiate us from objects," what Mander calls "life" or, after Walter Benjamin, "aura" (*Four Arguments*, 287). The television, in short, makes those broadcast on it merely hollow images. Unlike Mander, however, Carver's characters do not need a device to make them feel hollow. They have, after all, plenty of other problems to do the job, whether a dissolving marriage, alcoholism, or death of a loved one. Instead, then, the mediation—be it by television, window frame, camera viewfinder, or other device—works principally metaphorically. And yet, these are devices that need to be considered in light of the society about which Carver writes—what has been characterized as a spectator society by figures such as the French situationalists, especially Guy Debord in his book *Society of the Spectacle*, and later refined, if perhaps overstated, in the work of Jean Baudrillard, particularly *Simulacra and Simulation*, in which he explores how mass media calls into question "the distinction between cause and effect, between active and passive, between subject and object" (30). Baudrillard frequently comments on how the lines between viewer and viewed are blurred, just as the "Viewfinder" narrator is both watcher and watched. Much of Carver's fiction deals with this notion of watching and being watched, both of which, it might be argued, attribute to Carver's minimalism, which gives but sketches of characters, incomplete conceptions, as often as not based merely on the visible image and actions of these characters. Certainly, in light of the spectator society, driven to such a state largely by the proliferation of televised images, the connection of TV to these other framing devices is not a particularly inconceivable stretch. This is certainly a connection that Mullen makes when he notes that the young couple of "Why Don't You Dance?" is "Framed in the windows of neighbors like actors in a television drama" (107).

Clearly, these concepts of a spectator society, of mediated experience, of television as an impediment to personal, human interaction, paint a rather dire picture of TV in Carver's fiction. And perhaps there is some truth to this, especially for a collection such as *What We Talk about When We Talk about Love*, in which, as Mullen points out, "People . . . watch television because they have nothing more productive to do, lack the intelligence or motivation to do otherwise, or wish to repress or deflect the ennui and alienation of their class-bound lives" (102). Likewise, Arthur A. Brown's contention that television is one thing that "substitutes for communion and is used by [Carver's] characters to block out the realization that they are dissociated from themselves and from others, especially those with whom they should be most intimate" ("Raymond Carver," 126), is clearly manifested in some of Carver's stories. However, it is perhaps too simple to look at television as a strict negative in Carver's stories, and this is particularly true of the later stories, in which the author exhibits a growing ambivalence toward TV.

Much has been made of the increased stylistic complexity of Carver's later fiction. The stark minimalism of his early work gives way, by the time we get to *Cathedral*, to a richer, more detailed style. Although they can still be considered minimalist, the stories are not pared down to the level of those in *What We Talk about When We Talk about Love*. Instead, as Bruce Weber has noted, they "are fuller, more generous and more optimistic" ("Raymond Carver," 96). Carver claimed that these stories felt *"finished* in a way I rarely felt about my stories previously" (McCaffery and Gregory, "An Interview with Raymond Carver," 103). They may have felt more "finished" to Carver because these later stories tend to be much more pointed in their conclusions. They tend toward a much greater sense of resolution than the early stories do, as apparent in "A Small, Good Thing," a radical rewrite of "The Bath," from *What We Talk about When We Talk about Love*. Much has been written contrasting these stories; for example, while "The Bath" concludes with a great deal of ambiguity, "A Small, Good Thing" concludes with a much greater sense of resolution. Confrontations are settled, and previously anonymous characters are fleshed out and named. In addition, television, nowhere mentioned in "The Bath," appears significantly in "A Small, Good Thing."

The differences, in terms of plotting and style, are quite striking in these stories, and in considering the role of television in these later stories, we must consider the changes in Carver's approach to his fiction. Mullen clearly associates Carver's style with the style of broadcast television, writing, "The flavorless monotone of television language . . . reverberates in both the numb monosyllables Carver's working-class characters speak in and the flat, deadpan expository authorial voice" (104). However, Mullen is writing primarily of the early, bare-bones stories. What, then, are we to make of the richer voice of Carver's later work? Are the *Cathedral* stories less concerned with the role of television than the earlier stories are? It would seem not. Mullen, writing on *What We Talk about When We Talk about Love*, notes that "televisions run constantly throughout the stories, providing a dramatic echo or counterpoint to the 'real life' action" (106). However, a close consideration of these collections reveals that TVs make their presence felt considerably more in *Cathedral*, the "dramatic echo" greatly amplified. In fact, in *What We Talk about When We Talk about Love*, television receives direct mention in only six of the seventeen stories, though as I have suggested in my consideration of "Viewfinder," television aesthetic can be seen as reverberating throughout this book's pieces. By contrast, televisions appear or receive direct mention in all of the stories in *Cathedral* save one ("Chef's House"). Moreover, in some of the twelve stories, TV provides more than a "counterpoint" to the action and in fact becomes a central plot or thematic element.

In the opening story of *Cathedral*, "Feathers," for example, television almost seems to constitute an additional guest at the dinner party depicted, one that seems more welcome than the pet peacock that intrudes on the scene. Upon arriving at the party, the narrator and his wife, Fran, find their host, Bud, watching a stock car race, which they leave on as they drink their aperitifs. Even more interesting than what is on the screen is what sits atop the appliance, "an old plaster-of-Paris cast of the most crooked, jaggedy teeth in the world" (12). The object, a cast of the teeth of Bud's wife, Olla, before he paid to have them fixed, is worth considering in light of the story's interest in physical appearances, which, one could certainly argue, is also television's stock-in-trade. The "horror-show teeth on top of the TV" (14) play into the contrast between the splendor of the peacock's feathers and the ugly visage of Bud's new baby. The narrator imagines Bud's thoughts—"So okay if it's ugly. It's our baby. And this is just a stage. Pretty soon there'll be another stage. There is this stage and then there is the next stage. Things will be okay in the long run, once all the stages have been gone through" (24)—in such a way that could be compared to how television programming passes, with one moment having little connection to that before, as Raymond Williams would have it, "a single irresponsible flow of images and feelings" (*Television*, 92). Randolph Paul Runyon notes how questions of sequence are garbled in "Feathers," just as they are in Williams's evaluation of American TV broadcasting. Runyon writes, "The more closely we examine these teeth . . . the more slippery the notion of before and after becomes. The mold, of course, is just a copy of the original: Olla's teeth as they were before the treatment began. So the 'before' is a copy, while the 'after' is the (revised) original" (*Reading Raymond Carver*, 139).

Television also plays an important role in "Careful," which early on presents a scene in which the protagonist, Lloyd, sees his landlady lying on the floor of her living room: "She seemed to be asleep. Then it occurred to him she might be dead. But the TV was going, so he chose to think she was asleep. He didn't know what to make of it" (112). Runyon writes, "It's hard for us to know what to make of it either, for nothing happens later in 'Careful' to integrate it into the story" (161). There is indeed a kind of disjuncture between this scene and the story, and in fact there is also a disjuncture within the logic of the passage. What is it, after all, about the TV that should suggest that the woman is alive? As the story unfolds, as Lloyd is increasingly plagued by a buildup of wax in his ear, there does seem to be some connection drawn between the activity of the television and that of life. Indeed, Lloyd, unconcerned with the electricity bill, for which he is not responsible, frequently leaves the TV set on "all day and all night. But he kept the volume down unless he saw something he wanted to watch" (113). For Lloyd, in the throes of alcoholism, essentially evicted from his house and forced to move into a confining apartment, the TV serves as company, bringing a kind of activity, a kind of life to an existence otherwise increasingly lonely and isolated. The soundlessness of the TV set is part of a trifold presentation of silence in the story. It obviously parallels Lloyd's loss of hearing resulting from the wax, but it also duplicates the lack of communication between Lloyd and Inez, his wife. The rift between them, forced by his alcoholism, is exemplified by Lloyd's reception of Inez's final words to him before leaving his apartment. Inez has helped Lloyd clear his ear of the wax, but nonetheless, "He didn't listen. He didn't want to. He watched her lips move until she'd said what she had to say" (123).

While television's presence is especially strong in "Feathers" and "Careful," a quick gloss of some of the other stories in *Cathedral* shows that its presence is not exceptional; in fact, it permeates the collection. In "Preservation," for instance, TV is part of the paralysis that afflicts the husband, "who had been on the sofa ever since he'd been terminated three months ago" (35). In "Vitamins" the narrator asks a returned veteran, "Is all that shit about Vietnam true we see on the TV?" (104), drawing attention to the way social and historical understandings are developed, in part, by media representation. In "Where I'm Calling From" the narrator, confined to a "drying out facility," imagines on New Year's Eve that his girlfriend is "probably at home watching the same thing on TV that I've been watching" (143), suggesting the commonality of televised experience. In "A Small, Good Thing," Ann, whose son lies comatose after being hit by a car, thinks in terms of television. After telling the doctor that she cannot leave her son alone in the hospital, she thinks "how unfair it was that the only words that came out were the sort of words used on TV shows where people were stunned by violent or sudden deaths" (81). It is almost as if Ann (and perhaps Carver?) is apologizing for the sentimentality of her response, for the melodrama that is so commonplace on TV and yet also can exist, or so Carver seems to suggest, on the other side, the "reality" side of the screen. All of these examples show the complexity of Carver's treatment of television in this later work. There is no singularity to its use as there seems to be in the early work. Instead the purpose served by television changes given the circumstances and the characters involved. The stories, when taken as a body, are ultimately encoded with a decided ambivalence toward the medium.

This ambivalence toward TV is nowhere stronger than in the title story, "Cathedral." In this story television's purpose seems to shift; even as it threatens to impede communication, as it does frequently elsewhere in Carver's fiction, it also serves as a kind of communal device. The story opens with the narrator explaining that an old friend of his wife's, a blind man, is coming to visit. He quickly reveals his trepidations about the visit, as well as his prejudices about the blind: "I wasn't enthusiastic about his visit. He was no one I knew.

And his being blind bothered me. My idea of blindness came from the movies. In the movies, the blind moved slowly and never laughed. Sometimes they were led by seeing-eye dogs. A blind man in my house was not something I looked forward to" (209). That the depiction of the blind in movies is a driving force in the narrator's preconceptions is striking in a story in which the related medium of TV plays such a large role. Mass media, to a great extent, feeds the narrator's prejudices, quite appropriately for a character who is depicted as a consistent consumer of media. He watches TV while waiting for Robert, the blind man, to arrive since he feels he has nothing else to do in the interim (214). Then, when he feels that the uncomfortable after-dinner conversation has run down, he leaves the table and turns on the TV, which provides a kind of escape from his discomfort, irritating though this act might be to his wife (218).

The narrator's embracing of visual media is given a sharp counterpoint in the form of his wife, who, it is revealed, has a kind of affinity toward the written and spoken word. We are told, for instance, how the wife first met Robert working for him as a reader of case files and reports at his office. The significance of this is not lost on Brown, who notes, "That her job was reading and her work with the blind man was performing a kind of social service are details that show that Carver wants us to be aware of reading and its humanist possibilities" (134). Additionally we are told that "She was always trying to write a poem. She wrote a poem or two every year, usually after something really important had happened to her." By contrast, the narrator, after revealing to the reader his dislike of his wife's poem about letting Robert touch her face, explains, "Maybe I just don't understand poetry" (210).

From these details, one could argue that "Cathedral" is yet another story that simply dismisses television as an impediment to communication and human relationship, a metaphor for disconnect. However, "Cathedral" does far more with the medium than this. Television actually serves as common ground between the narrator and Robert. This begins when Robert tells the wife that he has two TVs: "I have a color set and a black-and-white thing, an old relic. It's funny, but if I turn the TV on, and I'm always turning it on, I turn on the color set." The narrator is left speechless: "I didn't know what to say to that. I had absolutely nothing to say to that. No opinion. So I watched the news program and tried to listen to what the announcer was saying" (218–19). Ironically the inability to respond, to speak, provides the opening for the communion between the narrator and Robert that occurs at the end of the story. The narrator's expectations of the behavior of a blind man, created in part by messages conveyed by the media, have been undercut by the reality that even a blind man can "watch" a TV, and that this particular blind man does so, by his own admission, quite often. Television, the device if not the programming into which the narrator retreats, then, serves almost as a kind of Socratic dialogue, forcing the narrator to confront the falseness of his assumptions.

The story is brought to its climax when Robert joins the narrator in front of the television, watching, for lack of any other engaging program, "Something about the church and the Middle Ages. . . . Not your run-of-the-mill TV fare" (222). Carver devotes more verbiage to describing the images of cathedrals on the TV screen, complete with the motion of the cameras capturing the images, than he typically does describing the "real-world" settings of his stories. He is certainly able to describe the cathedrals in more detail than does his narrator, who finds himself quite limited in his attempts to explain to the sightless man the experience of seeing the pictures on the TV. His descriptions are partly undercut by a simple lack of knowledge, as when he is unable to answer Robert's question about whether the paintings on walls are frescos. "That's a good question. I don't know," he responds, revealing that seeing is not analogous with knowing (223). Finally the narrator gives up, telling Robert, "You'll have to forgive me. . . . But I can't tell you what a cathedral looks like. It just isn't in me to do it. I can't do any more than I've done. . . . The truth is, cathedrals don't mean anything special to me. Nothing. Cathedrals. They're just something to look at on late-night TV. That's all they are" (225–26). Yet, they come to mean considerably more, when Robert has the narrator draw a cathedral, Robert's own hand riding the narrator's in order to get a sense of the shape. It is here that true communion occurs between these two characters, by way of human touch. It is also true that the television is instrumental in leading the characters to this point of contact.

Notably, as they draw this image, the TV station goes off the air for the night, and yet the drawing and the communion continue. The analogy between the concluded television programming and the narrator, who shuts his eyes at Robert's instruction, is obvious. Beyond vision, be it televised images or biological processes, there is still human contact. Perhaps nowhere else does Carver's fiction seem so optimistic. Turning away from the comfort of vision ends up being a liberating experience for the narrator, but it should also be noted that there is no way that television can really be seen as any kind of villain in this story. The story seems to argue that while television ought not be a substitute for human interaction, it can in some cases be an enabler. This is parallel to the evolution of food in Carver's works, as cited by Brown: food is an obstacle to communication in "The Idea" (from *Will You Please Be Quiet, Please?*) and a means to communication at the end of "A Small, Good Thing," in which the formerly sinister baker reaches out to Scotty's parents, proclaiming, "Eating is a small, good thing in a time like this" (88). Television, "Cathedral" suggests, can also be a "small, good thing" if employed appropriately. "Cathedral" is by no means a celebration of TV's greatness; instead, the ambivalence of its treatment demonstrates that the television is ultimately powerless when faced with the power of humans' ability to reach out to one another, which is something that characters in Carver's fiction often fail to do. The TV is instrumental in the forging of the bond between the narrator and Robert, but by the same token, it is something that is clearly in the hands of the characters, that does not simply manipulate but is itself used as the tool it was first developed to be. Thus does Carver undercut the simplicity with which many critics treat the media; media is no more simplistic than the enormously complex topic of human relationships.

Most of the writing that has been done on the topic of television's impact on literary fiction has focused on the high postmodernists, writers of outlandish fictions such as those of Vonnegut, Barth, Pynchon, and their literary descendants, including Don DeLillo and David Foster Wallace. Certainly it seems fair to suggest that the relatively recent rise of TV technology in the world has had some effect on the wild experimentation employed by these writers. It has been less easy for critics to consider through the same lens the kind of "neorealism" employed by Raymond Carver. He seems more in the tradition of Stephen Crane, Sherwood Anderson, or Ernest Hemingway (often cited as an influence and the author with whom Carver is most often, perhaps unfairly, compared) or that of the Russians—Chekhov, Tolstoy, Turgenev—for whom Carver frequently expressed his admiration. Carver can, in fact, be seen as part of the reaction to postmodernism's experimentation, which "substituted the surreal and the fantastic" for realism and which "mixed the weird and the far-out with a relentless and sometimes disquieting nihilism" (Carver, *No Heroics, Please*, 148). In his own literary criticism and interviews, Carver clearly favored the realism of the prepostmodernists, though he acknowledged the skill of many postmodern writers. Moreover, Carver, by revealing his preferences so clearly, gave credence to those who considered the author a kind of strictly realist writer. Yet, it is vital to recall that Carver was writing in the postmodern age, the television age. The new aesthetics that came with the proliferation of media, it seems, must certainly have had an influence on his fiction, an influence strong enough for television to receive considerable attention in his work, and consequently to deserve the attention of critics considering the role of TV in American fiction. The more flamboyant manifestations of televisual aesthetic in high postmodern writing might be eschewed in Carver's fiction, but enough remains that we can clearly identify Carver, his themes and rhetorical approaches, with the age into which he was born as a writer.

Not surprisingly, a few critics have seen beyond the surface of his fiction and treated Carver as a postmodern writer, if a different kind than, say, Thomas Pynchon. This seems apt, given that Carver's work, like that of other postmodern writers, often makes use of television but always seeks to transcend it, to become something distinct. In the essay "Steering by the Stars," Carver makes a direct comparison of literature—and here he is discussing "bad writing"—to media's approach to communication, disparaging the use of "language only to convey some kind of fast-forward information better left to the daily papers or the talking heads on the evening news" (*No Heroics, Please,* 132). In light of this critique, it is clear that Carver has no interest in merely emulating televisual language in his fiction, but the parallels, as detailed by Mullen, are nevertheless quite interesting when we consider the frequent appearances of TV in these stories, as an object and a conveyer of information. Could it be that Carver's style lifts a part of its technique from the language of the media age in order to offer a commentary on that age? Certainly, if Carver's fiction does indeed draw from such language, it does so not in imitation but rather attempting to do considerably more.

Works Cited

Baudrillard, Jean. *Simulacra and Simulation.* 1981, trans. Sheila Faria Glaser. Ann Arbor: University of Michigan Press, 1994.

Brown, Arthur A. "Raymond Carver and Postmodern Humanism." *Critique* 31, no. 2 (Winter 1990): 125–36.

Carver, Raymond. *Cathedral.* 1983. New York: Vintage, 1989.

———. *No Heroics, Please.* New York: Vintage, 1992.

———. *What We Talk about When We Talk about Love.* New York: Vintage, 1981.

———. *Will You Please Be Quiet, Please?* 1976. New York: Vintage, 1992.

Gentry, Marshall Bruce, and William L. Stull, eds. *Conversations with Raymond Carver.* Jackson: University Press of Mississippi, 1990.

Mander, Jerry. *Four Arguments for the Elimination of Television.* New York: Quill, 1978.

McCaffery, Larry, and Sinda Gregory. "An Interview with Raymond Carver." In *Alive and Writing: Interviews with American Authors of the 1980s,* ed. Larry McCaffery and Sinda Gregory, 66–82. Urbana: University of Illinois Press, 1987. Also in *Conversations,* ed. Gentry and Stull, 98–116.

Mullen, Bill. "A Subtle Spectacle: Televisual Culture in the Short Stories of Raymond Carver." *Critique* 39, no. 2 (Winter 1998): 99–114.

Runyon, Randolph Paul. *Reading Raymond Carver.* Syracuse: Syracuse University Press, 1992.

Weber, Bruce. "Raymond Carver: A Chronicler of Blue-Collar Despair." *New York Times Magazine,* June 24, 1984, 36–50. Also in *Conversations,* ed. Gentry and Stull, 84–97.

Williams, Raymond. *Television: Technology and Cultural Form.* New York: Schocken Books, 1975.

Tamas Dobozy

McCarthy's Mailmen

The Cold War, Raymond Carver, and "What Do You Do in San Francisco?"

The cold war (1945–91) was the longest war fought by America in the twentieth century, being "waged" throughout most of Raymond Carver's life (1938–88). Since Carver is arguably America's preeminent short story writer of the cold war period, it is time critical attention were paid to the possible impact and influence of the cold war, especially in its domestic manifestation, on his fiction. It is my argument that Carver's stories not only are a record of America's quotidian struggles but also are about the way in which the quotidian is frequently an expression of, or response to, larger, even international, political conflicts.

This article thus participates in a growing trend in Carver criticism: addressing the ways in which his fiction is contingent on social context. Josephine Hendin, for instance, has argued that Carver's stories reflect the 1980s in America and that decade's emphasis on the "materialism of experience" ("Fictions of Acquisition," 228–29), or the determination of meaning along a quantitative register, in keeping with the economic orientation of Reagan's decade. As well, Charles Newman (*The Postmodern Aura*, 94) and Joe David Bellamy (*Literary Luxuries*, 80) regard Carver's work, for good or ill, as exemplifying a "literary Republicanism," the aesthetic manifestation of Reaganomics. Likewise, Frank Lentricchia dismisses Carver as another writer whose view of a helpless, socially atomized citizenry ignores the responsibility of authors to defy capitalism, to make political agency possible ("The American Writer," 241). My aim is to contest these notions, suggesting that Carver, far from being an unwitting dupe of Reaganism, is at least as politically conscious in his writing as Don DeLillo and the other writers whom Lentricchia valorizes.

Carver's work is capable of conceiving the larger political scene without resorting to the overwhelming narrative scale of *Gravity's Rainbow* or *Underworld* or *JR*. Indeed, like G. P. Lainsbury, I hope to show that Carver's work makes "visible a discrete historical moment in the ongoing project that the world knows as America" ("A Critical Context," 87). In addition, like Martin Scofield, I hope to probe how Carver's use of the pastoral—or "negative pastoral," as he puts it—is an irony-laden commentary on "democracy" in America, where personal freedom is merely another "cliché" ("Negative Pastoral," 255). In this case Carver has much in common with his more overtly political peers—such as Thomas Pynchon, Don DeLillo, and William Gaddis—in that all of them are very much products of, and writers whose aesthetics are informed by, the cold war.

Focus here is on one of Carver's early short stories—"What Do You Do in San Francisco?"—suggesting that it offers an acute critique of, and commentary on, the surveillance of the American populace inaugurated in the 1950s by the Eisenhower/Nixon regime via Senator McCarthy and the House Un-American Activities Committee (HUAC). My article therefore begins with probing the discursive paradigms set up and sustained by cold-war policy makers, and their cultural impact and relevance, and then discusses how these paradigms are embedded within, and interrogated by, "What Do You Do in San Francisco?"

A Story Called Containment

Don DeLillo refers to the assassination of President Kennedy on November 22, 1963, in Dallas, Texas, as the signal moment of American postmodernity. This event, more than any other, continues to represent the crisis of confidence in the social and cultural narratives by which postwar America operated: "Our culture changed in important ways. . . . There's the shattering randomness of the event, the missing motive. . . . Our grip on reality has felt a little threatened. Every revelation about the event seems to produce new levels of secrecy, unexpected links" ("The Art of Fiction," 299). As the quote indicates, the assassination displaced the "open" story that was America with a sense of randomness, uncertainty, and secrecy, conditions that obstructed the sorting, selecting, and ordering necessary for narrative and, by extension, historical consciousness. Simply put, it allowed too many possibilities for expression within a singular, encapsulating narrative: "It took seven seconds to kill the president and we're still collecting evidence and sifting documents and finding people to talk to and working through the trivia" (292). In the wake of the assassination, Americans were left—as Carver's many interrogative titles suggest—at a loss for the story. Were the Soviets behind the murder? Was the Mafia involved? Was the state leaving out its involvement in the assassination? Could any one story possibly contain such a vast body of evidence? The legacy of the cold war appeared as a narrative indeterminacy, the impossibility of containment.

In *Containment Culture: American Narratives, Postmodernism, and the Atomic Age*, Alan Nadel argues that the cold-war story of democracy not only "contained" the spread of communism by empowering U.S. policy makers in most undemocratic ways but also "contained" life in the United States—contained it conceptually, artistically, and ethically (7–8). The notion of containment, as an official government policy, is believed to have begun with George Kennan's 1947 essay "The Sources of Soviet Conduct." This document—meant to address strategies for "the patient but firm and vigilant containment of Russian expansive tendencies" (Kennan, 575)—everywhere informs the cold-war zeitgeist, including its aesthetic. Most important, for this aesthetic and for Carver's story, is the notion that one of the crucial advantages (illusory, as we shall see) of Western cold warriors was their relative freedom from ideological pressure, their ability to work within "free institutions," and their agency, because of this, to grasp and convey reality "objectively" (Kennan, 576). Thus, the cold warriors of the west were realists in opposition to those beguiled by the "magical attraction" of Soviet ideology (Kennan, 577). At the same time, Kennan praised the "general culture of production and technical self-respect which characterizes the skilled worker of the west" (578) and evinced the same confidence in the imminent collapse of communism as communism evinced regarding capitalism (580). This suggests a level of chauvinism no less ideological than that of the Soviet intellectuals he criticized. By the end of the article, Kennan espouses the same faith in capitalism that he identifies as "ideology" in Soviet practice: "The United States can create among the peoples of the world generally the impression of a country which knows what it wants, which is coping successfully with the problems of its internal life . . . and which has a spiritual vitality capable of holding its own among the major ideological currents of the time" (581). Here the response to the cold war fully becomes an aesthetic one, in which "seeming" and "impression" are mobilized in favor of ideological parity. American capitalism becomes a narrative founded on principles of "production," "freedom," "technical self-respect," "internal" integration, and unity on the parts of the American citizenry—all of which, coupled with "spiritual vitality," raise capitalism to the level of myth. Containment was not just a military strategy to be implemented overseas; it was also the aesthetic informing a cultural narrative of "unity," fixing or containing Americans within a tightly defined category of American-ness. In a sense, containment worked not only to reinforce core American values but also to isolate dissidents so as to make them appear antithetical to those values, thus reinforcing the definition of America upheld by cold-war policy makers. We shall see the aesthetic of containment acted out by Henry Robinson, the narrator of "What Do You Do in San Francisco?"

Kennan's article is crucial in the political and cultural background of a cold war that led authors such as Carver to deal on a narrative level with the failure of "containment." If narrative is the way we know, the way we process information, the way we sort relevant from irrelevant and right from wrong, then events such as the Kennedy assassination were indicative of the way in which a narrative of "containment" no longer worked. McCarthyism; the Bay of Pigs; the assassinations of the Kennedys, Martin Luther King Jr., and Malcolm X; Vietnam; and the death of protestors at Kent State all suggest that the "story" of Kennan's America was diffracting into competing versions of what it was to be American, capitalist, democratic, and anti-Communist. Just as containment was failing militarily in southeast Asia, so it was failing, as a cultural narrative, back home.

Strategies of Hypocrisy

The word "narrative" is important since it was the notion of democracy as a "discourse" that engaged many authors coming out of the 1960s. Critics such as Nadel, Tom Engelhardt, Stephen J. Whitfield, and Thomas Hill Schaub discuss the culture of the cold war as a *narrated* culture; and it was the notion of the state as an aesthetic construct that occupied authors who came of age in the 1960s. Like *The Warren Commission Report*, this construct attempted to reconcile a mass of incongruent elements within a seamless narrative. Cold war discourse represented America as the home of the free while explaining away such rampant curtailments of freedom as racial segregation,[1] McCarthyism, interference in the autonomy of foreign nations, and governmental censure. Apart from the most infamous examples of hypocrisy—such as the blacklisting of the Hollywood Ten—historical moments in which the narrative of American democracy and the actions taken in its name did not coincide include the need to safeguard democracy by supporting foreign antidemocratic, but also anti-Communist, movements and dictators in places such as Cuba (Batista); the "desire to use limitless [atomic] force in the interests of establishing the peaceful limiting of force" (Nadel, 166); the ban on Communist speakers at Berkeley in the 1960s in order to safeguard "traditional principles of [American] democracy," which presumably included "freedom of speech" (Nadel, 212–13); and the drafting of military alliances with Meo tribesmen against Communist insurgents in Laos in return for helping the Meo gain "control of the lucrative opium traffic in Southeast Asia's 'Golden Triangle'" (Whitfield, *The Culture of the Cold War,* 207).

These examples provide only some of the "incongruent elements" of cold-war discourse. In each case, respectively, two "mutually exclusive" stories clashed—anticommunism versus prodemocracy, nuclear brinkmanship versus nuclear deterrence, censorship versus freedom of speech, military alliance versus illegal drug trafficking—as the administration played it both ways. Hence, one of the signatures of the cold war was that American policy makers imposed a narrative on Americans that they felt no need to abide by themselves: "When it became necessary to explain to the Russians what made American society so praiseworthy, even rabid anti-Communists were compelled to highlight the civil liberties that they themselves had sought to curtail. The Bill of Rights that Vice President Nixon claimed abroad was operating in the United States was not a document that he and his allies sought to reinforce when he was at home" (Whitfield, 25).

The administration engendered an awareness of a contradiction at the heart of cold-war discourse. The much celebrated "Bill of Rights" proclaimed by Nixon abroad became, paradoxically, a pretext for curtailing deviation among the American people. That is to say, such texts, like the notion of democracy enshrined in the Constitution, became ideological weapons more important for their symbolic rather than actual function. They became enshrined ideals that needed to be safeguarded even at the cost of annulling what they stood for. Terms such as "democracy" were no longer valuable for what they enabled but in and of themselves, not because they made possible a beneficent nation-state but because they could serve coercion. American ideals became a discourse Americans lived "for" rather than "by."

What came out of the cold war was a notion of "American-ness" that—in the name of democracy, freedom of speech, and plurality—enforced conformity to a political norm, censured certain discourses, and rabidly superintended non-compliance with the behavior expected of Kennan's citizens. What Nadel calls the "common narrative" of the cold war refers to America as an anti-ideological, permissive, progressive, and democratic nation of free speech, Christian values, and capitalist munificence. This "common narrative" served to explain away military aggression as "looking out for America's interests (i.e., democracy) abroad," the building up of a nuclear arsenal as the keeping of world peace, the censure of radicals as a means of preserving free speech, and the forging of one-sided alliances as a maintenance of the political integrity and lawful security of countries from Soviet influence. Moreover, such policy makers fully expected Americans to substantiate this narrative, to ignore the contradictions that gave them such wide-ranging license.

Arcadia in the Time of the Cold War

By the 1960s, however, it was becoming increasingly apparent that the mobility of the cold–war administration of the 1950s—and the "common narrative" on which this mobility rested—was flawed. Hypocrisy was the very means by which various state strategies were implemented. The looseness of the "story" had given the Eisenhower/Nixon administration the necessary room to be totalitarian and democratic, advocates of free speech and censorship, lawful and illegal—as the moment required. In Raymond Carver's story we witness this discursive mobility in the character of the mailman, Henry Robinson, who, as a faithful employee of U.S. Mail, serves to safeguard appropriate (that is, federal) channels of information. Robinson's movements along the streets of his hometown, Arcata, witness the cold-war imposition of governmental censure on individuals. At the same time, Robinson's hypocrisy illustrates how he operates in immunity from the discourse he imposes, implicating Carver in an exposé of cold-war culture.

"What Do You Do in San Francisco?"—included in Carver's first substantial story collection, *Will You Please Be Quiet, Please?*—focuses on "a young couple [the Marstons] with three children" (111) who move from San Francisco to

Arcata, in northern California. The narrator, a mailman called Henry Robinson, uses the word "Beatnik" (rather than "hippie") to describe the couple, placing us squarely in the 1950s. The story sketches the arrival of the Marstons and their refusal to conform to Arcata's social expectations. Midway through the narrative, Marston and his female companion part ways; the woman disappears with the children, leaving Marston to linger around the mailbox waiting for a message. The story ends with Marston's sudden departure and the mailman resuming his mail delivery, as before.

Ostensibly the story is an objective record, told from the viewpoint of the mailman, who informs us from the first that the story is not about him. However, although we witness the activities of the "Beatniks" (111)—including their spurning of "work" (since the couple are visual artists they do not "work" in Robinson's sense of the term) (114); their "coolness" to Robinson's social overtures (114); their unwillingness to identify themselves on their mailbox (115); the rumors that suggest they are parolees (116); their playful but unruly children (115); the domestic untidiness that characterizes their home (117); the disappearance of the woman and, subsequently, Marston (118–21)—"What Do You Do in San Francisco?" really tells us nothing about the Marstons. Instead, the story enacts an allegory of surveillance. Just as HUAC set out the conditions that identified one as an American (or un-American), Robinson's speculations and suppositions confine the story of the Marstons to his own framework, to his own determination of what is and is not "proper." Like the cold-war policy makers, Robinson ultimately configures the family and subsequently passes a verdict on them, according to his own model of what is American and un-American, what is domestic and alien to Arcata. By the end, the story has doubled back to critique the engine of surveillance itself. Along the way Carver implicates the town of Arcata in Robinson's modus operandi.

In fact, Arcata subverts the paradisial promise evident in its allusion to "Arcadia," just as the system of cold-war surveillance subverted the promise of a "pastoral arcadia, for implementing schemes for moral and social perfection" (Bercovich, "The Puritan Vision," 35) that had been part and parcel of the American myth since the arrival of the Puritans. Instead of an Arcadian language of distilled essences, transcendent poetry, and utopian transparency, what Arcata offers is a language of reification and ideological coercion. However, on the surface the town seems to extend the plenitude associated with a literary Arcadia: escape from the "trouble" (117) of San Francisco's city life, the offer of gainful employment (114), the friendliness of the local "Welcome Wagon" (116), the cozy intimacy of a mailman who has worked the "route" since 1947 (111) and knows where everyone has lived and for how long (112). Arcata lives up to the allusion on which its name plays, reproducing the cultural imaginary of small-town plenitude—one of prosperity, social ease, and democratic permissiveness (Whitfield, 72–74).

However, beneath the surface Arcata is anything but an Arcadia: the story illustrates how "large, multifarious, national policies became part of the cultural agenda of a citizenry" (Nadel, 8) and how the American "federal civil servant," the mailman, effects, through narrative, a policy of containment that reproduces, in the words of Engelhardt, "a domestic iron curtain" (*The End of Victory Culture*, 91). Although Engelhardt's phrase refers to the social containment of African Americans—specifically Malcolm X—during the 1950s and 1960s, Carver's story illustrates that this containment was indeed a "cultural agenda" of the U.S. "citizenry" and that it extended not only to African American radicals but also to those who failed to conform to normative standards. In this sense, Marston and his family become the suspicious, indeterminate other that McCarthyism attempted to expose and eradicate. Everywhere, Carver hints at the difference between Arcata "proper"—Arcata as a discourse—and Arcata the actual—as lived conditions.

In fact, every supposed "plus" offered by Arcata is countered by a deeper "minus." For instance, gainful employment does not arrive with the scenery; nor is it simply the result of one's willingness to work, the supposed promise embedded in the American Dream. Robinson reveals to Marston how to obtain work: "I can tell you who to see at Simpson Redwood. A friend of mine's a foreman there. He'd probably have something" (114). In other words, the getting of work involves neither willingness nor experience nor aptitude—none of the qualities that capitalism defines as preconditions for economic success. Work in Arcata depends on nepotism. This lack of opportunity in Arcata is further foregrounded where Robinson admits that the previous owners of the Marston home "just moved out. . . . He was going to work in Eureka" (115). Arcata is not a place to find work; nor does it offer ground for setting down "roots," for finding permanence. In fact, Arcata suggests that small-town America is populated with itinerants wandering after available jobs, establishing an economic instability that troubles the narrative of capitalist prosperity. This is an America defined by transience, disenfranchisement, and undemocratic privilege.

To be sure, the only "permanent" job in Arcata is that of the "federal civil servant," Robinson, whose route of zip codes is the only stable element in an America constantly on the move. Thus, official discourse conceives of an ideal America through a terminology (the zip code) that assumes a stability and permanence obscuring the fluidity of its citizens' day-to-day movements. The zip code attests to a rooted, stable, ideal America, to which its uprooted, destabilized citizens must conform if they want their share of the mail, if they want a place in the discursive network of the nation. To be listened to, one must speak in the modality of the government, even if this modality inscribes rather than reveals the condition of American society. In this way, Robinson's hegemony suggests that official discourse constructs a system whose primary purpose is to reproduce, reinforce, and continually reinstate its own values and sense of reality.

The federal arm of the American government, in its spokesperson Henry Robinson, can present America as a place where people settle, put down roots, and live in established modes of life because its discourse uses terminology that presupposes permanence: the statistical equation of citizens with addresses. Here, America becomes a bunch of houses along a "route," while between the houses wend the shiftless, roving masses of the American working class. As Graham Clarke suggests, this mobility is not "celebratory" but rather "a larger condition of displacement" reflecting a culture in which there is "no rhetoric of freedom" ("Investing the Glimpse," 107). Thus, the national image fostered by federal policy makers functions not because of but in spite of social conditions. In this climate almost anyone can come under suspicion, since a significant portion of the populace refuses to corroborate, and thus appears to oppose, the dominant discourse characterizing America. In truth, however, the problem is with the discourse that unself-consciously superimposes itself on conditions it cannot represent. The "discourse" of Arcata reifies rather than substantiates America; Arcata is no Eden.[2]

No Fixed Address

This opposition, between official discourse and daily life, is further evinced when Marston tells Robinson that they "don't expect to get any mail for a while, yet" (114) as an excuse for not changing the "name on the [mail] box" (114). The name on the box never does get changed (115), suggesting that Marston and company do not want to be located or named within the economy of the postal system (a refusal that is one of Robinson's major complaints regarding the family). Letters, when they do finally begin arriving, coincide with the departure of the majority of the Marston family. Here, Marston appears more a fugitive from mail than from the people sending it. When a letter arrives from a friend (118), it causes delight, although the letter bears no stamp. The "Marston woman," who receives the mail, says that she does not mind paying for the postage since the letter comes from a friend (118), meaning that she will buy into the system insofar as it suits her but not because she feels any compunction to corroborate or support it. The unstamped letter signifies the Marstons' position outside the system, their membership in a subculture exterior to the operations of the administration. However, the missing postage ultimately justifies Robinson's violation of the Marston home with the demand that they pay the postage fee. This occasions the mailman's view into the home and his summary verdict on the manner in which the Marstons conduct their lives: "I . . . wish I'd paid the nickel myself," says Robinson (118). Government surveillance becomes the "trouble" that the Marston family cannot escape, continually reminding them of its watchful eye over a mode of life it does not approve of, as well as demanding that they assume and abide by its designations.

The infiltration of the family proceeds to a greater and greater degree in the story, following shifts in the *type* of mail they receive. First, Robinson tells us, only "circulars" arrive (117)—circularity suggesting how the Marston family operates outside of the advertising circuit (that is, circulation of capital). Then, Marston begins receiving a "few" letters, "maybe one or two a week" (117)—which affirms his status within the postal grid. Shortly thereafter, the letter arrives from Jerry (118), which eventuates Robinson's direct view into the home and the subsequent dissolution of Marston and the woman's relationship (there is nothing in the story to suggest marriage between Marston and the woman, except Robinson's projection of nuclear family values). Following this, the letters stop altogether, and Marston begins to pace back and forth in front of the mailbox waiting for mail (119), indicating the extent to which he has become dependent on, or managed by, the official network. After a short while another "circular" arrives, one qualified this time by Robinson as addressed only to "occupant" (119), indicating that Marston has now been put in his place, has had his individuality stripped away in conformity with his status as a personified zip code. He has been absorbed into a category. The final letter that arrives, and Robinson's reaction to it, suggests the extent to which Marston has become the anonymous figure on whom a cold-war discourse inscribed terms that ultimately fed back into, and supported, that discourse. Throughout, Marston's silence remains the only option of a man who, if he speaks, whether in affirmation or denial of Robinson's narrative, will only confirm his status as an outsider. Carver's story begins with the Marstons as exterior to the status quo and ends with their inscription according to the terms and values of that status quo (but which still leaves them, in their actuality, outside of it).

When Robinson hands over that final letter to Marston, he says: "This time I had a hunch I had what it was he'd been looking for. I'd looked at it [the letter] down at the station this morning when I was arranging the mail into packets" (120). Robinson has figured Marston out; the mailman's suspicions culminate in the arrival of this letter with the "woman's curlicue" (120) handwriting. The use of the word "hunch"—that is, Robinson *assuming* the story—suggests the general tenor of the cold war, where citizens were "guilty by suspicion," and where HUAC rarely needed proof to make its accusations (Whitfield, 188), inverting the standard logic of American justice—"a man is innocent until proven guilty"—into the necessity of proving one's innocence (Whitfield, 24). Marston's "guilt" becomes evident, in Robinson's mind, "not by evidence but by association and failure to confess" (Nadel, 84). The silence with which Marston and the woman greet Robinson's overtures facilitates Robinson's narrative. As in the case of those men and women who pleaded the Fifth before HUAC, and who failed to take the required loyalty oath, silence proved the most incriminating option of all: it meant that one did not corroborate the discourse that was America (as opposed to naming names, which suggested that one recognized his or her outsider status and wanted to be absolved and permitted reentry). Those who remained silent had something to hide, and what they hid, HUAC assumed, was a confession of guilt.

In a similar vein, Robinson regards Marston as guilty by association, since it is his name written in the "woman's" curlicue writing on the envelope. Of course, Robinson cannot know that the writing belongs to a "woman," and yet he assumes that it does so because the penmanship suggests the decorative, which Robinson associates with the feminine. The letter therefore accords with the narrative of female infidelity that Robinson blurts out to Marston near the end of the story (120), reinforcing his belief (arising from personal experience, as we discover through the course of the story that Robinson is divorced) that the woman is a no-good philanderer intent on breaking up the family. The "curlicue"[3] also suggests the self-reinforcing narrative of containment, as the story circles around to Robinson's initial suppositions. If Robinson has an aesthetic, and as the storyteller he certainly does, then it is in every way identical to that of the cold warriors. Marston goes from anonymous citizen—a recipient of circulars—to a suspect of the inquisition, a man guilty by association, and, guilt determined, transferred, as an "occupant," into the civic discourse. In the course of this inquisition we have actually not heard anything of Marston's story from Marston himself. He is a subject of a distinctly cold-war America:

> a world of people looking *at* one another . . . fixed in a wholly separate and distanced personal space and otherness . . . amidst a society which surrounds them with a constant stream of images reflecting imagined lives and myths of an idealized American materialism. We glimpse them caught within this culture . . . a momentary realization of their histories as wholly displaced from the fictions of the culture in which they exist. (Clarke, 105)

While Clarke is not speaking of cold-war America exactly, his description is eerily reminiscent of it in this case. As "What Do You Do in San Francisco?" demonstrates, Marston's story exists in silence, determined by the fact that it is never articulated, as if the only way to resist the culture that speaks *for us*—whose determinations leave us at the mercy of unsubstantiated principles—is to neither confirm nor deny. The only way to resist is to plead the Fifth and not incriminate oneself by refusing disclosure. At the same time, this leaves Marston on the outside, doomed to inscription by the nature of his protest. His atomization is evidence of cold-war alienation: he is an object of surveillance determined by the conditions of that surveillance.

The Home Front

If Robinson is the agent of the federal government, then the Welcome Wagon of Sallie Wilson figures as the home front in the battle against subversives. Sallie serves as the representative of a "citizenry" willing to adopt the "agenda" of national policy in lowering a "domestic iron curtain." She provides the "evidence" (116) that the "woman" with Marston is "a dope addict," a narrative which Robinson calls the "most horrible" (116), even worse than Marston being a "criminal" (116). Taking, or addiction to, "dope" runs even more contrary to the ethos of Arcata than conventional criminal activity: "The story most folks seemed to believe, at least the one that got around most, was the most horrible" (116), Robinson tells us. Carver's sentence encapsulates the public mood during the cold war, when hearsay and gossip became forms of valid testimony, and when the "story" that got around "was" usually "the most horrible." As the wording of Carver's quote suggests, one could only "seem" to believe in, and adhere to, the "common narrative" since, as Nadel points out, loyalty could not be reliably tested, even with an oath (77), given that communists were so untrustworthy. In Arcata, Sallie Wilson "has been snooping and prying for years under cover of the Welcome Wagon" (116), and her judgment on the woman is as arbitrary—as "belief" driven, as dependant on "seeming"—as the observations of HUAC, which, paradoxically, maintained the notion of American loyalty by gathering the names of as many *disloyal* Americans as it could. Sallie proves her loyalty by "seeming" to buy into the story of subversives operating within Arcata; by naming names she stabilizes her own status within Arcata's system of values. In order to retain her power and privilege within the town, she "seems to believe" the story and proves her loyalty to it by naming names.

Clearly, Robinson decides to include Sallie's testimony because it gels with his own: "there was something funny about [the Marstons]—the woman [in] particular" (116). Like Robinson, who turned against the Marston woman "from the first" (113), Sallie pinpoints the anonymous female co-occupant of Marston's household as the especially "funny" person in the rented house. Sallie's criticism of the woman hinges on the fact that she ignores Sallie, treating her "as if Sallie wasn't there" (116), which is a silence similar to pleading the Fifth, a refusal to corroborate with and legitimize the surveilling body (HUAC), and hence the discourse by which that surveillance operates. The primary reason for mistrust becomes a superficial physiological feature: "Well, just the way her eyes looked if you came up close to her, Sallie said" (116). Sallie's "snooping" and "prying" result in no information at all, perhaps the most damning fact where the Marstons are concerned. Similarly Robinson's judgment of the woman follows from a superficial trait: "But put me down for saying she wasn't a good wife and mother. She was a painter" (112). Robinson deems the woman's artistic calling proof of her failure as wife and mother, two areas in which he has no evidence to question her competence.

Arcata proves to be an inversion of the pastoral Eden suggested by its name; instead, the town delimits a site of mistrust, suspicion, quick judgments, moral rectitude, and a dominant narrative so exacting, offering so little room for deviation,[4] that the set of one's eyes is enough evidence for a damning verdict. Here, even a marginally subversive couple such as the "Beatniks," the Marstons, cannot "pursue happiness" in peace, precisely because the maintenance of traditional, "same old," American values necessitates their containment in a narrative that smothers the exercise of the liberty it safeguards. The principle of doubling—the two-facedness of Arcata—informs the modus operandi of the federal agent and the local citizenry.

The Other Side of the Official Side of the Story

The double-facedness of cold-war discourse is visible throughout the story. Carver continually draws our attention to acts of evasion—in the unanswered title, in Robinson's announcement that the story is not about himself, in the failure of Marston to speak—until we realize that the story is really about the liberty of a narrator who excuses himself—*but only himself*—from living up to the values he enforces: "I'm not a frivolous man, nor am I, in my opinion, a serious man. It's my belief a man has to be a little of both these days. I believe, too, in the value of work—the harder the better. A man who isn't working has got too much time on his hands, too much time to dwell on himself and his problems" (111).

Here Robinson revels in hypocrisy. He would like Marston to work, and yet Marston's indolence fuels Robinson's self-image and moral rectitude. In other words, he needs Marston *not to work*. Not having "time" to dwell on himself proves exactly Robinson's problem, because through work he displaces his own unease onto the other, onto the "customers" he serves. Robinson's conservatism, his belief in work as moral force, his valorizing of behavioral norms (being neither serious nor frivolous, the opposite poles of a binary he claims to straddle) provide convenient cover for his excess of time, violating inquisitiveness, and total solipsism.

Later we learn that Robinson sublimates personal trauma into work and, through work, projects that trauma onto the people on his mail route. Near the end of the story he yells at Marston: "It was work, day and night, work that gave me oblivion when I was in your shoes and there was a war on where I was" (120). Morality screens Robinson's overwriting. The very enforcement of moral rectitude (working) absolves him from living by it himself. Robinson's mail "route" becomes the continual delivery of his own story to himself, as the mailman turns his "subject" status, as mere mailman or transmitter of communication, into the all-powerful position of "author." His hypocrisy allows him to apply a set of normative rules that he feels no compunction to live up to himself. Robinson regards Marston as "distinct" in that the younger man has failed to grasp the moral lessons life has taught Robinson, while at the same time this regard originates in an identification with Marston (experiencing a similar "war").[5] By viewing others strictly through his own story, Robinson remains a locus of power, an "enterprise" that capitalizes by forcing others to reproduce his discourse. He is successful in maintaining power because he both tells the story that is reality and misses out on reality altogether.

In short, Robinson polices Arcata, rooting out those whose views and beliefs do not correspond to his cold-war ideals, while at the same time transgressing those very ideals in the way he roots out these subversives. In "Raymond Carver's Monologic Imagination," Miriam Marty Clark suggests that Carver's stories frequently investigate the way in which identity is determined by resistance to or exclusion (245) of those "menacing" discourses not identified with, or created by, the self (241). More to the point, Michael Trussler characterizes Carver's characters as "restricted to" or "ensnared" by discourse and unable—or, as in Robinson's case, *unwilling*—to recognize possibilities beyond those available to previously established modes of articulation ("The Narrowed Voice," 29). In other words, "What Do You Do in San Francisco?" details the ways in which discursive authority, and the version of reality it authorizes, depends on delimiting and excluding alternative discourses, or stories.

This way of thinking about discourse—how it constrains the subjects who have no choice but to accept and use it—illuminates how the narrative of containment in "What Do You Do in San Francisco?" conditions the subject position of Robinson, agent of a governmentally sanctioned information exchange, and Marston, the "ordinary man," who is denied any articulation of himself outside the view of him given by Robinson. Thus, while Robinson becomes the author of Marston's tale, Marston is left only with recourse to a means of resistance that is silent, outside of discursive articulation. Throughout, Marston's gestures, stances, and silences riddle the story with the uneasy sense that, whatever his story might be, it is certainly not the one Robinson is telling. Thus, while "common people," such as Marston, have a limited agency in the extratextual realm of gesture, action, and silence, their power is transitory, achieved only in the openings offered by official discourse, which, in this case, is the story told by the mailman. Marston cannot, finally, avoid inscription by Robinson, who overwrites his subjectivity. Instead, Marston—during the course of the story—disturbs Robinson's story with a glimmer, a suggestion of interpretations other than those Robinson comes up with, while at the same time being primarily an object determined by governmental censure. This glimmer is most notable at the end, where Robinson follows Marston's gaze over the countryside but cannot discern the object of Marston's concern, seeing only "the same old" (121), which suggests that he is culpable of missing out on the younger man's motives, and instead, subjecting him to the "same old," predetermined perspective. Carver's story therefore critiques both the discursive preeminence of Robinson and the idea of a "master narrative" overall, as well as using silence to substantiate the other story envisioned by Marston at the end. Marc Chénetier illuminates this strategy of silence by suggesting that the question evident in the story's title (among others) "linger[s] in the mind during and after the read-ing[,] . . . inciting one to look among the blanks and negations for answers" ("Living on/off the 'Reserve,'" 178). One such "answer," or, rather, a further "question," that the story presents, within its "blanks" and "negations," is the silent cry of Marston, whose story is that of the people silenced by a discourse within which they are trapped, or contained.

Like the cold-war administrations of Eisenhower and, later, Johnson and Nixon, Raymond Carver's mailman, Henry Robinson, embeds a system of val-ues within a narrative he feels no compunction to abide by, operating in com-plete freedom from it. Like Whitfield's cold warriors, he contains people such as Marston in his system of values without being contained in it himself. This act of containment, however, provides a matrix wherein another, albeit silent, narrative begins to proliferate. Thus, in the character of Robinson, Carver gives us an implicit critique of the cold-war aesthetic of containment, its implemen-tation and effects.

While this would appear to make a protest writer of Carver, it is important to note that, in the words of Bill Buford, Carver's are not stories of protest but of "the occasion for it" ("Editorial," 5). By this I mean that Carver's story demonstrates the internalization of cold-war discourse rather than its program-matic critique. It presents the occasion out of which 1960s protests arose with-out voicing protest or being topically political. From the very first sentence the story draws attention to this internalized discourse: "This has nothing to do with me" (111), Robinson tells us. Robinson's "story" asks us to buy into its premise of detachment and its apparent willingness—in true democratic fashion—to let us formulate our own opinions. He is, after all, just a mailman, just a messenger, and so the tale is not inflected with personal bias. However, in truth, Robinson's narration does not so much give us a story to read as read the story *for* us. By telling us that the tale does not concern him, his so-called democratic objectivity actually "classifies"—or puts "off-limits"—one particular reading (for example, that the story is actually about Robinson himself), removing it from the field of possible options. Therefore, Robinson's supposedly "democratic" narration—in which a record of plain, objective facts appears at our interpretative disposal—curtails our interpretation. Robinson's "democ-racy" becomes a consumer option, something we pay for (with our complicity), rather than a living, breathing, political practice. Robinson has become an example of a Joseph McCarthy–style demagoguery, the classifier of what belongs and does not belong inside Arcata, a sorter of our information in a way that does not want to call attention to himself as a sorter, because doing so would make him accountable to the principles whereby that sorting operates: intrusion, indolence, and forced conformity.

In making this apparent, Carver does not propose "political solutions . . . to social ills" but rather "widens our sympathies" (Scofield, 261). In other words, the solution he proposes is not programmatic, because it calls for empathy rather than a regulated responsive action. It calls for our deprivileging of one frame of reference (Robinson's or our own) over another (that of Marston, and of the American underclass in general), which is essential if we are to conceive a world in which community and democracy are actually practiced. As Charles May has pointed out, one of the purposes of a short story is "to show us how to deal with all that which we cannot understand" ("Do You See What I'm Saying?," 41), and thus, Carver's task here is not to create understanding by invoking an ideology opposed to Robinson's but to allow Marston's silence to linger as a form of resistance to discursive incorporation, and thus normalizing, and thus conformity. Indeed, his story is a resistance to discourse altogether. Democracy, for Carver, is an openness to Marston's silence, to that which resists our knowing, as well as our own willingness to grant this silence, to permit the liberty and independence it negatively signifies. This, of course, means that we must live with our incomprehension of the other.

Conclusion: The Story of America

McCarthy's story, too, was not about himself but about America, which was a useful way of distracting Americans from the fact that he was operating in complete subversion of the principles he supposedly safeguarded. Like McCarthy, Robinson wants the freedom of invisibility, of not being accountable to the principles he imposes on others. By the end of "What Do You Do in San Francisco?" Carver has reproduced the cold war's distinctly undemocratic discourse to expose the hypocrisy whereby that discourse functioned. In this sense, like DeLillo, Ellison, and other cold-war authors, he also lent his talent to scrutinizing the cultural implications of Kennan's policy of "containment," and McCarthyism, on a generation of Americans.

Notes

1. Ralph Ellison, in "Beating that Boy" (1945), in *Shadow and Act* (New York: Vintage, 1995), directly addresses the race issue in the context of the American narrative of "democracy," illustrating a central contradiction of postwar America: "For since 1876 the race issue has been like a stave driven into the American system of values, a stave so deeply imbedded in the American ethos as to render America a nation of ethical schizophrenics. Believing truly in Democracy on one side of their minds, they act on the other in violation of its most sacred principles; holding that all men are created equal, they treat thirteen million Americans as though they were not" (99). Ellison's statement illustrates the simultaneous function of "two sides" within a single "mind" or "set of principles"; yet, as Ellison notes, this "stave" does not hinder the function of American democracy—at least its function as a self-image, as a *discourse*—but in fact characterizes the way American democracy "acted." Hypocrisy, as Ellison notes, served as the mode of American policy.

2. Relevantly the sections of William L. Stull and Maureen P. Carroll's biography of Carver, *Remembering Ray: A Composite Biography of Raymond Carver* (Santa Barbara,

Calif.: Capra, 1993), that deal with Carver's own life in Arcata range under titles that reflect the dystopian character of cold-war America: "Weedy Logic," "The Most Unhappy Man," "Bad News," "Secret Places," "All-American Nightmares," and "A Nothing Generation." The one exception to the rule is "Tell Me More about Salmon Fishing," which suggests pleasures found in escaping from town.

3. Circularity appears throughout the story, not only in the delivered "circulars" or the woman's "curlicue" handwriting, but also in the "curly-headed girls" (114), presumably Marston's daughters.

4. In *Reading Raymond Carver* (Syracuse: Syracuse University Press, 1992), Randolph Paul Runyon attempts to uncover, from the scant evidence provided by the story, what previous event in San Francisco Marston ran from. Runyon argues that the title of the story has little to do with the exchange between "Mrs. Marston" (he, like Robinson, assumes that Marston and the woman are a conventionally married couple) and the postman (113); "The story merits its title not," Runyon says, "surely, because of what the *mailman* may have done there" (41). At the same time, it is possible to read that what the mailman did or did not do in San Francisco is the very crux of the story: Mrs. Marston's lack of interest in the mailman's life, her refusal to *hear* his narrative, seals her fate *within* that narrative. By not expressing interest in Robinson's "story," "Mrs. Marston" effectively sets herself against it, whether she intends to or not; by not participating in its recounting—as the witnesses called by HUAC pleaded the Fifth and therefore neither confirmed nor denied the hearings—she becomes its antagonist. In my interpretation, the story very much hinges on what the mailman did or did not do in San Francisco, and Carver's title elaborates the question that an isolated Robinson would like others to ask *of him*.

5. Alan Nadel (*Containment Culture: American Narratives, Postmodernism, and the Atomic Age* [Durham, N.C.: Duke University Press, 1995), too, says that American discourse viewed the Soviet Union as same and other—"same" in the sense that it was a possibly capitalist nation that had fallen off the true path to which it had to be returned, and "other" in the sense that it was a wholly alien culture intent on infiltrating and undermining America (20).

Works Cited

Bellamy, Joe David. *Literary Luxuries: American Writing at the End of the Millenium.* Columbia: University of Missouri Press, 1995.

Bercovich, Sacvan. "The Puritan Vision of the New World." In *The Columbia Literary History of the United States,* ed. Emory Elliott, 33–44. New York: Columbia University Press, 1988.

Buford, Bill. "Editorial." *Granta* 8 (1983): 4–5.

Carver, Raymond. *Will You Please Be Quiet, Please?* New York: Vintage, 1992.

Chénetier, Marc. "Living on/off the 'Reserve': Performance, Interrogation, and Negativity in the Works of Raymond Carver." In *Critical Angles: European Views of Contemporary American Literature,* ed. Marc Chénetier, 164–90. Carbondale: Southern Illinois University Press, 1986.

Clark, Miriam Marty. "Raymond Carver's Monologic Imagination." *Modern Fiction Studies* 37, no. 2 (1991): 240–47.

Clarke, Graham. "Investing the Glimpse: Raymond Carver and the Syntax of Silence." In *The New American Writing: Essays on American Literature since 1970*, ed. Graham Clarke, 99–122. New York: St. Martin's, 1990.

DeLillo, Don. "The Art of Fiction CXXXV." Interview with Adam Begley. *Paris Review* 128 (April 1993): 274–306.

Ellison, Ralph. "Beating That Boy." In Ralph Ellison, *Shadow and Act*, 95–101. New York: Vintage, 1995.

Engelhardt, Tom. *The End of Victory Culture: Cold War America and Disillusioning of a Generation*. New York: HarperCollins, 1995.

Hendin, Josephine. "Fictions of Acquisition." In *Culture in an Age of Money: The Legacy of the 1980s in America*, ed. Nicolaus Mills, 216–33. Chicago: Ivan R. Dee, 1990.

Kennan, George (X). "The Sources of Soviet Conduct." *Foreign Affairs* 25, no. 4 (July 1947): 566–82.

Lainsbury, G. P. "A Critical Context for the Carver Chronotope." *Canadian Review of American Studies* 27, no. 1 (1997): 77–92.

Lentricchia, Frank. "The American Writer as Bad Citizen—Introducing Don DeLillo." *South Atlantic Quarterly* 89, no. 2 (1990): 239–44.

May, Charles E. "'Do You See What I'm Saying?': The Inadequacy of Explanation and the Uses of Story in the Short Fiction of Raymond Carver." *Yearbook of English Studies* 31 (2001): 39–49.

Nadel, Alan. *Containment Culture: American Narratives, Postmodernism, and the Atomic Age*. Durham, N.C.: Duke University Press, 1995.

Newman, Charles. *The Postmodern Aura*. Evanston: Northwestern University Press, 1985.

Runyon, Randolph Paul. *Reading Raymond Carver*. Syracuse, N.Y.: Syracuse University Press, 1992.

Schaub, Thomas Hill. *American Fiction in the Cold War*. Madison: University of Wisconsin Press, 1991.

Scofield, Martin. "Negative Pastoral: The Art of Raymond Carver's Stories." *Cambridge Quarterly* 23, no. 3 (1994): 243–62.

Stull, William L., and Maureen P. Carroll, eds. *Remembering Ray: A Composite Biography of Raymond Carver*. Santa Barbara, Calif.: Capra, 1993.

Trussler, Michael. "The Narrowed Voice: Minimalism and Raymond Carver." *Studies in Short Fiction* 31, no. 1 (1994): 23–37.

Whitfield, Stephen J. *The Culture of the Cold War*. Baltimore: Johns Hopkins University Press, 1996.

Chad Wriglesworth

Raymond Carver and Alcoholics Anonymous

A Narrative under the "Surface of Things"

When Raymond Carver met Richard Ford in 1978, Carver had already crossed over into what he spoke of as the second of "two lives." June 2, 1977, marked Carver's "line of demarcation," the day he entered into a new life without alcohol (Weber, "Raymond Carver," 89). Ford remembers that in those days of instability Carver "had inched his way out of shadows and into light, and he was as thankful, and as determined to stay in the light—my light, your light, the world's light—as any convert to a feasible religion" ("Good Raymond," 73). Ford's memory suggests that Carver was something of a convert, a changed man on a pilgrimage to physical and spiritual recovery. However, while critics may recognize that "something" happened to Carver's life and work, few are willing to consider Carver's transformation as a spiritual awakening. This reluctance causes Carver's comments on the sacred to be handled with skepticism, as spiritual imagery and confessional language are typically dismissed as an alcoholic's restored hope in humanity rather than a possible encounter with a sacred "other." In contrast to the postmodern way of suspicion, Dennis Taylor advocates for an authentic engagement with spirituality in literature. Taylor goes so far as claiming that some texts in the Western canon actually demand a religious interpretation; when this possibility is squelched, "what is left-over is a nagging spiritual question" ("The Need," 125). Concurring with Taylor, I suggest that a truly judicious approach to Raymond Carver's life and work will create the necessary theoretical space for a spiritual reading.

Perhaps the most significant article concerning Carver's spirituality is William L. Stull's "Beyond Hopelessville: Another Side of Raymond Carver." In this essay Stull contrasts the bleakness of Carver's earlier work with the optimism found in *Cathedral*. Stull's close and comparative reading of "The Bath" and "A Small, Good Thing" suggests that the ominous uncertainty of "The Bath" becomes revised from chaos "into an understated allegory of spiritual rebirth" that culminates as a "symbol of the Resurrection" (12, 13). Although Stull cites specific allusions to the Bible in "A Small, Good Thing," Carver makes no claims of biblical literacy or confessional faith, making it problematic to suggest that he was using Christian imagery and typology as deliberately as Stull suggests.[1] When asked about literary influences during his childhood years, Carver explains that growing up, "we had the Bible in our house but the family did not read" books on a regular basis (Tromp, "Any Good Writer," 79; Sexton, "David Sexton Talks," 121). Perhaps for this reason both Randolph Paul Runyon and Mark A. R. Facknitz reject Stull's interpretation. They, in turn, assert that the ending of "A Small, Good Thing" is not designed to elicit a sense of Christian communion but rather is a self-generated *human* communion that is genuine but also godless (Runyon, *Reading Raymond Carver*, 149–51; Facknitz, "The Calm," 295–96). Although these observations make a valid rebuttal, the overwhelming rejection of structured Christianity also negates the possibility of a spiritual awakening that is evident in Carver's postrecovery work. To dismiss an encounter with the sacred on the grounds that it does not correlate with popular expressions of Christianity leads to yet another misreading. When the problem of interpreting the spiritual aspects of Carver's work is revisited, it becomes clear that his vision of the sacred is far more nuanced than critics have formerly realized, as he simultaneously refuses to be aligned with confessional Christianity or the material limitations of secular humanism.

As an alternative approach, Hamilton E. Cochrane contends that Carver's predilection toward spirituality arises from his association with Alcoholics Anonymous.[2] As previously stated, Carver's relationship with the sacred is not systematic or easily definable—for it is not bound by orthodox creed or specific doctrine. In a similar way, the Alcoholics Anonymous Twelve Steps to Recovery program is described as "a spiritual rather than a religious program," a means of generating space for physical, relational, and spiritual recovery (Wilcox, *Alcoholic Thinking*, 64). Cochrane asserts that examining Carver's redemption "in light of the AA experience is illuminating and more accurate than locating his new sensibility in some other, say, Christian perspective" ("Taking the Cure," 81). Although Cochrane's observations are convincing, it is worth noting that Carver on more than one occasion actually denied the influence of AA. When asked about the influence of Alcoholics Anonymous, Carver informed one interviewer, "I can't honestly say I've ever consciously or otherwise patterned any of my stories on things I've heard at the meetings" (Simpson and Buzbee, "Raymond Carver," 40). However, this rejection should be interpreted with care. If Carver was a genuine participant in the Alcoholics Anonymous program, it is possible that he practiced the AA pledge of anonymity and confidentiality, which promotes reticence and group solidarity over any type of public recognition or misuse of personal testimonies (*Twelve Steps*, 189–92). Even if Carver did not reproduce specific material from AA meetings in his work, an examination of key stages in the AA program's Twelve Steps to Recovery illustrates that the optimism of Alcoholics Anonymous created an environment that fostered a spiritual awakening in Carver's life and work.[3]

In 1977 Carver was living in San Francisco, where he visited St. James Episcopal Church and went to "at least one and sometimes two [AA] meetings a day for the first month" (Simpson and Buzbee, 39). During Carver's early drying-out period, he continued to attend meetings for what he calls "the longest while—six or eight months" (*Carver Country*, 106). Apart from these few references to AA, it is difficult to assess the level of participation Carver maintained with Alcoholics Anonymous throughout his life; nevertheless, it is evident that the general presence of AA remained with him. For example, Tess Gallagher recalls that by 1980 Carver was secure enough in his sobriety to attend AA meetings with friends who were struggling with alcoholism (*Soul Barnacles*, 219). Gallagher remembers that in 1988, during a time when Carver found himself tempted to drink again, he "started out for an AA meeting" but returned home, as he was unable to find the exact location of the meeting (*Soul Barnacles*, 209). That same year, when Carver passed on, his daughter, Chris, remembers how the Lord's Prayer was offered at the conclusion of her father's funeral, "as they do at the end of AA meetings, in respect and gratitude for my dad's sobriety" (Halpert, *Raymond Carver*, 183).

Taking all of this into consideration, the objective of this article is to offer an illustrative study that compares key stages of Alcoholics Anonymous with the spiritual aspects of Carver's postrecovery writings. As with any structured program, all steps within the Alcoholics Anonymous sequence are vital—none can be circumvented or left out. Although each step is interdependent on the others, key stages are marked by critical moments of confessional participation and active decision making. I have deliberately privileged an examination of these steps, not necessarily because they are the most important stages in the program, but because the active participation embedded within these steps is palpable in Carver's life and writing. When these particular stages are examined collectively, it is evident that Carver's rehabilitation brought sense and order to a chaotic personal narrative and that, beneath "the smooth (but sometimes broken and unsettled) surface of things" (Raymond Carver, *Fires*, 26), Carver's own life and work coincide with the patterns of Alcoholics Anonymous, suggesting that this recovery program contributed significantly to his spiritual and literary transformation.

Step Three: "Cathedral" and the Possibility of *Something*

Made a decision to turn our will and our lives over to the care of God *as we understood Him*. (*Twelve Steps*, 34)

When a person enters Alcoholics Anonymous, the only confessional requirement is that the new member must be willing to recognize that alcoholism has bent his or her mind "into such an obsession for destructive drinking that only an act of Providence can remove it" (*Twelve Steps*, 21). The second step recognizes that this healing force of Providence is not antagonistic but desires wholeness and restoration—which leads to the third, and perhaps most critical, step of the program. Through acts of faith, alcoholics must cross a threshold, turning their lives over to the care of the higher power as they "understand Him," content to receive renewal based on the limited revelation they have received. This act of unhinging and self-emptying proves to be the most significant stage of the recovery program, as all future steps return to this initial encounter with the higher power. Reading a story such as "Cathedral" in this context suggests that the ambiguous "higher power" of Alcoholics Anonymous surfaces in the form of an ineffable "something" that is mysteriously revealed to the narrator of "Cathedral."[4]

When one probes below the surface of "Cathedral," characteristics of Carver's "God as he understood Him" become clearer. In the story, a blind man named Robert, an old friend of the narrator's wife, comes to visit the couple. The narrator, as Kirk Nesset observes, is "hemmed in by insecurity and prejudice, buffered by drink and pot and by the sad fact, as his wife says, that he has no 'friends,' is badly out of touch with his world, his wife, and himself" (*The Stories of Raymond Carver*, 66). Despite jealousy and a wealth of stereotypes concerning blindness, this insular narrator actually becomes dependent on Robert, a character whose vision reaches far deeper than the narrator could ever imagine.

As the evening conversation fades, Robert and the narrator are watching a late program, "something about the church and the Middle Ages" (Raymond Carver, *Cathedral*, 222). The blind man leans toward the screen with his ear cocked, hearing what he fails to see. Together the two men listen to a droning Englishman describe cathedrals and their symbolic ability to reach for transcendence. The narrator suddenly becomes aware of a communication gap, and the rhythm of the story shifts toward possibility. In a series of rapid questions, he asks the blind man: "Do you have any idea what a cathedral is? What they look like, that is? Do you follow me? If somebody says cathedral to you, do you have any notion what they're talking about? Do you know the difference between that and a Baptist church, say?" (223–24). Although Robert knows something of cathedrals, he has no idea what one actually looks like. Yet, as the narrator stares at the various cathedrals on the television screen, he realizes that words will not capture or translate the image. He gropes for language but stops as he "wasn't getting through to him" (225). In frustration, the narrator simply states that "in those olden days, when they built cathedrals, men wanted to be close to God. In those olden days, God was an important part of everyone's life. You could tell this from their cathedral-building" (225). In response, the blind man asks a question that leads to the narrator's confession of disbelief:

> "Hey, listen. I hope you don't mind my asking you. Can I ask you something? Let me ask you a simple question, yes or no. I'm just curious and there's no offense. You're my host. But let me ask if you are in any way religious? You don't mind me asking?"

I shook my head. He couldn't see that, though. A wink is the same as a nod to a blind man. "I guess I don't believe in it. In anything. Sometimes it's hard. You know what I'm saying?"

"Sure, I do," he said.

"Right," I said. (225)

Through these unpredictable shifts in conversational rhythm, it is probable that the hovering and breaking of silence are not merely indicators of what is described as Carveresque reticence but rather the origins of genuine conversation, a spacious invitation from the "higher power" designed to negotiate a passage into spiritual awakening. As Martin Buber suggests, authentic conversation reflects an unpredictable pattern of silence and spontaneous upsurge, perhaps cultivated by a spiritual presence. Buber writes,

> it is not necessary for all who are joined in a genuine dialogue actually to speak; those who keep silent can on occasion be especially important. . . . No one, of course, can know in advance what it is that he has to say; genuine dialogue cannot be arranged beforehand. It has indeed its basic order in itself from the beginning, but nothing can be determined, the course is of the spirit, and some discover what they have to say only when they catch the call of the spirit. (*The Knowledge of Man*, 87)

Mirroring Buber's assertion, silence encroaches on the two men again, until the narrator is moved to clarify his nonreligious stance even further. He explains, "'The truth is, cathedrals don't mean anything special to me. Nothing. Cathedrals. They're something to look at on late-night TV. That's all they are.' It was then that the blind man cleared his throat" (226). In Carver's typical "spare style that tells nothing, but shows everything," readers are called to interpret meaning from actions rather than words (Cochrane, 79). The blind man "cleared his throat." Is this just coincidental timing, or was the blind man somehow offended by the narrator's indifference toward a sacred "other"? Whatever the case, Robert's throat clearing shifts the control of the narrative, as, in this moment, the power of knowledge transfers so that it is now the blind who somehow see.

Robert directs the narrator to gather up some heavy paper and a pen. After they clear a space to draw, Robert closes his hand over the narrator's and politely orders, "Go ahead, bub, draw. . . . Draw. You'll see. I'll follow along with you. It'll be okay. Just begin now like I'm telling you. You'll see. Draw" (227). These directions speak a prophetic irony. Twice the blind man repeats, "you'll see," in the context of you'll *see how things work*. However, the expansive conclusion of the story reveals that the narrator, who previously claims he does not believe in "it" or "anything" that inhabits cathedrals, actually *sees* "something" through the creation of this makeshift drawing (225, 228). As instructed, the narrator draws. He begins timidly, drawing a box that "could have been the house [he] lived in." Yet, after some encouragement, something takes over, and he remembers how he "couldn't stop" (227). Even when the program about cathedrals goes off the air, the two men continue. In a rapid series of sequential commands, the blind man offers another series of directions to his pupil: "Put some people in there now. What's a cathedral without people? . . . Close your eyes now" (227–28). Without questioning, the narrator continues to draw. With eyes closed, he is guided to a moment that transports him to an encounter with "something" ineffable:

> So we kept on with it. His fingers rode my fingers as my hand went over the paper. It was like nothing else in my life up to now.
>
> Then he said, "I think that's it. I think you got it," he said. "Take a look. What do you think?"
>
> But I had my eyes closed. I thought I'd keep them that way for a little longer. I thought it was *something* I ought to do.
>
> "Well?" he said. "Are you looking?"
>
> My eyes were still closed. I was in my house. I knew that. But I didn't feel like I was inside anything.
>
> "*It's* really *something*," I said. (228, emphasis added)

Through participation in volitional blindness, the narrator is able to see "something" beyond what his restrictive limitations formerly allowed. In the presence of "something," he remains prayerfully silent, as though it was "something" he ought to do. Although Carver builds this final moment through lines that are abstract and seemingly elusive, the narrator's memory clarifies the moment's significance, eliminating the possibility of this being a purely mundane experience. As if transported by the spires he has drawn, the narrator remembers a sensation "like nothing else in [his] life." Without language or speech to fully interpret the encounter, he turns to silence. In such a moment, Paul Tillich postulates the possibility of an authentic encounter with the "other," recognizing that there are "those who feel that they cannot find the words of prayer and remain silent towards God. This may be lack of Spirit. It may also be that their silence is silent *prayer*, namely, the sighs which are too deep for words" (*The New Being*, 138).

Traditionally, critics have attributed the expansive conclusion of "Cathedral" to the interpersonal connectivity between the narrator and the blind man. An alternative reading acknowledges this relational transformation but also proposes that Carver's repetition of "something" is a significant, yet ambiguously open expression that also creates linguistic space for an encounter with an ineffable "higher power," a force that neither Carver nor his narrator could adequately define through language. As Susan Lohafer observes, the word "something" appears "twenty-nine" times in the story, propelling the narrative into what she calls an example of "lay scripture" (*Reading for Storyness*, 104, 94). Paul Doherty moves in a similar direction, offering an insightful commentary on the rhetorical significance of the word "something" and its paradoxical relationship to sacred confession:

> "It's really something." Those words are the honest best the [narrator] can make of his new experience. In its vague generality, the sentence simultaneously conveys both the inadequacy of language to describe the experience which the [narrator] is having, and the validity of that experience. "*It,*" the experience of moving beyond language, is "*real*" it is "*some thing.*" ("A Note," 340)

When previously questioned about his religious convictions, the narrator replied that he did not believe in "*it. In anything*" (225, emphasis mine). In contrast to professing belief in a voidlike "nothing," after seeing the makeshift cathedral through volitional blindness, the narrator suddenly recants, testifying that "*It's* really *something*" (226, 229, emphasis mine). As Doherty observes, what was formerly "no thing" is now perceived as "some thing" plausible that pulls both the narrator and readers toward the possibility of a sacred encounter.

Like a medieval icon, the text and drawing become an opening to another dimension, a place where the human being meets something of the ineffable. In his essay "The Blind Man of Siloe," Jean-Luc Marion distinguishes between highly stylized images that invite voyeurism and traditional icons, which actually pull the viewer into a sacred dialogue through their banality or even ugliness. In this way, an overtly attractive image has the potential to lead to one-sided spiritual blindness, while an icon creates mutual sight, allowing the viewer "to see" and "be seen" by a sacred other (Marion, 66–68). Although the narrator's cathedral lacks aesthetic merit, its blunt and haphazard features may be capable of pulling the creator-observer to a point where he can "see" and "be seen" by the significant "something" that remains ineffable. This aspect of "Cathedral" is particularly curious, as readers illustrate how, as a text, "Cathedral" bears qualities of an icon. This is particularly true of the final lines, as the conclusion of the story has generated moments of spiritual transference for readers. Here we see what Paul Ricoeur describes as a phenomenon where "everyday reality is metamorphosed by means of what we would call the imaginative variations that literature works on the real" (*Figuring the Sacred*, 43).

Tobias Wolff remembers reading "Cathedral" for the first time. At the illuminating conclusion, he recalls metaphorically entering the text and feeling as if he were "levitating" (Halpert, 53). In a similar way, Tess Gallagher remembers that after working through revisions of the story with Ray, the last lines of the final version "just took the top off the whole story. I could feel it physically, as if the roof had lifted off that imaginary house" (Stull and Carroll, "Two Darings," 475). Largely because of this expansive effect, Edward Duffy ventures to call "Cathedral" a story of "unambiguous salvation . . . as if by attending to [the story], a reader with ears to hear and eyes to see could be lifted up toward the heavens" ("Word of God," 331). While there is certainly validity in this observation, Duffy's interpretation also suppresses the role that human interaction and conversation play in the story. As the conclusion suggests, an encounter with the sacred is not about escaping a physical dimension but is a response to "new possibilities of being-in-the-world" by embracing an existence that extends beyond the self (Ricoeur, *Figuring the Sacred*, 43). As Lohafer observes, in a story charged with both reticence and rhythm, "Conversion is conversation" (112).

While Carver did acknowledge a renewed sense of self-esteem through his recovery from alcoholism, he also suspected the influence of "something" else that he was unable to name. When asked about his "more generous" writing, Carver could only state, "I'm more sure of my voice, more sure of *something*. . . . I don't have that sense of fooling around, of being tentative. . . . When I go to my desk now and pick up a pen, I really know what I have to do. It's a totally different feeling" (McCaffery and Gregory, "An Interview," 103). Although Carver may not couch his spirituality in an orthodox system of faith, it is not overstatement to suggest that this unnamed "something" in Carver's life and work is the manifestation of a sacred reality. For Carver and the narrator of "Cathedral," this "something" is essentially ineffable, a force to be encountered and experienced rather than harnessed and possessed.

Carver was a writer deeply concerned with spiritual matters, one who spoke of the unnameable "higher power" that entered his life through grace. As Carver's personal narrative references a "higher power," his later fiction functions as a testament to this gracious force that rescued him from the isolation of alcoholism. In opposition to such an interpretation, Facknitz recognizes grace in Carver's fiction and yet attributes it to nothing beyond the restoration of human compassion. Facknitz states:

> Grace, Carver says, is bestowed upon us by other mortals, and it comes suddenly, arising in circumstances as mundane as a visit to the barber shop. . . . [It is] not Grace in the Christian sense at all, it is what grace becomes in a godless world—a deep and creative connection between humans that reveals to Carver's alienated and diminished creatures that there can be contact in a world they supposed was empty of sense or love . . . in the cathedrals we draw together, we create large spaces for the spirit. (295–96)

Considering Carver's acknowledgment of the "higher power," Facknitz's strictly humanist interpretation illustrates what now stands as a normative misreading of Carver's work. While Facknitz correctly asserts that grace in Carver's work is not traditionally "Christian," his interpretation fails to consider the possibility of an "other," or what both Carver and his narrator call "something." Despite Facknitz's polished speculation, it seems plausible that even in the midst of a "godless world," Carver had given himself over to this "higher power," a force that desired his restoration and recovery. As Tess Gallagher affirms, Raymond "never heaped credit upon himself for having overcome his illness. He knew it was a matter of grace, of having put his trust in what AA identifies as 'a higher power,' and of having miraculously been given the will to turn all temptation to drink aside" (*Soul Barnacles*, 208–9). Healing and possibility were offered to Carver as a gift. As part of his response to sobriety, Carver's later fiction follows patterns of Alcoholics Anonymous, as he seeks to reconcile the past and communicate possibilities of hope and expansive living to others.

Step Nine: Redeeming the Past through Re-Vision

Made direct amends to [people we have hurt] wherever possible, except when to do so would injure them or others. (*Twelve Steps*, 83)

In a 1983 review of *Cathedral*, Anatole Broyard perceptively recognizes that "like a missionary, Mr. Carver seems to be gradually reclaiming or redeeming his characters" ("Diffuse Regrets," 27). After Carver's initial rehabilitation from alcoholism, he felt an increased burden to revisit the past, holding himself responsible to reconcile division and broken relationships on personal and textual levels. Tess Gallagher remembers that in 1979 Carver wrote a letter to her explaining that "writing" was what he had left of "religion and soul making" (*Soul Barnacles*, 240). Through writing, Carver was determined to reconcile the past by creating new possibilities in the present. As a result, Gallagher suggests, "He carried some burdens of guilt about 'what had happened,' and he worked out his redemption and consequently some of ours in his art" (*Soul Barnacles*, 59). Through an almost obsessive gift for revision, Carver revisited his characters over extended periods of time, offering hope for recovery to those formerly left stranded in the text.

The redemptive quality of Carver's fiction is particularly evident when comparing "The Bath" to "A Small, Good Thing." Although "The Bath" was published two years before "A Small, Good Thing," Tess Gallagher asserts that "A Small, Good Thing" was actually written first but was severely cut and published as "The Bath" under the direction of Gordon Lish, Carver's editor at the time. Carver had been sober for about two years when he wrote the stories for *What We Talk about When We Talk about Love*, and Gallagher states that during this time of initial sobriety, "Ray's alcoholism had made him malleable and too accepting of Lish's editing" ("A Conversation," 96). Although Carver was unhappy with Lish's editorial decisions for the stories in *What We Talk about When We Talk about Love*, Gallagher explains that Carver allowed the book to be published and that he eventually revised backwards, as his confidence as a writer increased through sobriety. She explains, "[Ray] decided not to put his sobriety in jeopardy by going to battle to keep the book from being published in the Lish edited version. When Lish wouldn't agree not to publish the book, Ray didn't stop him. He just revised the stories backwards for his final collection" ("A Conversation," 96).

When asked to compare "A Small, Good Thing" and "The Bath," Carver suggested that the two versions are not related but are entirely separate stories that came from different sources. Although Carver did not mention Lish's influence explicitly in a 1984 interview, he did indicate that after "The Bath" there was "unfinished business" to deal with, largely because the story was not told correctly the first time. Comparing the two stories, Carver stated:

> In my own mind I consider them to be really two entirely different stories, not just different versions of the same story; it's hard to even look on them as coming from the same source. I went back to that one, as well as several others, because I felt there was unfinished business that needed attending to. The story hadn't been told originally; it had been messed around with, condensed and compressed in "The Bath" to highlight the qualities of menace that I wanted to emphasize . . . so in the midst of writing these other stories for *Cathedral* I went back to "The Bath" and tried to see what aspects of it needed to be enhanced, redrawn, reimagined. (McCaffery and Gregory, 102)

In the case of "A Small, Good Thing," it is probable that Carver returned to the story in order to tell the truth of his own recovery—a decision that would separate his work from Lish's editorial influence and communicate the possibility of hope that was offered to Carver through sobriety.

It is helpful to consider Carver's return to "A Small, Good Thing" in conjunction with Paul Ricoeur's theory of "new possibilities of being-in-the-world." Ricoeur suggests that writers and interpreters of texts are

> concerned with the permanent spirit of language. By the spirit of language we intend not just some decorative excess or effusion of subjectivity, but *the capacity of language to open up new worlds*. Poetry and myth are not just nostalgia for some forgotten world. They constitute a disclosure of unprecedented worlds, an opening on to other *possible* worlds which transcend the established limits of our *actual* world. (Ricoeur, *A Ricoeur Reader*, 489–90)

Applying Ricoeur's theory to Carver's life and work suggests that when Carver's own narrative of self-destructive alcoholism intersected with the healing offered through the "higher power," a new horizon opened to him. As the spirit of language led Carver to the possibility of this new world, he was transported beyond his own limitations into a new and healing vision of hope. In this context, Carver's process of revision actually becomes a "re-visioning" toward this new reality, as "through fiction and poetry" characters and content are transformed toward "new possibilities of being-in-the-world . . . within everyday reality" (Ricoeur, *Figuring the Sacred*, 43).

Alcoholics Anonymous states that seeking reconciliation "is the beginning of the end of isolation from our fellows and from God" (*Twelve Steps*, 82). This statement is particularly significant when one considers that characters in "The Bath," as edited by Lish, illustrate complete isolation, whereas in "A Small, Good Thing" broken lines of communication are reconnected through numerous appeals for forgiveness and reconciliation.[5] Carver not only reconciles the characters of "A Small, Good Thing"; he also leads the disconnected parties into a meal reminiscent of the Eucharist, which leads Ewing Campbell to suspect that at this moment "a conversion follows" (*Raymond Carver*, 55). In the midst of what should be anger and fractured communication, Carver joins these disconnected people through confession, sunlight, and the breaking of bread. For this reason, despite the same characters and general plot progression, Carver could honestly say that "The Bath," as edited by Lish, was not related to "A Small, Good Thing" at all. As a man living a new and re-visioned reality, Carver was no longer content with the message of "The Bath" and found himself compelled to proclaim the largesse communicated in "A Small, Good Thing," a reality that more accurately aligned with his own redemptive experience.

A similar illustration of recovery surfaces through the posthumous publication of "Kindling" in *Call If You Need Me*. The story, one of five previously uncollected, was found in Carver's writing desk in Port Angeles, Washington. "Kindling" becomes increasingly significant when contextualized within the larger Carver corpus, as the main character, Myers, is a figure who reappears in several collections. In "Put Yourself in My Shoes," published in 1976, Myers is temporarily liberated from writer's block at the expense of a family's tragic circumstances.[6] Years later he reappears In "The Compartment." This time, on a train trip to visit his estranged son in Strasbourg, the struggling writer is edgy, for he has not seen his son in eight years. When the train stops in Strasbourg, Myers realizes that a watch he bought for his son has been stolen. In this moment he suspects that the whole reunion is wrong; he wanders around the train, looking out windows, hoping not to see his son. In a daze, Myers exits through a door and finds himself in the wrong compartment. During the confusion the train uncouples and reattaches, carrying Myers in a new and unknown direction. Without a map or his possessions, Myers gives himself over to a long sleep, a passenger without any sense of guidance or purpose.

In *Call If You Need Me*, Myers makes a final appearance in "Kindling." It is evident nearly twenty years after Carver's death that the author-creator went back to reimagine Myers in light of a new horizon of possibility. Carver begins "Kindling" by stating, "It was the middle of August and Myers was between lives. The only thing different about this time from the other times was that this time he was sober" (7). The Myers we meet in "Kindling" is shaky but a man changed for the better. Although still terse and insular, he is humble, open to some degree of conversation and relationship. In contrast to the isolation of previous endings, readers finish "Kindling" knowing that Myers is on a path to recovery and stability.

Step Eleven: Wordless Prayer and Sacred Sources

> Sought through prayer and meditation to improve our conscious contact with God as we understood Him, praying only for knowledge of His will for us and the power to carry that out. (*Twelve Steps*, 96)

Alcoholics Anonymous states that in group meetings and personal life, "there are really no required prayers. Although most feel that some form of prayer or meditation is necessary to maintain sobriety, specific prayers are only suggestions" (Wilcox, 73). As a participant in Alcoholics Anonymous, Carver might have been expected to incorporate a method of meditative prayer in his life. The fact that he did so suggests that he took Step Eleven of the Twelve Steps to Recovery seriously. Carver's reverence toward words makes his meditation practices compressed, even wordless, as natural images rather than words become the vehicle for communicating with an ineffable "something."

Near the end of his life Carver received an honorary doctor of letters degree from the University of Hartford. At the convocation he offered an address that was later titled "Meditation on a Line from Saint Teresa." Written in 1988, it stands as the last piece of published prose that Carver completed. He opens his address by quoting a line by Saint Teresa, which was used as an epigraph by Tess Gallagher for her collection of poems titled *Amplitude*. By quoting Saint Teresa, Carver rededicates himself to a belief that "Words lead to deeds. . . . They prepare the soul, make it ready, and move it to tenderness" (Raymond Carver, *No Heroics, Please*, 223). After commenting on the beautiful truth of the phrase, Carver repeats the passage, noting how the text may seem foreign to an age that no longer imagines words bearing the full weight of meaning. Particularly moved by "soul" and "tenderness," Carver confesses, "There is something more than a little mysterious, not to say—forgive me—even mystical about these particular words and the way Saint Teresa used them, with full weight and belief" (223). Carver then moves toward a closing passage, a benediction that stands as closure to both life and text:

> Long after what I've said has passed from your minds, whether it be weeks or months, and all that remains is the sensation of having attended a large public occasion . . . try then, as you work out your individual destinies, to remember that words, the right and true words, can have the power of deeds. Remember too, that little-used word that has just about dropped out of public and private usage: tenderness. It can't hurt. And that other word: soul—call it spirit if you want, if it makes it any easier to claim the

territory. Don't forget that either. Pay attention to the spirit of your words, your deeds. That's preparation enough. No more words. (225)

Those who knew Carver well have commented on his almost sacred handling of words. Jay McInerney, a former student under Carver, remembers that as an instructor, Carver mumbled when he spoke. McInerney recalls, "if it once seemed merely a physical tic, akin to cracking knuckles or the drumming of a foot, I now think it was a function of deep humility and respect for the language bordering on awe, a reflection of his sense that words should be handled, very, very gingerly. As if it might be almost impossible to say what you wanted to say. As if it might be dangerous, even" ("Raymond Carver, Mentor," 119). In a similar way, Geoffrey Wolff remembers "that Ray believed in the power of language so profoundly, it was so sacred to him, that he understood, as few people understand, that words are loaded pistols. Sometimes to say something, to name it, is to enact it. So there were certain words he would not say" (Halpert, 184–85). It is this reverence for language, the suspicion of its mystical and incarnational power, that causes Carver's spirituality to depend on ineffable encounters with nature rather than the spoken word.

Encounters with natural sources such as wind and water lead Carver, as well as his fictional characters, toward an engagement with the sacred, as the actions of these sources communicate what language on its own fails to describe. Tess Gallagher remembers that for Ray, rivers "were places of recognition and healing" that opened to possibilities of renewal and expansion" (*Soul Barnacles*, 84). *Twelve Steps and Twelve Traditions* uses the healing image of water to describe the power of prayer, explaining how "The persistent use of meditation and prayer . . . did open the channel so that where there had been a trickle, there now was a river which led to sure power and safe guidance from God as we were increasingly better able to understand Him" (109). It does not take long to encounter water in Carver's work, particularly in his poetry. There are watery titles to nearly every volume. Then there are the poems themselves, moving with turbulent or rippling allusions to water. There is rain; there are lakes; there are springs; there are references to straits and oceanic bays; but more than anything else, there are rivers and creeks.

Carver's affection for rivers is unabashedly proclaimed in *Where Water Comes Together with Other Water*, in which a particular creek, Morse Creek, becomes the hinging metaphor of Carver's life, pulling him into moments of past, present, and future reality. In the poem that serves as the title for this collection, "Where Water Comes Together with Other Water" (63),[7] Carver announces how he "loves creeks and the music that they make." All forms of water touch him— the "rills," the "streams," the "open mouths of rivers where they join the sea"— but the sites where one body of water joins another stand out like "holy places." Carver confesses that he holds an affinity for coastal rivers, such as Morse Creek.

These currents, which gather everything before spilling into the ocean, mesmerize him. They are not all the same; Carver claims that, like the uniqueness of each human being, there is no river "like any other"; each has its own past, present, and future state of being. In a moment of meditation, he collapses his own existence into the mystery and movement of Morse Creek. He tells us, "I have a thing / for this cold swift water. / Just looking at it makes my blood run / and my skin tingle." The signs of life within his own body parallel the running of the current before him; its history is not entirely separated from his own. He imagines traveling upstream, which takes him back in time. At thirty-five, he remembers, his heart was "empty and sere"; yet, after five years it began to "flow again." Like an expansive current, Carver stands at the water's edge, fused into its flowing and mysterious purpose. As part of a mutual mystery, he is overwhelmed with affection for the new life flowing in him. He tells us:

> I'll take all the time I please this afternoon
> before leaving my place alongside this river.
> It pleases me, loving rivers.
> Loving them all the way back
> to their source.
> Loving everything that increases me.

"Where Water Comes Together with Other Water" is set at Morse Creek, along which Carver walked, sometimes daily, with Tess Gallagher. Gallagher recalls that late in his struggle with cancer, before a trip to Alaska, "Ray wanted to go to Morse Creek once more" (*Soul Barnacles*, 84). Debilitated by lung cancer, Carver walked with his wife as they proceeded on a slow and deliberate journey. When they reached the mouth of the creek and gazed on the fullness of water entering the sea, they experienced a moment of spiritual and personal connectivity. In a moment that metaphorically communicated an experience of new life, Gallagher remembers:

> without saying anything, we began to walk toward the mouth where this freshwater river joins the Strait of Juan de Fuca. . . . [Ray] was traveling on his remaining right lung, but carrying himself well in the effort, as if this were the way to do it, the way we had always done it. When we made it to the river mouth, there was an intake of joy for us both, to have crossed that ground. It was one of those actions that is so right it makes you able in another dimension, all the way back to the start of your life. We savored it, the river's freshwater outrush into salt water, that quiet standing up to life together, for as long as it was going to last. (*Soul Barnacles*, 84)

For Carver, flowing water was a sacred voice of active hope. Intent on communicating its message to others, he did not confine the healing presence of rivers to his own life but used the voice of water to guide his characters as well. Throughout "Kindling," Carver provides numerous allusions to a nearby river; the sound of the Little Quilcene River communicates something sacred to an emptied Myers, a dried-out man who desires restoration. It is a powerful river that "rushes down through the valley, shoots under the highway bridge, rushes another hundred yards over sand and sharp rocks, and pours into the ocean" (Raymond Carver, *Call If You Need Me*, 13). Although the river is fast and purposeful, its central power comes through its mystical ability to speak to Myers, the main character.

Myers comes into town and rents a room from a couple named Sol and Bonnie. As the couple show Myers the prepared room, he hears the water for the first time. Myers, known for being terse, simply states, "I hear water" (9). Sol tells him about the Little Quilcene River, but Myers offers no response. However, when the couple leave, Myers returns to the voice of water: "He opened the window all the way and heard the sound of the river as it raced through the valley on its way to the ocean" (10). Desiring more of its presence, Myers shifts the furniture in his room and moves his desk in front of the open window; he then stares at a blank page and writes a phrase reminiscent of Alcoholics Anonymous, "Emptiness is the beginning of all things." Cursing what he imagines to be his own foolishness, he turns out the light and stands in darkness—listening to the river's purposeful movement (10).

Myers's healing begins when he finds a purpose. A flatbed truck dumps two cords of wood in the yard, and he offers to cut the wood. Sol teaches Myers how to use a saw and how to split the kindling. After a day's work, Myers returns to his desk and is able to write about the simple pleasures of life: "I have sawdust in my shirtsleeves tonight. . . . It's a sweet smell" (18). He stays awake into the night, thinking about the wood and what he accomplished. Again, the voice of water leads Myers out of bed, and his eyes are drawn up the river. "When he raised his window the sweet, cool air poured in, and farther off he could hear the river coursing down the valley" (18). This passage contains spiritual significance for Myers, as Carver combines the voice of the water with the presence of wind, two traditional sources of the sacred.[8] In this moment Myers is circled by the presence of something beyond himself. As the cool air pours "in" and fills his being, Myers moves further toward recovery.

After cutting the wood, Myers decides to leave. However, he hesitates and opens the window again. In the darkness of night Myers looks to the pile of sawdust and listens to the river for a while. He then returns to his table and writes a final passage that documents this stage of his recovery: "The country I'm in is very exotic. It reminds me of someplace I've read about but never traveled to before now. Outside my window I can hear a river" (20). After finishing his entry Myers decides to stay one more night. Before crawling into bed Carver writes that Myers "left the window open . . . it was okay like that" (20).

"Something" happened to Myers that bears the marks of an encounter with the sacred. In his final entry Myers alludes to what is a common pattern in conversion narratives. He finds himself in an Edenic or "exotic" country. Like T. S. Eliot, who writes that the end of our searching "Will be to arrive where we started / And know the place for the first time" ("Little Gidding," in Eliot, *Four Quartets*, 241–42), Myers experiences a similar encounter that leads to revelation. He has read about this place, this river, but not fully known it until now. For this reason, Myers stays another night, not because he is tired or defeated but because this place feels like the home he has intuitively known and longed for his entire life.

Step Twelve: "Bearing Witness" and Concluding Thoughts

Having had a spiritual awakening as the result of these steps, we tried to carry this message to alcoholics, and to practice these principles in all our affairs. (*Twelve Steps*, 106)

The testimonial component of Alcoholics Anonymous requires that the recovered alcoholic carry the message of redemptive hope to others. Reflecting on Carver's generous spirit, Jay McInerney remembers that Carver participated in this call, as he often "accompanied friends in need to their first AA meetings" (122). In addition to attending meetings with struggling friends, Carver also wrote to those who found themselves dismantled by alcoholism. Gallagher includes one such letter in *Carver Country*. In this letter Carver provides a personal testimony of his own struggle with alcohol and offers words of encouragement to Mr. Hallstrom, an unstable writer who has written to Carver with concerns about sobriety and the temptation to drink. Carver concludes this lengthy letter in the following way:

Listen, I'm glad you wrote to me. I'm sorry if this seems hasty, or not very considered and thoughtful, but I wanted to get some kind of response back to you before any more time had elapsed.

Stay well. Don't drink, as they say. Think of me if ever you feel like you want to drink. I know if I can kick it, well, then there is hope for just about anybody. I had the world's worst case of it.

Write me again in a month or two, or whenever it's right, and tell me how you are and what you're doing.

This is with every good wish.

Warmly,

Ray Carver

("Letter to Mr. Hallstrom," 107)

Apparently this letter to Mr. Hallstrom was only one of many responses that Carver offered to those in need. As Gallagher indicates, "there's no way to tell how many writers and readers who'd connected with his escape from alcoholism were helped by him through the mails or through just learning of his escape" (*Soul Barnacles,* 219). Gallagher explains how many people "who have escaped alcoholism come [to Carver's grave]" after almost twenty years. They leave notes or a word of thanks, "like it's a kind of shrine" (Koch, *There Is in the Soul*). Jim Harbaugh, a Jesuit and Twelve Steps retreat leader, envisions using Carver's fiction and poetry to communicate hope to clients who are resistant to the religious or philosophical language present in the Twelve Step literature. Particularly optimistic about the use of "A Small, Good Thing," Harbaugh suggests, "The 'spiritual' qualities found in ['A Small, Good Thing'] might be a good way to describe spirituality without defining it in a way that puts off either religious or non-religious people . . . [the story's spiritual qualities] are very consonant with the qualities of the recovering person as described in 12 Step literature" ("Literature," 39).

Carver's vision of the sacred is spacious. However, without compartmentalizing his message into an explicit theological construct, it is worth considering that Carver's transformation may place him in the threshold of what Karl Rahner alludes to as anonymous Christianity. Rahner states:

> There is such a thing as anonymous Christianity. There are men who merely think that they are not Christians, but who are in the grace of God. And hence there is an anonymous humanism inspired by grace, which thinks that it is no more than human. . . . When we affirm as a doctrine of faith that human morality even in the natural sphere needs the grace of God to be steadfast in its great task, we recognize . . . that such humanism, wherever it displays its true visage and wherever it exists, even outside professed Christianity, is a gift of the grace of God and a tribute to the redemption, even though as yet it knows nothing of this. ("Poetry and the Christian," 366)

Rahner's insights remain both controversial and thought-provoking, as his observations seek to unify the "humanist" versus "religious" debate that continues to haunt Carver's work. However, when applied to Carver, Rahner's vision is by no means perfect, for the concept of "anonymous Christianity" still makes an explicitly religious claim on Carver's eclectic, or more specifically, "anonymous," spirituality. Nevertheless, seeking to reconcile humanism with theology is a move in the right direction, as any subsequent approach to the spiritual dimension of Carver's life and work will require a methodology that is sensitive to both spiritual and humanistic concerns. As scholars seek to reconcile these seemingly contradictory views, a long-standing dualism between "human" and "sacred" domains may begin to collapse. This can happen only as interpreters of religious thought and literature begin to investigate the material concerns of humanism, while those who have rejected spiritual traditions also consider how and why immanent grace may still lurk in our world.[9]

Although Carver never claimed to be religious, he believed that his own life testified to "miracles and the possibility of resurrection" (Simpson and Buzbee, 46). This peculiar affirmation of new life outside of institutionalized faith becomes plausible when contextualized within the Alcoholics Anonymous program. Entering Alcoholics Anonymous simply requires that substance abusers confess that they "do not own the truth to categorically state that there is no God . . . [however], as members recover, they no longer are in a position to argue whether or not [God] exists," for any denial of the sacred negates their own miraculous transformation (Wilcox, 80–81). In the midst of Carver's spiritual ambiguity, perhaps only two things are completely clear. First, "something" transformed Raymond Carver's life and work. Second, the structural patterns of at least some of the Twelve Steps of the Alcoholics Anonymous recovery program have proved to be a far larger influence on Carver's life and work than critics have previously recognized. For those seeking more definitive answers concerning Carver's personal beliefs, we are ultimately left with spiritual possibility rather than confessional certainty, as Carver alone may claim knowledge of these answers. When we push for spiritual certainties beyond what Carver has offered, we are reminded of his echoing phrase "No more words." Silence must answer what our words cannot.

Notes

1. Peter S. Hawkins offers some insightful comments on the relationship between Christianity and "A Small, Good Thing" in his introduction to the story in *Listening for God: Contemporary Literature and the Life of Faith*, ed. Hawkins and Paula J. Carlson (Minneapolis: Augsburg Fortress Press, 1994), 71–73.

2. After noting the autobiographical aspects of Carver's fiction, Cochrane, in "'Taking the Cure': Alcoholism and Recovery in the Fiction of Raymond Carver," *University of Dayton Review* 20, no. 1 (Summer 1989), discusses the debilitating aspects of alcoholism in "One More Thing," an early story published in *What We Talk about When We Talk about Love*. He then turns to *Cathedral* and *Where I'm Calling From*, noting how many of the stories are shaped by the spiritual message of rebirth, which is prevalent in Alcoholics Anonymous. Cochrane explains how "Where I'm Calling From," "Fever," and "A Small, Good Thing" are explicitly linked to the principles of the AA program.

3. Although this article focuses on Carver's spirituality in light of Alcoholics Anonymous, I should say up front that I do not intend to present the AA program as the sole narrative in Carver's recovery. Alcoholics Anonymous remains the focal point of this particular study; however, I am convinced that Carver's relationship with Tess Gallagher, his second wife, remains the most significant influence in his spiritual and relational recovery. This topic is yet another line of inquiry that is worthy of careful investigation.

4. Steve Mirarchi has compiled a variorum edition of "Cathedral" that compares the 1981 *Atlantic Monthly* version with the 1983 Knopf edition; see his "Conditions of Possibility: Religious Revision in Raymond Carver's 'Cathedral,'" *Religion and the Arts* 2, no. 3 (1998): 299–309. Although these revisions are not addressed in this essay, Mirarchi makes the assertion that "Carver's specific revisions ultimately bring about a new discourse on religion" (299).

5. In "A Small, Good Thing," the desire for forgiveness is particularly strong in the character of the baker, who repeatedly says how sorry he is as he seeks forgiveness for what he has done (287–88). For a comparative reading of "The Bath" and "A Small, Good Thing," see William L. Stull, "Beyond Hopelessville: Another Side of Raymond Carver," *Philological Quarterly* 64, no. 1 (Winter 1985): 1–15; and Kathleen Westfall Shute, "Finding the Words: The Struggle for Salvation in the Fiction of Raymond Carver," *Hollins Critic* 24, no. 5 (December 1987): 1–10.

6. In addition to "Put Yourself in My Shoes," "The Compartment," and "Kindling," I also suspect that "The Lie" is a story about Myers (Raymond Carver, *Fires: Essays, Poems, Stories* [1983; New York: Vintage Books, 1989], 141–43). Although the persona of the story is unnamed, the plot progression, literary allusions, and general tone of dialogue between the unnamed couple allow "The Lie" to be read as an extension of "Put Yourself in My Shoes." With four identified stories about Myers, it seems worth investigating and applying some of the theoretical concerns of the short-story sequence. For example, to what extent do these four stories read as a unified or extended narrative about one character and his physical, social, and spiritual transformations? Essays such as Robert M. Luscher's "The Short Story Sequence: An Open Book," in *Short Story Theory at a Crossroads*, ed. Susan Lohafer and Jo Ellyn Clarey (Baton Rouge: Louisiana State University Press, 1989), provide some solid insight concerning the possibilities and limitations of reading a body of short fiction as a cohesive unit, rather than as strictly isolated pieces of literature (209–16).

7. All references to Carver poems are from *All of Us: The Collected Poems*, ed. William L. Stull, introduction by Tess Gallagher (New York: Knopf, 1998), reprinted by permission of Tess Gallagher.

8. For a discussion of sacred aspects of wind (spirit/breath) and water in ancient traditions and texts, see Mircea Eliade, *The Sacred and the Profane: The Nature of Religion*, trans. Willard R. Trask (New York: Harcourt, Brace, 1959), 129–32; and Paul Ricoeur, *Figuring the Sacred: Religion, Narrative, and Imagination*, ed. Mark I. Wallace, trans. David Pellauer (Minneapolis: Fortress Press, 1995), 52–55.

9. A recent methodology that seeks to reconcile the division between religious and humanist thought is a project described as "Theological Humanism." For an overview of the methodology, see David E. Klemm, "Introduction: Theology of Culture as Theological Humanism," *Literature and Theology* 18, no. 3 (September 2004): 239–50. Klemm defines theological humanism as "a normative stance in life committed to the integrity of human life in its moral, ethical, and theological dimensions" (239). The trans-religious nature of theological humanism is indicated in this special issue of *Literature and Theology*, where an interdisciplinary collection of scholars engage literature and film through Christian, agnostic, and Buddhist perspectives.

Works Cited

Broyard, Anatole. "Diffuse Regrets." *New York Times,* September 5, 1983, 27.

Buber, Martin. *The Knowledge of Man: A Philosophy of the Interhuman,* ed. Maurice Friedman, trans. Maurice Friedman and Ronald Gregor Smith. New York: Harper and Row, 1965.

Campbell, Ewing. *Raymond Carver: A Study of the Short Fiction.* New York: Macmillan, 1992.

Carver, Chris. In Halpert, *Raymond Carver,* 183–84.

Carver, Raymond. *Call If You Need Me: The Uncollected Fiction and Other Prose,* ed. William L. Stull. New York: Vintage, 2001.

———. *Carver Country: The World of Raymond Carver.* Introduction by Tess Gallagher. Photography by Bob Adelman. New York: Charles Scribner's Sons, 1990.

———. *Cathedral.* New York: Alfred A. Knopf, 1983.

———. *Fires: Essays, Poems, Stories.* 1983. New York: Vintage, 1989.

———. "Letter to Mr. Hallstrom." In Carver, *Carver Country,* 105–7.

———. *No Heroics, Please: Uncollected Writings.* New York: Vintage, 1992.

———. *Where Water Comes Together with Other Water.* New York: Vintage, 1986.

———. *Will You Please Be Quiet, Please?* New York: McGraw-Hill, 1978.

Cochrane, Hamilton E. "'Taking the Cure': Alcoholism and Recovery in the Fiction of Raymond Carver." *University of Dayton Review* 20, no. 1 (Summer 1989): 79–88.

Doherty, Paul C. "A Note on the Function of Language in 'Cathedral.'" *Religion and the Arts* 2, no. 3 (1998): 337–42.

Duffy, Edward. "Word of God in Some Raymond Carver Stories." *Religion and the Arts* 2, no. (1998): 311–36.

Duranti, Riccardo. "A Conversation with Tess Gallagher." In *Cathedrals,* ed. Gianluca Bassi and Barbara Pezzopane, 89–109. Rome: Leconte Editore, 2002.

Eliade, Mircea. *The Sacred and the Profane: The Nature of Religion,* trans. Willard R. Trask. New York: Harcourt, Brace, 1959.

Eliot, T. S. *Four Quartets.* 1943. New York: Harcourt Brace Jovanovich, 1971.

Facknitz, Mark A. R. "'The Calm,' 'A Small, Good Thing,' and 'Cathedral': Raymond Carver and the Rediscovery of Human Worth." *Studies in Short Fiction* 23, no. 3 (Summer 1986): 287–96.

Ford, Richard. "Good Raymond." *New Yorker* 74, no. 30 (October 5, 1998): 70–76, 78–79.

Gallagher, Tess. *Soul Barnacles,* ed. Greg Simon. Ann Arbor: University of Michigan Press, 2000.

Gentry, Marshall Bruce, and William L. Stull, eds. *Conversations with Raymond Carver.* Jackson: University Press of Mississippi, 1990.

Halpert, Sam, ed. *Raymond Carver: An Oral Biography.* Iowa City: University of Iowa Press, 1995.

Harbaugh, Jim. "Literature (and Other Arts): What We Talk about When We Talk about Spirituality and Recovery." *Dionysos: Literature and Addiction TriQuarterly* 11, no. 1 (2001): 35–46.

Hawkins, Peter S., and Paula J. Carlson, eds. *Listening for God: Contemporary Literature and the Life of Faith*. Minneapolis: Augsburg Fortress Press, 1994.

Klemm, David E. "Introduction: Theology of Culture as Theological Humanism." *Literature and Theology* 18, no. 3 (September 2004): 239–50.

Koch, Alfred. *There Is in the Soul a Desire for Not Thinking: The Double Life of Raymond Carver*. Lea Redfern, English Translation Producer, Australian Broadcasting Corporation. Transcript. Third Coast International Audio Festival. Chicago Public Radio: www.thirdcoastfestival.org/transcripts_koch.asp

Lohafer, Susan. *Reading for Storyness*. Baltimore: Johns Hopkins University Press, 2003.

Luscher, Robert M. "The Short Story Sequence: An Open Book." In *Short Story Theory at a Crossroads*, ed. Susan Lohafer and Jo Ellyn Clarey, 148–67. Baton Rouge: Louisiana State University Press, 1989.

Marion, Jean-Luc. "The Blind Man of Siloe." Trans. Janine Langan. *Image: A Journal of the Arts and Religion* 29 (Winter 2000–2001): 59–69.

McCaffery, Larry, and Sinda Gregory. "An Interview with Raymond Carver." In *Alive and Writing: Interviews with American Authors of the 1980s*, ed. Larry McCaffery and Sinda Gregory, 66–82. Urbana: University of Illinois Press, 1987. Also in *Conversations*, ed. Gentry and Stull, 98–116.

McInerney, Jay. "Raymond Carver, Mentor." In *Remembering Ray: A Composite Biography of Raymond Carver*, ed. William L. Stull and Maureen P. Carroll, 119–26. Santa Barbara, Calif.: Capra, 1993.

Mirarchi, Steve. "Conditions of Possibility: Religious Revision in Raymond Carver's 'Cathedral.'" *Religion and the Arts* 2, no. 3 (1998): 299–309.

Nesset, Kirk. *The Stories of Raymond Carver: A Critical Study*. Athens: Ohio University Press, 1995.

Rahner, Karl. "Poetry and the Christian." In *Theological Investigations*, vol. 4, trans. Kevin Smyth, 357–67. New York: Crossroad, 1982.

Ricoeur, Paul. *Figuring the Sacred: Religion, Narrative, and Imagination*, ed. Mark I. Wallace, trans. David Pellauer. Minneapolis: Fortress Press, 1995.

———. *A Ricoeur Reader: Reflection and Imagination*, ed. Mario J. Valdés. Toronto: University of Toronto Press, 1991.

Runyon, Randolph Paul. *Reading Raymond Carver*. Syracuse, N.Y.: Syracuse University Press, 1992.

Sexton, David. "David Sexton Talks to Raymond Carver." *Literary Review* 85 (July 1985): 36–40. Also in *Conversations*, ed. Gentry and Stull, 120–32.

Shute, Kathleen Westfall. "Finding the Words: The Struggle for Salvation in the Fiction of Raymond Carver." *Hollins Critic* 24, no. 5 (December 1987): 1–10.

Simpson, Mona, and Lewis Buzbee. "Raymond Carver." In *Writers at Work: The Paris Review Interviews*, 7th series, ed. George Plimpton, 299–327. New York: Viking, 1986. Also in *Conversations*, ed. Gentry and Stull, 31–52.

Stull, William L. "Beyond Hopelessville: Another Side of Raymond Carver." *Philological Quarterly* 64, no. 1 (Winter 1985): 1–15.

Stull, William L., and Maureen P. Carroll. "Two Darings." *Philosophy and Literature* 22, no. 2 (1998): 468–77.

Taylor, Dennis. "The Need for a Religious Literary Criticism." *Religion and the Arts* 1, no. 1 (Fall 1996): 124–50.

Tillich, Paul. *The New Being.* New York: Charles Scribner's Sons, 1955.

Tromp, Hansmaarten, trans. Stephen T. Moskey. "Any Good Writer Uses His Imagination to Convince the Reader." In *Conversations,* eds. Gentry and Stull, 72–83.

Twelve Steps and Twelve Traditions. New York: Alcoholics Anonymous World Services, 1981.

Weber, Bruce. "Raymond Carver: A Chronicler of Blue-Collar Despair." In *Conversations,* ed. Gentry and Stull, 84–97.

Wilcox, Danny M. *Alcoholic Thinking: Language, Culture, and Belief in Alcoholics Anonymous.* Westport, Conn.: Praeger, 1988.

Wolff, Geoffrey. In Halpert, *Raymond Carver,* 184–88.

Wolff, Tobias. In Halpert, *Raymond Carver,* 153–59.

Paul Benedict Grant

Laughter's Creature

The Humor of Raymond Carver

Who doesn't feel the world brighten when they've had a few good from-the-belly laughs? (Raymond Carver, "On Longer Stories")

Taken out of context, this statement is innocuous enough, but some readers would be forgiven for doing a double take when they register the name of the author. Of all the words that critics habitually employ to characterize Raymond Carver's writing, "humor" is conspicuous by its absence: with few exceptions, far from provoking "a few good from-the-belly laughs," his work is commonly described as being dark, dismal, and depressing. Carver's longtime editor Gordon Lish, for example, believes that the value of his work lies in "his sense of a peculiar bleakness" (quoted in Weber, "Raymond Carver: A Chronicler," 87). Bruce Weber, in turn, senses a "vast unhappiness" in Carver's characters (87), a judgment shared by Larry McCaffery and Sinda Gregory: "Carver writes about troubled people on the outs," full of "emotional turmoil, and hopelessness" ("An Interview," 99, 101). While valid to a degree, assessments like these have painted Carver into a corner and "won him a reputation as a rootless chronicler of working-class despair" (Gentry and Stull, Introduction, xv).

Interestingly, these images contradict the impressions provided in personal portraits by Carver's family and friends. Despite their marital troubles, Carver's first wife, Maryann, considered him "a very funny man" (Halpert, *Raymond Carver*, 64). Close friend Richard Ford agrees: "When Ray was around there was such a sense of mirth and good humor in the air" (Halpert, 163). Another close friend, Tobias Wolff, describes Carver as "very, very funny" (244) and by way of illustration recounts an episode in which he and Carver literally lost control of themselves laughing: "I don't know which of us laughed first, but in a moment we were helpless with it, Ray bent double in his chair, pounding the floor with his feet" (247). On meeting Carver for the first time, Tobias's brother, Geoffrey, was also struck by his humor: "in no time at all we were laughing. Ray was a great laugher" (Halpert, 107). This impression is endorsed by Stephen Dobyns: "He had a great laugh. His whole body would collapse backwards as if he had been struck in the chest with something happy and his face would wrinkle and a high raspy noise would burst out again and again. There was nothing restrained about it. For a moment he was laughter's creature" (110). Many more acquaintances, including James D. Houston (16), Dennis Schmitz (49), and Morton Marcus (53), mention Carver's infectious laugh; indeed Dorothy Catlett considers Carver's "wonderful laugh" to be one of her most vivid memories of the man (198). Carver's second wife, Tess Gallagher, highlighted this aspect of his personality in her introduction to Bob Adelman's photographic retrospective *Carver Country:*

> If I could add one element to Bob Adelman's portraits of Ray, it would be something impossible to show in photographs—his infectious laughter. In his years with me the house was full of this laughter, which came out of him as a stored-up gladness, a hilarity that ignited spontaneously while he talked on the phone to friends, or sat in his bathrobe reading aloud from a letter. (19)

Given its prominence in his daily life, it would be surprising if this "infectious laughter" had not infected Carver's art to some degree, and close analysis of the texts confirms that this is indeed the case. His work may dwell on the desperate and the disenfranchised, but as Fred Moramarco notes, he is "never one to miss an opportunity for humor in the midst of gravity" ("Carver's Couples"). Examining Carver's use of humor in his poetry and fiction will shed light on what Gallagher calls "a much-overlooked element of his work" ("Carver Country," 12), enabling us to reassess his art and regain some ground from those who persist in positioning him as a painter of the darker shades of life.

Carver was well aware of the critical consensus—"I've been beaten over the head by some critics . . . saying that the picture I portray of America is not a happy one . . . that I'm concentrating on showing the dark underbelly of things" (O'Connell, "Raymond Carver," 147)—but he felt that this was an unfair assessment of his work:

> The tone is serious, by and large, though obviously some of the stories are humorous in places. . . . I think my stories often have to do with loss, and as a result the tone is, well, not somber, but severe. Grave, maybe, and somewhat dark—especially the early stories. . . . I suppose generally the tone is *grave*. But life is a serious business, isn't it? It's *grave* . . . tempered with humor. . . . I don't feel I'm emphasizing the dark side of things. (Alton, "What We Talk About," 155–56, 159)

As these comments show, Carver clearly recognized the humor in his work, and lamented the fact that many readers tended to focus on the darker elements at the expense of the lighter aspects. When Kay Bonetti mentioned the fact that few critics had remarked on the humor in his stories, he was pleased to put the record straight:

I'm glad you brought it up, because I feel that there is plenty of humor in them. There was a good long review of *Will You Please Be Quiet, Please?* in *Newsweek* when the book first appeared. And the reviewer did talk about the humor in the stories, and I was very glad to see that, because I think that there *is* humor in the stories—a little black humor maybe, but humor. ("Ray Carver," 58)

David Sexton elicited a similar response; when asked if his "humor is close to pain," Carver replied:

That's life, is it not? In a lot of instances the humor has a double edge to it. We laugh at it because if we didn't laugh at it . . . we could bawl our eyes out. I'm glad somebody does find humor in these stories. A story in *Cathedral* called "Careful," about a guy who has his ear plugged up, is on the face of it a grim and desperate situation, but I read the story aloud at Harvard University last month . . . and the people howled. They found it terribly funny in parts. They were not laughing at the last pages of the story, but there are places that are very funny. It's not the *Saturday Night Live* kind of humor, it's dark humor. ("David Sexton Talks," 131)

In one of Carver's last interviews, Gail Caldwell, commenting on the way "critics often grab onto a darkness of vision as a way of talking about the work," asked him if he found the world "as bleak a place as his stories suggest." In reply, Carver again drew attention to the response he had when reading his stories to an audience:

I don't [find it bleak] . . . I used to hold to that much more rigidly and steadily than I do now. And it's not just because my own circumstances have changed, which they have. I still think it's a bitter—a grim scene out there. But I feel a little more affirmative, a little more cheerful. . . .

All my stories are a little bit dark. . . . But there's humor in them, too, often. I think "Elephant" is funny. I read it aloud once, and it was hard to get through the story because of the laughter. ("Raymond Carver: Darkness," 245–46)[1]

The "grim and desperate situation[s]" Carver writes about may not seem conducive to comedy, but humor often springs from pain, loss, and conflict of some kind, as a coping mechanism. As Carver admits, his humor is decidedly "black": "life is a serious business," "bitter" and "grim," but humor helps to temper its "grave" aspects, moderating its hardships, toughening the spirit against adversity, and offering a means of emotional escape. In this respect, it corresponds to the theory of black humor, or gallows humor, propounded by Freud in *Jokes and Their Relation to the Unconscious* (1905) and "Humour" (1927). In Freud's opinion, humor acts as a safety valve, a way of releasing repressed feelings. It is evasive, a way of distancing or displacing negative emotions, but it also has a heroic function in the sense of liberation it achieves in allowing us to stand aloof from the trials and tribulations of life:

> Humor has something liberating about it; but it also has something of grandeur and elevation. . . . The grandeur in it clearly lies in the triumph of narcissism, the victorious assertion of the ego's invulnerability. The ego refuses to be distressed by the provocations of reality, to let itself be compelled to suffer. It insists that it cannot be affected by the traumas of the external world; it shows, in fact, that such traumas are no more than occasions for it to gain pleasure. (Freud, "Humour," 162)

When questioned by David Applefield on the way in which many of his characters "reflect certain classic psychological tendencies," Carver admitted to having no detailed knowledge of Freud's works ("Fiction & America," 212), but his conception of humor as a palliative against pain—"We laugh at it because if we didn't laugh at it . . . we could bawl our eyes out"—accords with Freud's theory of humor as displaced emotion. Freud's idea of humor as a heroic force that allows us to "triumph" over "the traumas of the external world" is also germane. Carver's personal traumas appear in refracted form throughout his work: alcoholism, dysfunctional relationships, financial hardship. Nevertheless, as Kirk Nesset notes, "while such scenarios reflect to an extent the darkest periods of Carver's early married life, they also attest to his triumph, to that miraculous recovery of sorts, and to Carver's uncanny capacity for transforming life into art, for erecting a monument to pain even as he learned to transcend it" (*The Stories of Raymond Carver*, 2). Even while acknowledging his preoccupation with the disappointments that life occasionally affords, Carver stressed that he was "also interested in survival, what people can do to raise themselves up when they've been laid low" (Boddy, "A Conversation," 199). In "His Bathrobe Pockets Stuffed with Notes" (262),[2] a poem that "reveal[s] humorously the haphazard nature of creation itself" (Gallagher, introduction, in Carver, *A New Path to the Waterfall*, 316), one of the fragments that Carver supplies derives from the television series *Star Trek*: "We've sustained damage, but we're still able / to maneuver." Despite its seeming flippancy, Gallagher sees this snippet as representative of Carver's oeuvre: "It's this attempt to maneuver, with and in spite of damage, which constitutes the heroic in Carver Country" ("Carver Country," 10). Humor was an important tool in this process: it helped Carver maneuver his way through the difficult terrain of his own life and those he chose to depict, retaining his composure—and at times enabling his characters to retain theirs—in the face of events that would have otherwise proved emotionally crippling. In doing so, Carver was able to "throw some light on what it is that makes us, and keeps us, often against great odds, recognizably human" (Carver, "All My Relations," 137).

In her introduction to Carver's collected poems *All of Us*, Gallagher likens his prosodic style to that of Lao-tzu, author of *Tao Te Ching*, as being "radiant with humor" (xxiii). In truth, his humor sounds only intermittently in his poetry, and when it *is* there, it usually functions as a means of offsetting an encroaching, darker vision. There are humorous flashes that fall outside this definition—the list of mechanical mishaps in "The Car" (151), the rueful remarks on composition in "Reaching" (77), or the following excerpt from his first published poem, "The Brass Ring" (297), which describes a couple riding a merry-go-round: "the young woman laughed / all the time, he said. The husband laughed / too, even though he had a moustache." However, these are exceptions to the rule; for the most part, humor appears in the midst of minor (and not so minor) disasters, as a means of displacing pain. This is not to undersell its importance; on the contrary, it is a testament to Carver's comic spirit that he could wrest humor from influences and events that had such a negative impact on his life.

Foremost among these negative influences is alcohol. "There's no way to make a joke out of this," says the narrator of "Where I'm Calling From," referring to his alcoholism and his second spell at a drying-out facility (242), but Carver does precisely that: despite the fact that alcohol had such a damaging effect on his own life, he manages to extract some humor from the situations he describes. In "For Semra, with Martial Vigor" (11), the speaker, in an effort to amuse his date, careens around the kitchen in mock military guise and accidentally knocks over a teapot. A shamed sense of drunkenness mitigates the humor of the poem's last lines, but they are funny nonetheless:

> I'm sorry I said
> to the teapot
> Semra I mean
> Hell she said
> I don't know why the hell
> I let you pick me up.

In a later poem, "You Don't Know What Love Is" (16), the humor is broader, as befits its subject. Written in the form of a drunken monologue by Charles Bukowski, the poem is a parodic tour de force—Donald Justice calls it "a masterpiece of comedy" (Halpert, 32)—and suggests that despite the ravages wreaked by alcohol, Carver was occasionally able to see the funny side of the subject.

According to Maryann, she and Carver were able to laugh about their drunken exploits before his descent into alcoholism: "occasionally we did get drunk . . . it was only on occasion, and when it happened we thought it was funny" (Halpert, 73). Later their drinking led to some frightening incidents, but as Chuck Kinder observes, they always managed to laugh about their misfortunes:

it would be interesting to see how he and Maryann would talk about horrific things they had gone through. Bill Kittredge has a terrific story about a couple of old funky barroom ladies who have learned to cut their losses to jokes. And that's what happened with Ray and Maryann. They'd tell these horrific stories and they'd be laughing about them. (Halpert, 38)

Many years later, having achieved sobriety, Carver was still able to laugh at his former drunken "hi-jinks"; as Gallagher recalls, "I can remember wonderful evenings with the painters Susan Lytle and Alfredo Arreguin in Seattle, during which Ray and Alfredo would be in tears with laughter while sharing some near-catastrophic tale of their separate drinking days" ("Carver Country," 13). Carver behaved the same way with Lewis Buzbee: "He laughed out of control at his own stories, as much amused by the sordid tales of his past as exhilarated by the changes in his life" (117). In Carver's fiction some alcoholics do the same. In "Where I'm Calling From," one of the narrator's fellow inmates, Tiny, tells "nutty stories" in order to minimize the seriousness of his situation (238): "Tiny . . . began telling about something that had happened on one of his drinking bouts. People at the table laughed and shook their heads. . . . We'd all done things just as bad and crazy, so, sure, that's why we laughed" (228). The narrator of "Where Is Everyone?" reacts similarly when listening to confessions at AA meetings: "I would listen and shake my head and laugh in recognition of the awful stories I heard" (159). Adding insult to injury, his children use his alcoholic mishaps to entertain their friends, "regaling their pals with the most frightful stories, howling with laughter as they spilled out the lurid details of what was happening to me and their mother" (158).

This concept of cutting one's losses to jokes is distinctly Freudian. Like their father, the children in "Where Is Everyone?" are distancing themselves from a hurtful home life by joking about a situation that, in reality, is anything but humorous. The inmates in "Where I'm Calling From" also use humor to achieve a sense of liberation, asserting their invulnerability in face of the facts, refusing to be, as Freud has noted, "distressed by the provocations of reality" and insisting that they "cannot be affected by the traumas of the external world" ("Humour, "162). Indeed, in recounting jokes based on their drunken exploits, they maintain "that such traumas are no more than occasions . . . to gain pleasure." However, their humor is essentially evasive—the laughter of forgetting. While applauding the impulse, Carver is careful to emphasize the poignancy of the situation. Tiny's seizure, which follows close on the heels of his jokes, serves as a reminder of the reality that he and his fellow alcoholics seek to escape.

Other poems testify to Carver's ability to find humor in otherwise awful situations. In "Our First House in Sacramento" (67), the speaker opens a long list of domestic disasters by recounting the night when a stranger appeared at the door brandishing a baseball bat, only to break down weeping in frustration when he realized that he had mistaken the new owner for the old one. "None of this," notes the speaker ruefully, "had anything to do / with Beatlemania." The same comic sensibility is present in another poem from the same collection, "Next Year" (68), which chronicles the downfall of an alcoholic couple. The poem moves from one calamity to the next in a mounting crescendo of catastrophe; yet, the speaker still manages to find humor in the experience: "she took the microphone / from the singer's hands and crooned her own / torch song. Then danced. And then passed out / on the table."

The humor in these late poems may be dependent on Carver's changed circumstances at the time of writing. The original situations were surely anything but humorous, but the intervening years had allowed him to, in a Wordsworthian sense, recollect his emotions in tranquillity, that is, from a sure-footed position of sobriety and restored order. As Arthur Saltzman notes, "a provisional ease has been won which makes relationships a bit less consternating and tempers memories of family misunderstandings, burned-out passions, or alcoholic wreckage with opportunities for renewal" (*Understanding Raymond Carver*, 166–67). This newfound "ease" would account for the droll sense of humor, suggesting that Carver's years of sobriety enabled him to mine past events with an eye for the amusing remains buried beneath the tragic.

This process is at work in the late fiction too. In "Intimacy," a successful writer revisits his ex-wife and is subjected to a huge harangue. The situation is hardly humorous, but Carver's mode of telling renders it so. While admitting that "the emotion of the story is true, in every line," he denied that it had any basis in reality (Stull, "Matters of Life and Death," 188); still, this is another occasion where he transcends original emotions via humor, mollifying a harrowing state of affairs. As Ford writes, "I would say that if that story originated in anything like what it represents to be, that when the original events were taking place there was no humor in it. When he wrote it, though . . . I can't believe that he didn't know there were many funny things in this story" (Halpert, 160).

Humor's ability to temper past experience and offer refuge in the midst of present troubles achieves particular poignancy in "Distance." Urged by his daughter, a father relates a story from the early days of his marriage, when he and his now estranged wife were happy and content. Cracks were already showing, however, and the fault line was revealed when he chose to go on a hunting trip instead of staying with his wife and their crying child. He returns, and they are reconciled. She prepares breakfast, but as he is sitting down to the meal, he overturns his plate, and they burst out laughing. Years later the narrator looks back on this moment of shared laughter as a haven of happiness: "They had laughed. They had leaned on each other and laughed until the tears had come, while everything else—the cold and where he'd go in it—was outside, for a while anyway" (160). The title of the story refers not only to the distance in space and time but also to the emotional detachment required to maintain composure in the face of subsequent events. Here, laughter is almost talismanic, a weapon used to ward off external forces, but it ultimately proves powerless to prevent them from entering. In this respect, the humor in many of Carver's stories might be seen as an attempt not only to smooth over present difficulties but also to recapture the emotion of that earlier laughter, which represents a state of lost innocence.

In Carver's fiction, alcoholism is often attended by instances of infidelity, separation, and divorce, but despite the anguish these events occasion, the stories are not without humor. The howls of the Harvard audience attest to the humor in "Careful," but its combination of farce and anguish is also present in "A Serious Talk," in which the estranged husband, in moments of manic impulsiveness, burns his wife's collection of Christmas logs, steals her home-baked pies, and saws through the telephone line with a carving knife. Similar scenes occur in "One More Thing," in which the husband hurls a jar of pickles through a window and then, having been given his marching orders from his wife, proceeds to steal extraneous toilet items—including her eyelash curler. Frustrated, and unable to communicate on a civilized level, these men resort to petty thievery. Carver invites us to laugh at their actions but compels us to recognize their ridiculous acts of revenge as poignant forms of self-preservation.

Infidelity is treated humorously in "Sacks," in which the narrator visits his adulterous father. An ironic tone is established as they enter an airport bar and he readies himself to listen to the old man's confession: "I leaned back in the seat and drew a long breath, inhaling from what I took to be the air of woe that circled his head" (38). During their conversation, he fingers an ashtray that contains the comically incongruous reading "HARRAH'S CLUB / RENO AND LAKE TAHOE / GOOD PLACES TO HAVE FUN" (39). Even more incongruously, he must listen to the constant laughter of a female patron while his father is trying to unburden himself of his guilt. The woman's laughter is prompted by her seduction by two men at the bar, a situation that mirrors his father's story, for jokes initiated his affair with Sally: "pretty soon she gives a little laugh at something I'd said. . . . Then she asks if I'd heard the one about the travelling shoe-salesman who called on the widow woman. We laughed over that one, and then I told her one a little worse. So then she laughs hard at that. . . . One thing's leading to another, is what's happening" (42). Laughter was a bridge that brought them together. No such bridge will be built with his son, but the ironic tone with which the latter relates the episode prefigures the narrator's eventual acceptance of the situation and suggests that he has begun to reevaluate his opinion of his father—even empathize with him. The story is being told in flashback: a year has passed. Now his own marriage seems to be floundering. It is significant that the last line of the story ends with a joke at the expense of his wife.

Carver exploits the comic side of marital miscommunication to much greater effect in "Fever." Carlyle's wife, Eileen, has left him for another man and a "bohemian" life in California: "after eight years of being married to him, Eileen had pulled out. She was, she said in her letter, 'going for it'" (254). Carlyle receives "long, rambling letters" from her, full of silly statements on the strength of their spiritual attachment: "She wrote, 'That which is truly bonded can never become unbonded.' . . . He hated the word *bonded*. What did it have to do with the two of them? Did she think they were a corporation?" (253). From her telephone calls, it would appear that Eileen has been dabbling in Buddhism: "She wanted to talk about his head and his karma. She'd looked into his karma. It was going to improve any time now, she said. Carlyle listened, hardly able to believe his ears" (254). Eileen seems to have lost all conception of practical matters:

> "I'd better get off the phone now. I don't want to run up your nickel."
> Eileen laughed. "It's only money. Money's not important except as a necessary medium of exchange. There are more important things than money. But then you already know that."
> He held the receiver out in front of him. He looked at the instrument from which her voice was issuing. (256)

While Carlyle is recovering from his fever, Eileen tells him to record his thoughts in writing so he will have "an hour-by-hour account of [his] sickness" (267). Again, Carlyle cannot credit what he is hearing: "He pressed his fingertips against his temple and shut his eyes. But she was still on the line, waiting for him to say something. What could he say? It was clear to him that she was insane" (268).

The narrator of "Menudo" has a similar problem, caught between his current wife, Vicky, an affair with a neighbor, and the memory of his ex-wife, Molly, a woman who, like Eileen, seeks some kind of higher meaning as a result of a broken marriage. Like Eileen, Molly sends her ex-husband bizarre letters full of new-age philosophy:

> They were full of talk about "auras" and "signs." Occasionally she reported a voice that was telling her something she ought to do or some place she should go. And once she told me that no matter what happened, we were still "on the same frequency." She always knew exactly what I felt, she said. She "beamed in on me," she said, from time to time. . . . She also had a new word for destiny: *Karma*. "I'm following out my karma," she wrote. "Your karma has taken a bad turn." (379)

The narrator's affair with Vicky caused Molly's first nervous collapse: "It was after I took her home that I began hearing about 'higher power' and 'going with the flow'—stuff of that sort. Our destiny had been 'revised'" (376). He balks at this behavior and leaves her. In an effort to make sense of what has happened, Molly wound up going to fortune-tellers, palm readers, *crystal ball gazers*, looking for answers, trying to figure out what she should do with her life. She quit her job, drew out her teacher's retirement money, and thereafter never made a decision without consulting the *I Ching*. She began wearing strange clothes—clothes with permanent wrinkles and a lot of burgundy and orange. She even got involved with a group that sat around, I'm not kidding, trying to levitate. (376)

Unable to let go of the past, Molly continues to contact the narrator at his new address:

Finally, she said, it didn't matter, it was of no real concern to her, if she and I lived together the rest of our lives or not. Our love existed on a "higher plane." That's what she said to Vicky over the phone that time, after Vicky and I had set up housekeeping together. Molly called, got hold of Vicky, and said, "You have your relationship with him, but I'll always have mine. His destiny and mine are linked."

My first wife, Molly, she talked like that. "Our destinies are linked." She didn't talk like that in the beginning. It was only later, after so much had happened, that she started using words like "cosmic" and "empowerment" and so forth. (375–76)

As funny as these descriptions are, they are also poignant. Molly's newfound interests are a result of the separation, a response to a situation she finds difficult to handle; the narrator, for his part, finds recourse in humor in the manner described by Freud: the comic way in which he relates the details of Molly's lifestyle and communications allows him to distance himself from an unpleasant set of circumstances and offset the guilt he feels over abandoning her.

In addition to his marital troubles, the narrator of "Menudo" has cash concerns due to a financially dependent mother. In this respect, the story has links to "Elephant." Financially drained by his mother, brother, son, daughter, and ex-wife, the narrator threatens to move to Australia in order to escape their influence. The responses he receives vary wildly. His aged mother, oblivious of the irony, considers returning to waitressing, while his son, who had previously considered drug dealing to make ends meet, threatens suicide:

For one thing, he was allergic to cocaine. It made his eyes stream and affected his breathing, he said. This meant he couldn't test the drugs in the transactions he'd need to make. So, before it could even begin, his career as a drug dealer was over. No, he said, better a bullet in the temple and end it all right here. Or maybe hanging. That would save him the trouble of borrowing a gun. And save us the price of bullets. (393)

Predictably the narrator continues to provide money. In the meantime, he has two vivid dreams. In one he imagines himself drinking alcohol, the root of his worst experiences; in the other he recalls the way in which, when he was a child, his father used to support him on his shoulders, an experience that imparted a feeling of security. The significance of these dreams—which are analogous to his present situation vis-à-vis his family—is not lost on him, and the morning after he reassesses his situation:

> all of a sudden, I could imagine how it must have sounded to my family when I'd threatened them with a move to Australia. They would have been shocked at first, and even a little scared. Then, because they knew me, they'd probably started laughing. Now, thinking about their laughter, I had to laugh, too. *Ha, ha, ha.* That was exactly the sound I made there at the table—*ha, ha, ha*—as if I'd read somewhere how to laugh. (398–99)

Feeling better, he sets off for work and bumps into a coworker, George, who is driving a souped-up car. George's guffaw echoes the narrator's laughter: "He laughed—*ha, ha, ha*" (400); just as significantly, he refers to his car as a "baby" (401) for whom he had to borrow money to have overhauled, recalling the family commitments that had hitherto plagued the narrator. As Nesset notes, "George has discovered, as his coworker has, that not only do responsibilities and obligations sometimes fail to drag one down, they even afford uncanny liberty" (90). The tale ends on a note of exhilaration, as the narrator climbs aboard and casts off his worries. Laughter once again acts as a form of emotional release in the manner described by Freud. Both men are still bound to reality, but their laughter offers temporary relief from the pressures under which they have been living.

"Fever," "Menudo," and "Elephant" are stories of survival: Carlyle survives his fever and his broken marriage; the narrator of "Menudo," instead of fleeing his emotions as he had done previously, finally seems to take responsibility for his actions; the narrator of "Elephant" reconciles himself to his obligations and, as a result, experiences a feeling of euphoria. They all face difficult trials but are able to face them with a degree of humor. That humor derives from Carver himself, who had lived through similar experiences and survived them. As he recognized, the tone of these late stories is more positive than that in his previous work. "Cathedral" marked the turning point: "I knew that story was different from anything I'd ever written, and all of the stories after that seemed to be fuller somehow and much more generous and maybe more affirmative" (Sexton, 125). This newfound optimism seems to have heralded a corresponding change in Carver's humor, which finds fuller expression. Marilynne Robinson, for example, describes his last stories as "more rueful and humorous" ("Marriage," 40), despite the fact that they deal with subjects familiar to his earlier work.

As Nesset notes, one of these subjects was "present in Carver's work from the beginning" but "emerges concretely only in the later work," where he "confront[s]" death and mortality head-on" (74). One might expect Carver's treatment of this subject to be solemn, but it is invariably humorous. In "I Could See the Smallest Things," for example, the death of Sam's wife, Millie, is reported with comical understatement: "She was only forty-five when she did it. Heart failure. It hit her just as she was coming into their drive. The car kept going and went on through the back of the carport" (33). The same type of humor is present in "Boxes," in which the narrator relates the death of his partner, Jill's, second husband: "he drove their car through a bridge into the Elwha River. He didn't have life insurance, not to mention property-damage insurance. Jill had to borrow money to bury him, and then—can you beat it?—she was presented with a bill for the bridge repair" (333). In "Where Is Everyone?" the narrator's account of his father's death, as recalled by his mother, manages to be both macabre and funny: "She said later she noticed nothing out of the ordinary except maybe his snoring seemed heavier and deeper and she couldn't get him to turn on his side. But she went to sleep. She woke up when my dad's sphincter muscles and bladder let go. It was just sunrise. Birds were singing" (162–63).

In all of these examples death is presented in a farcical fashion that robs it of its sting. The same can be said of the depictions of death in "Put Yourself in My Shoes." Atypically for Carver, the story concerns a writer, Myers, and the sometimes felicitous alchemy involved in artistic inspiration. It opens with Myers's wife informing him of the suicide of Larry Gudinas, who used to work with him but had gotten "canned" (74). When the Myerses visit the Morgans, Mr. Morgan relates a story of an adulterous professor who was ordered out of his house by his wife; while he was leaving, his son threw a can of tomato soup at him, causing a serious concussion that led to hospitalization. The two tales seem unrelated, but as Randolph Runyon points out, they "are connected by Carver's outlandish pun: both [men], after a fashion, got 'canned'" (*Reading Raymond Carver*, 45). More black humor follows. The Morgans are fuming over the way the Myerses abused their privileges while staying at their home, but rather than confront them directly, they relate an analogous episode that occurred during their trip to a museum in Germany. While there, Mrs. Morgan lost her purse, which contained a check and a large sum of cash. Mrs. Attenborough tracked them down and returned it, minus the cash, but as she was about to leave, she had a heart attack. Mrs. Morgan describes the death melodramatically, but Myers's laughter punctures the pretentiousness:

"Fate sent her to die on the couch in our living-room in Germany," Mrs. Morgan said.

Myers began to laugh. "Fate . . . sent . . . her . . . to . . . die . . . in . . . your . . . living . . . room?" he said between gasps.

"Is that funny, sir?" Morgan said. "Do you find that amusing?"

Myers nodded. He kept laughing. He wiped his eyes on his shirt sleeve. "I'm really sorry," he said. "I can't help it. That line '*Fate sent her to die on the couch in our living-room in Germany.'* I'm sorry. Then what happened?" he managed to say. "I'd like to know what happened then." (86)

The story has a sting in its tail: in an effort to locate Mrs. Attenborough's address, Mrs. Morgan had opened her purse and discovered the missing money. Again, Myers cannot control his laughter:

> Myers giggled.
>
> "If you were a real writer, as you say you are, Mr. Myers, you would not laugh," Morgan said as he got to his feet. "You would not dare laugh! You would try to understand. You would plumb the depths of that poor soul's heart and try to understand. But you are no writer, sir!"
>
> Myers kept on giggling.
>
> Morgan slammed his fist on the coffee table and the cups rattled in the coasters. "The real story lies right here, in this house, this very living room, and it's time it was told! The real story is *here*, Mr. Myers," Morgan said. . . . He stopped to glare at Myers, who was holding his forehead and shaking with laughter. (86–87)

In his belief that "real" writers would not dare to laugh at such a thing, Morgan betrays his humorlessness and instinctive bent toward tragedy; Myers's response, by contrast, could be seen as a metatextual comment against those critics who accuse Carver of being overly serious and refuse to credit his comic side. Like Myers, Carver dares to laugh at death—even when his characters do decide to "plumb the depths."

This is ably demonstrated in "Whoever Was Using This Bed," a story that "provides a humorous, comprehensive look at human powerlessness in the face of oblivion, as well as our strategies for compensating for such debility" (Nesset, 91). Woken in the night by a wrong number, Jack and Iris are unable to get back to sleep and fall to discussing terminal illnesses while ironically working their way through a pack of cigarettes. "I feel as if I've come to a place I never thought I'd have to come to," Jack thinks, "a place where a little harmless dreaming and then some sleepy, early-morning talk has led me into considerations of death and annihilation" (361). The ironic tone is apt, for the manner in which they consider these subjects results in some comical dialogue:

> "Who knows what we'll die of?" Iris says. "It could be anything. If we live long enough, maybe it'll be kidney failure, or something like that. . . . That's what can happen to you sometimes if you're lucky enough to get really old. When your kidneys fail, the body starts filling up with uric acid then. You finally turn a whole different color before you die."
>
> "Great. That sounds wonderful," I say. "Maybe we should get off this subject . . . ?" (354–55)

At one point, Jack admits to having sharp pains in his side:

> "Maybe it's my gallbladder. Or else maybe a gall*stone*, whatever the hell that is."
>
> "It's not really a stone," she says. "A gallstone is like a little granule, or something like that. It's about as big as the tip of a pencil. No, wait, that might be a *kidney* stone I'm talking about. I guess I don't know anything about it." She shakes her head.
>
> "What's the difference between kidney stone and gallstone," I say. "Christ, we don't even know which side of the body they're on. You don't know, and I don't know. That's how much we know together. A total of nothing. But I read somewhere that you can pass a kidney stone, if that's what this is, and usually it won't kill you. Painful, yes. I don't know what they say about a gallstone."
>
> "I like that 'usually,'" she says. (357)

Things escalate when they address the question of whether they will unplug each other should they ever be on life-support systems. Jack decides against it:

> "As long as people can stand the sight of me, just so long as they don't start howling, don't unplug anything. Let me keep going, okay? Right to the bitter end. Invite my friends in to say good-bye. Don't do anything rash."
>
> "Be serious," she says. "This is a very serious matter we're discussing." (360)

Returning from work later the same day, Jack gives Iris the answer he failed to deliver the night before: "I'll pull the plug for you. . . . But what I said about my plug still stands" (361). As they are making up, the phone rings; it is the mystery caller of the night before. As Jack vents his anger on her, Iris unplugs the telephone, and "the line goes dead." Runyon has drawn attention to "the more or less hidden pun" here "between unplugging a phone and unplugging a life-support system" (194), but another pun escapes his notice: Iris's accompanying comment—"The *gall* of that woman" (362)—echoes the earlier conversation on gallbladders and gallstones, reinforcing the link between telephone plugs and life-support machines. Iris has, in a sense, broken her promise and pulled the plug on Jack. These sly puns, slipped into a story that might have suffered from a surfeit of seriousness in someone else's hands, are symptomatic of Carver's comic spirit and typify the tone of his late fiction. Nesset's appraisal of "Errand," another late story that also deals with death, is applicable: "it is not grimness that we come away with but triumph, a sense of the triumphs of imagination, the limited yet inspirational victories of the human mind over cessation" (97).

These triumphs are also present in Carver's poems, which "deal much more specifically, and autobiographically," with death (Nesset, 91). In keeping with their autobiographical nature, however, the humor in the poems is more conscious of its function as a means of displacing a subject Carver would perhaps rather not consider too closely. In "Fear" (60), for example, the speaker ends a long catalog of apprehensions by replicating the line "Fear of death" and then reprimands himself for the repetition—"I've said that"—suggesting that death is very much on his mind. At times poems that begin light-heartedly darken as they progress, as in "Woolworth's, 1954" (53), in which a comic play on the mispronounced word "Linger-ey" (for "lingerie") segues into a meditation on mortality, as the speaker admits that some of the lovers from whom he stripped said lingerie are now most probably dead.

Other poems move in the opposite direction, as if to escape death's dominion. In "Ask Him" (92), which deals with a visit to a cemetery in Montparnasse, the speaker and his son are accompanied by a guard, and he and the boy "joke together" as they wander among the graves. They stop by the grave of Baudelaire. Puzzled by the number of inscriptions on the tombstone, the speaker, via his son, asks the guard to provide an explanation; the guard places "One hand over the other. Grinning," as his son translates: "'Like a sandwich, Pop,' my son says. 'A Baudelaire sandwich.'" The light-hearted talk abruptly stops when the speaker tells his son to ask the guard if he has plans to be buried in the cemetery: "He looks from one to the other of us. / Who are we kidding? Are we making a bad joke? / He salutes and walks away. / Heading for a table in an outdoor café. / Where he can take off his cap, run his fingers / through his hair. Hear laughter and voices."

The guard's need to put thoughts of death behind him and return to a zone of light and laughter recurs in a later poem, "Wake Up" (287), in which the speaker and his partner visit a castle dungeon. All of the torturer's tools are on display: the rack, the iron maiden (engraved "with a little noncommittal smile"), and the executioner's block. On a whim, the speaker kneels and rests his head in the block, and his partner, playing along, reenacts a mock execution. What begins as a joke ends in an unnerving experience:

> I push myself up off my knees, and I look at her,
> neither of us smiling, just shaky
> and not ourselves. Then her smile and my arm going
> around her hips as we walk into the next corridor
> needing the light.

This poem appears in Carver's last collection of poetry, *A New Path to the Waterfall*, composed in part during the last months of his life. For obvious reasons, death is a major preoccupation. Many of the poems are openly elegiac, but Carver did not let death stand in the way of laughter: as Gallagher records, "His humor, lashed as it was to pain, positively unraveled me" (*All of Us*, xxviii). One of the most harrowing poems, "Lemonade" (284), deals with the drowning of a young boy. In Gallagher's opinion, it exemplifies Carver's "genius for transmitting subtle inflections of emotion, including humor at the saddest moments. For when a sorrow is too relentlessly pursued, we can't help ourselves—we laugh, refreshing ourselves for the hardest truths" (*All of Us*, 367). The hardest truth that Carver had to face was the news of his imminent death, but his response reveals that humor had not deserted him. "What the Doctor Said" (289) deals with Carver being given the news of the lung cancer that would kill him:

> I just looked at him
> for a minute and he looked back it was then
> I jumped up and shook hands with this man who'd just given me
> something no one else on earth had ever given me
> I may even have thanked him habit being so strong

Tobias Wolff sees this poem as an example of Carver's "very macabre sense of humor" (Halpert, 192), but it also exemplifies the way his "self-humor steadily redeems him" (Gallagher, *All of Us*, xxiii). This humorous self-deprecation is also on show in "No Need" (293), in which a somber tone is comically displaced by the colloquial questions that follow: "I see an empty place at the table. / Whose? Who else's? Who am I kidding?"

   Although Carver often dealt humorously with death in his work—even deriving humor from his own fatal illness—he was not inclined to discuss it in person, according to Geoffrey Wolff:

> I had written something about [my heart] operation and the events leading up to it. And very characteristic of me, the seriousness in that piece came from what I hoped was a comic imagination. . . . So Ray had taken some pleasure from the piece, but when I spoke to him about the origin of the piece and explained some of the details of the illness, it was the only time I ever noticed him uneasy around me. . . . The subject of illness or death was not at all welcome. On the page, it was a different matter, but not face to face. (Halpert, 184)

Tobias Woolf had the same impression when seeing Carver while he was recovering from his first operation for lung cancer: "He never let people talk about it when they'd come over to the house. We'd sit around and joke and laugh. He'd laugh and gossip and ignore his sickness" (Halpert, 192). Olivier Cohen had a similar experience when he visited Carver a few months before his death: "He gave no sign of his suffering and joked around as usual" (164). In his unwillingness to dwell on his condition and deflect its seriousness with jokes, Carver's behavior evokes Freud's theory of humor and accords with his customary treatment of such themes in his work; in particular, it recalls his poignant portrait of the dying Chekhov in "Errand": he "continued to insist there was nothing seriously wrong. 'He laughed and jested as usual . . . while spitting blood into a large vessel'" (419–20).

Dick Day visited Carver five weeks before he died and testifies to his continued good humor: "We laughed until tears came" (Halpert, 196). For Gallagher, that laugh is one of the most missed aspects of her late husband's presence:

> When I think "never again" of that beautiful sound that was most him for me, I have to be crushed, crushed and uplifted at once. Crushed because it is too beautiful. Uplifted because it is too beautiful to sacrifice to mourning, but must be treasured . . . entrusted to all who shared rooms and hearts with that laughter while he lived. ("Carver Country," 19)

Critics must treasure and entrust the sound of that laughter to Carver's future readers in order to rescue his work from a preponderance of one-sided appraisals and misapplied notions; his humor is too important to sacrifice to such limited interpretations. Beneath the ostensibly murky material of Carver Country, a place of crushed aspirations and broken lives, lies a vision that is ultimately uplifting and redemptive. For all its darkness, Carver's humor is humane and sympathetic to the foibles of human nature. It may offer only a temporary means of emotional escape, a haven from life's hardships, but therein lie its poignancy and its importance. This essay has merely offered an overview of the subject, and there is much more to be written, but in time the author who has been called "A Chronicler of Blue-Collar Despair" may come to be regarded as one of American literature's more improbable humorists.

Notes

1. Tess Gallagher refers to this episode in one of her reminiscences: "When, in his last public reading in the Northwest, he read "Elephant" aloud in a small Seattle bookstore . . . there was so much laughter he had to stop again and again, gazing up once in a while with a shy smile on his face" ("The Ghosts of Dreams," 106–7). Other commentators testify to the laughter Carver's readings elicited. Lewis Buzbee records how Carver's "wry humor drew me even farther into the stories" (115), and David Carpenter comments on the enthusiastic response Carver received when he read "Whoever Was Using This Bed" to an initially reticent, rain-soaked Saskatchewan audience: "Soon, more than a hundred sodden people are howling with laughter" (175).

2. All references to Carver poems are from *All of Us: The Collected Poems*, ed. William L. Stull, introduction by Tess Gallagher (New York: Knopf, 1998), reprinted by permission of Tess Gallagher.

Works Cited

Alton, John. "What We Talk about When We Talk about Literature: An Interview with Raymond Carver." *Chicago Review* 36 (Autumn 1988): 4–21. Also in *Conversations*, ed. Gentry and Stull, 151–68.

Applefield, David. "Fiction & America: Raymond Carver." *Frank: A Journal of Contemporary Writing and Art* 8/9 (Winter 1987–88). Also in *Conversations*, ed. Gentry and Stull, 204–13.

Boddy, Kasia. "A Conversation." *London Review of Books* 10, no. 16 (September 15, 1988). Also in *Conversations*, ed. Gentry and Stull, 197–203.

Bonetti, Kay. "Ray Carver: Keeping it Short." *Saturday Review* 9 (September/October 1983): 21–23. Also in *Conversations*, ed. Gentry and Stull, 53–61.

Caldwell, Gail. "Raymond Carver: Darkness Dominates His Books, Not His Life." *Boston Globe*, June 1, 1988, 25, 27. Also in *Conversations*, ed. Gentry and Stull, 243–48.

Carver, Maryann. In Halpert, *Raymond Carver: An Oral Biography*, 54–77.

Carver, Raymond. "All My Relations." Introduction to *The Best American Short Stories 1986*, xi–xx. Boston: Houghton Mifflin, 1986. Reprinted in Carver, *No Heroics, Please*, 134–45.

———. *All of Us: The Collected Poems*. London: Harvill Press, 1996.

———. *Carver Country: The World of Raymond Carver*. Photographs by Bob Adelman. Introduction by Tess Gallagher. New York: Scribner's, 1990.

———. *Fires: Essays, Poems, Stories*. Santa Barbara, Calif.: Capra Press, 1983.

———. *No Heroics, Please: Uncollected Writings*, ed. William L. Stull. London: Harvill Press, 1991.

———. "On Longer Stories." Introduction to *American Fiction 88*, ed. Michael C. White and Alan Davis. Farmington, Conn.: Wesley Press, 1988. Reprinted in Carver, *No Heroics, Please*, 154–59.

———. *What We Talk about When We Talk about Love*. London: Collins, 1982.

———. *Where I'm Calling From: The Selected Stories*. London: Harvill Press, 1995.

Day, Dick. In Halpert, *Raymond Carver: An Oral Biography*, 195–96.

Dobyns, Stephen. "Remembering Ray Carver." In Runyon, *Reading Raymond Carver*, ix–xv.

Ford, Richard. In Halpert, *Raymond Carver: An Oral Biography*, 159–73.

Freud, Sigmund. "Humour." In *The Standard Edition of the Complete Psychological Works of Sigmund Freud*, ed. and trans. James Strachey. 1927. London, 1981, 159–66.

———. *Jokes and Their Relation to the Unconscious*, ed. and trans. James Strachey. 1905. Harmondsworth: Penguin Freud Library, 1983, vol. 6.

Gallagher, Tess. "Carver Country." Introduction to Carver, *Carver Country*, 8–19.

———. Introduction. In Carver, *All of Us*, xxiii–xxx.

———. Introduction. In Carver, *A New Path to the Waterfall*, xxii–xxxi. New York: Atlantic Monthly Press, 1989. Reprinted in Carver, *All of Us*, 311–20.

———. Note to "Lemonade." *Esquire* 112, no. 1 (1989). Reprinted in Carver, *All of Us*, 367.

Gentry, Marshall Bruce, and William L. Stull, eds. *Conversations with Raymond Carver*. Jackson: University Press of Mississippi, 1990.

———. Introduction. In *Conversations*, ed. Gentry and Stull, ix–xx.

Halpert, Sam, ed. *Raymond Carver: An Oral Biography*. Iowa City: University of Iowa Press, 1995.

Justice, Donald. In Halpert, *Raymond Carver: An Oral Biography*, 31–34.

Kinder, Chuck. In Halpert, *Raymond Carver: An Oral Biography*, 34–47.

Lish, Gordon. In Weber, *Raymond Carver: A Chronicler*, 87.

McCaffery, Larry, and Sinda Gregory. "An Interview with Raymond Carver." In *Alive and Writing: Interviews with American Authors of the 1980s*, 66–82. Urbana: University of Illinois Press, 1987. Also in *Conversations*, ed. Gentry and Stull, 98–116.

Moramarco, Fred. "Carver's Couples Talk about Love." October 10, 2004: www.whitman.edu/English/carver/moramarco.html

Nesset, Kirk. *The Stories of Raymond Carver: A Critical Study*. Athens: Ohio University Press, 1995.

O'Connell, Nicholas. "Raymond Carver." In *At the Field's End: Interviews with Twenty Pacific Northwest Writers*, 76–94. Seattle: Madrona, 1987. Also in *Conversations*, ed. Gentry and Stull, 133–50.

Robinson, Marilynne. "Marriage and Other Astonishing Bonds." *New York Times Book Review*, May 15, 1988.

Runyon, Randolph Paul. *Reading Raymond Carver*. Syracuse, N.Y.: Syracuse University Press, 1992.

Saltzman, Arthur. *Understanding Raymond Carver*. Columbia: University of South Carolina Press, 1988.

Sexton, David. "David Sexton Talks to Raymond Carver." *Literary Review* 85 (July 1985): 36–40. Also in *Conversations*, ed. Gentry and Stull, 120–32.

Stull, William L. "Matters of Life and Death." *Bloomsbury Review* 8 (January/February 1988): 14–17. Reprinted in *Conversations*, ed. Gentry and Stull, 177–91.

Weber, Bruce. "Raymond Carver: A Chronicler of Blue-Collar Despair." *New York Times Magazine*, June 24, 1984, 36–50. Also in *Conversations*, ed. Gentry and Stull, 84–97.

Wolff, Geoffrey. In *Raymond Carver: An Oral Biography*, ed. Halpert, 106–8, 184–88.

Wolff, Tobias. In *Raymond Carver: An Oral Biography*, ed. Halpert, 191–92.

Claire Fabre-Clark

The Poetics of the Banal in
Elephant and Other Stories

Carver's last stories, published first in a separate volume as *Elephant and Other Stories* (1988)[1] and shortly after in an anthology of selected stories entitled *Where I'm Calling From* (1989), have frequently led critics to remark on the enlarged field of vision with which their author was endowed in the last period of his life. Carver's later fiction indeed includes protagonists outside the limited sphere of the couple or of the individual. The best introduction to the collection is no doubt this statement by the author:

> Since I started writing fiction again, the stories have come very quickly. Now they deal not just with husband and wife domestic relationships but with relationships: son and mother, or father and children; and they go into these relationships more extensively. All these stories, with the exception of a Chekhov story in the *New Yorker* in June, were written in the first person. And they're all longer, more detailed and somehow more affirmative, I believe. And although the relationships are more complex, I'm somehow dealing with them in a more simplified or straightforward manner. (quoted in Applefield, "Fiction & America," 210)

In another interview, conducted by McCaffery and Gregory in 1984, Carver insisted that the opening up of his vision dated back to the publication of *What We Talk about When We Talk about Love* (1981), repeatedly justifying this change by referring to the improved circumstances of his life ("An Interview," 100–102). In this study, I would like to show that, in spite of these undeniable changes, Carver's writing can still be placed under the sign of continuity, and that the stories from *Elephant and Other Stories* are a radicalization of his work rather than a change of direction. This holds true especially where the representation of the banal is concerned, a motif Carver began to work on in the earlier collections. The close study of the stories from this collection, but also references to previous pieces compared with their unpublished versions, will be instrumental in this analysis, which is inspired by the works of the psychoanalyst and writer Sami-Ali on the banal and of the philosopher Clément Rosset on the real.

Carver's stories, dealing as they do mainly with ordinary situations, often evoke the notion of the banal. His writing is built on the poetics of the banal whose features remain to be defined. Moreover, the presence of more educated and articulate characters than in the author's earlier stories, and indeed of "writer-characters" such as the narrators of "Intimacy" and "Blackbird Pie" and the figure of Chekhov in "Errand," invites us to examine his writing's metatextual dimension, although Carver is always discreet and ironic when treading on those grounds.

Exploring the representation of commonness or banality in Carver's stories should therefore not limit itself to a thematic approach but lead us to examine all the facets of stereotyped representation. The history of stereotypes[2] has been admirably analyzed by Ruth Amossy and Elisheva Rosen: in its recent history—especially in contemporary fiction and criticism—stereotype is the material from which the writers must work but also from which they must differentiate themselves. An interesting case in point is the work of Roland Barthes, who never ceased to assert the vital need for literature to shun banality at all costs, to fight against the petrifying powers of the *doxa*, even if, in a final stage, Barthes's exploration of the fascinating powers of photography led him to a possible return to the "first degree" of experience. The purpose here is not to retrace the complex and nonlinear development of the stereotype in literature, but only to bear it in mind when approaching Carver's work, in which the status of banality is far from being unequivocal: the implicit attitude underlying it is neither a supercilious and ironic condemnation nor a purely "innocent" approval. If anything, it is marked by paradox and ambivalence, which can be observed in the characters, the narrators, the implicit author, and which finally prefigures the reaction of the implied reader. Triviality, clichés, and banality are represented extensively; however, they can also carry the poeticity of the story and not be exempt from both irony and empathy.

The Multiple Values of Clichés

By resorting to the extensive representation of clichés, which, at first sight, implies a negation of "literary language," Carver transforms everyday contemporary language into poetic material. The banality of dialogues or the insertion of clichés in the very texture of the narrative coexists with the assertion of a singular voice. Being capable of evoking without reproducing, stylizing without caricaturing—such are the demands of a writer who openly claims his filiation with the "realistic tradition" but who is nevertheless conscious of the complexities referentiality:

> Presumably my fiction is in the realistic tradition (as opposed to the really far-out side), but just telling it like it is bores me. . . . If you look carefully at my stories, I don't think you'll find people talking the way people do in real life. People always say that Hemingway had a great ear for dialogue, and he did. But *no one ever talked like they do in Hemingway's fiction.* At least not until they'd read Hemingway. (McCaffery and Gregory, 112)

Considered chronologically, Carver's stories start with a relatively discreet (and more conventional) use of cliché and move to a more aesthetical and stylized use in the later collections. In many cases, the corrections observed in the manuscripts show that Carver tended to favor expressions that were as close as possible to common language, rather than their witty or poetical variations. Since no duplicity in the narrating process is clearly perceptible, it is often difficult for the reader to interpret the status of clichés and stereotypes. Clichés are reproduced without any kind of distancing, and the reader needs to find the key to their understanding. All the same, their repetition or accumulation is sufficient in itself to produce a distanciation effect or, on the contrary, to carry a pathetic charge. The most spectacular use of clichés can be found in the last stories, in particular in "Elephant," "Boxes," and "Intimacy."

"Boxes" can be read as the intertwining of three voices characterized by clichés: those of the character-narrator, the mother, and Jill, the narrator's girlfriend. A sense of imminent threat hovers over the whole narrative, grafted onto the mother's departure. However, all emotional effusion is kept in check under the tight control of the narrative voice. To the emptiness that gradually invades the consciousness of the narrator—as he perceives things to be less and less significant—is opposed the presence of clichés as unique points of contact with the world. Nevertheless, polysemy inserts itself at some strategic points of the narrative. For instance, in the sentence "My mother is *packed* and ready to move," the idiomatic expression based on a metonymical substitution ("my mother" replaces "my mother's boxes") suggests that the mother herself is fantasmatically packed in a box (as if she were dead), but the "boxes" may also be interpreted as the preset arrangement of characters into stereotypical "categories" defined by each character's use of clichés.

First, let us look at the clichés in the mother's discourse: "They can go to hell"; "Why didn't you tell me this was the North Pole?"; "How else explain her being kept around on the face of the earth?"; "I hate this g.d. place"; and "she likes it just fine to be back in Sunny California." Naturally, these clichés are disseminated in the narrative, but when read in a sequence they help draw the stereotyped portrait of an abusive mother who spends her time criticizing her son and everyone else. Furthermore, the underlying imagery that connects them is that of spatial—even cosmic—references: "face of the earth," "g.d. place," "hell," "North Pole," "Sunny California"; through these images she reinforces her abusive character with the fantasy of infinite displacement and absolute mastery of space.

As for Jill, the narrator's girlfriend, the clichés she uses reveal a sort of pop psychology, or we might say "supermarket psychology" (a cliché that is cautioned by the metonymic presence of the supermarket in the story in the form of the Sears catalog), that she applies to her boyfriend's mother: "she's laying guilt trips"; "she says my mother is *negative* about everything and everybody ought to *find an outlet*, like other people in her *age bracket*." One recognizes here a very codified vocabulary that helps characterize Jill's voice—a common-sensical woman who uses ready-made psychological analyses—rather than offer new and illuminating insights into the situation. Finally, what is revealed through the clichés used by the narrator, such as "all hell broke loose," "she began to put the bad mouth," "I'm eating like a wolf," and "she is a heartache to me," is the sense of threat that the fear and desire provoked by the thought of leaving his mother are imposing on him. Therefore, the signifiers of suffering, even though they are contained in fixed expressions, impose themselves on the reader's consciousness through accumulation.

One of the functions of the clichés is this text is to constitute characters as types. Their speeches echo one another in a polyphony of recognizable topoi allowing hidden patterns of meaning to emerge in a story whose narrating voice seems to have renounced any kind of affect. The narrator of "Boxes," contrarily to the other characters, is but very little defined by his language, but his suffering caused by the need to leave his mother or simply coping with her existence is at once controlled and liberated by the clichés: smothered by the weight of dead words but reasserted by the interplay of the various expressions and the echoes they form. This network effect enables the semes of threat and pain to circulate again inside the text and nouns such as "hell," "wolf" or "heartache" to be resemanticized though the narration, which is otherwise devoid of affect.

The tone that emanates from the story "Elephant" is very close to the one studied in "Boxes," but the function of clichés is quite different. The structure of this story is conventional, with an ever-increasing tension to the very end of the story in the form of a liberating climax. The narrative segments are interspersed with short dialogues extracted from telephone conversations or letters that the narrator has exchanged with the various members of his family: his brother, mother, daughter, and son. They all regularly call him up to request money from him, and their demands, like their promises to pay him back, are usually formulated with the help of clichés: "I've gone belly up"; "you can help me pull out of it"; "things would pick up for her"; and "she wanted to stand on her two feet," for example. Regarding the density of stereotyped expressions, this text surpasses all of Carver's other stories.

The narrator's replies are also strewn with clichés: "But I was thinking if he paid the money he owed me it might take me off the hook there and let me breathe for a while"; "unless I had a stone in place of a heart"; or "My heart went out to him and I wished trouble hadn't knocked on his door. But my own back was against the wall now." From the point of view of psychological coherence, the use of clichés is justified here by its protective function: it enables the characters to attenuate the urgency of their demands and the depth of their dependency. However, its association with the isotropy of money in this text is all the more relevant formally, for it can be read as the linguistic equivalent of the money that passes from hand to hand. In fact, the only transactions that we witness are those of words exchanged through letters or on the telephone, and their linguistic exhaustion symbolically redoubles the strictly economic debasement. As was the case in "Boxes," the clichés in "Elephant" are present in both direct and indirect speech. The letters written to the narrator by his daughter are rendered verbatim, displaying her clichéd way of expressing herself: "My daughter would write these letters and say how they were living on oatmeal, she and her kids. . . . Things would turn around, she was sure, in the summer. If nothing else worked out—but she was sure it would; she had several irons in the fire—she could always get a job in the fish cannery that was not far from where she lived" (77–78).

The rhetoric of this summary of the daughter's letters, rendered in indirect speech, displays a double strategy on the daughter's part—provided that we read it as a faithful transcription of her letters. The narrative alternates moments destined to move the father—"they were living on oatmeal, she and her kids"—and clichés meant to persuade him—"she had several irons in the fire" and "they were going to be crying out for cold drinks." Thus, the passage fulfills the criteria of a perfect piece of oratory: it is both convincing and moving. Hence the clichés here remind one of the *endoxa* as defined by Aristotle, and of which Peter I. Von Moos writes as "sufficiently acceptable opinions (the positive contrary of *adoxa* and *paradoxa*, problematic or shameful opinions) relying on a general or at least representative consensus" (Von Moos and Plantin, *Lieux communs*, 7). Converging with this ancient conception of the "common place," the cliché is here valorized since its principal quality is persuasive rather than risible. However, since it is re-presented, it is also subjected to a certain form of distance perceptible by the reader. Indeed, one may question the reliability of the narrator—doesn't he transcribe and necessarily modify his daughter's words?—and once again, the subtle discrepancy and even the comic effect that stems from such an accumulation are reinforced. The narrator's reiterated assertions as to the exactitude of his transcriptions—"That's what he said. Those were his exact words"—are but signs that instill doubt and suspicion in the reader. Contrary to the characterizing function of cliché in "Boxes," clichés are unanimously shared in "Elephant"; so much so that the "origin" of the voice is often doubtful, or at least subject to confusion. All the voices seem to merge into an indefinite "one" that organizes echoes, opposes them, cancels, or repoeticizes the clichés.

When one looks closely at the way the characters' expressions echo one another in "Elephant," not just one but several isotropies take shape. A first semantic and lexical field is structured around the sea as a common seme. The echoes between these expressions and the repetition effect they produce help revive the clichéd nature of the collocations. They also provoke a slightly comic effect due to the conflictual metaphors thus brought close together: at the beginning, going into debt is implicitly metaphorized by the dying fish ("I've gone belly up") or the fish caught on a hook ("take me off the hook and let me breathe"), whereas the image later used to evoke bankruptcy is that of the drowning family ("I'm going under. You're all going under, and you're pulling me down with you"). Another contradiction, or at least tension, may be observed in the use of the phrase *to knock at the door*, which is successively applied to indicate bad luck for the narrator's brother ("I wished *trouble* hadn't *knocked* on his door") and good fortune for his daughter ("until *opportunity knocked*"). In other parts of the narrative, the meteorological metaphor—a privileged metaphor of verbal stereotyping—is recurrent, alternately used by the narrator: "I'd been mailing checks to her every month, rain or shine, for three years" (73); by his brother: "'When it rains, it pours,' he said"; or indirectly by his mother: "She'd thought this would be the year she could put some money back for the rainy days ahead" (85).

Water is obviously the common seme of most of the metaphorical networks that are implied in the clichés throughout the narrative of "Elephant" as a correlative of the narrator's fear of psychological submersion, a fear (temporarily) resolved at the end of the story by the narrator's salutary takeoff in the "unpaid-for car" (90). Thus are built structures of echoing phrases, which by their very excess suggest a metaphorical reading, while the contradictions question or disturb a real poeticization of fixed images. Such echoing discreetly evokes water as a structuring image in this story. Even more important, however, are the form of these expressions in the texture of the narrative: the proliferation of binary structures such as "rain or shine," "left or right," or "an arm and a leg" imparts a rhythmic pattern beyond the signified of the cliché.

The formal unity of "Intimacy" also relies on the interplay of clichés and stereotypes. The paradox of this story is that *intimacy* is both re-created and negated in the domestic scene during which the ex-wife literally assails the narrator with clichés and erratically tries to assuage (or revive) old wounds. The woman's words, as told retrospectively by the narrator, mix coherence and incoherence, syntax and parataxis in a sort of ecstatic and irrepressible flow:

> She says, Let go of the past, for Christ's sake. Those old hurts. You must have *some other arrows in your quiver*, she says.
>
> She says, You know something? I think you're sick. I think you're *crazy as a bedbug*. Hey, you don't believe the things they're saying about you do you? Don't believe them *for a minute*, she says. Listen, I *could tell them a thing or two*. Let them talk to me about it, if they want to hear a story.
>
> She says, are you listening to me?
>
> I'm listening, I say. *I'm all ears*, I say.
>
> She says, I've really had a *bellyful of it*, buster! Who asked you here today anyway? I *sure as hell* didn't. You just show up and walk in. *What the hell*

do you want from me? *Blood?* You want more blood? I thought you had
your fill by now. (46, emphasis added)

In the void left by their lost intimacy, fixed expressions insert themselves as
if to screen off emotion but also as if to enable another dialogue to inscribe
itself in filigree. In the second part of the extract, the monstrous figure of a
bloodthirsty, vampirical husband takes shape, even though the woman is the
one who has a "bellyful of it." Following the principle of a poetic contamina-
tion, a paradigmatic dimension is evoked along the syntagmatic chain formed
by the succession of clichés. Thus, in texts that are almost totally devoid of
metaphor, metaphorical shapes are evoked through the networks formed by
clichés, even though they are only fleetingly perceptible.

Moments of Crisis

The literal transcription of common language contributes to the originality of
Carver's characters and narrators: their singular voice is paradoxically made up
of common expressions that freely associate or are dissonant in the course of
the narrative. Rarely do the characters comment on their use of language (with
an exception in "Blackbird Pie"), and the reader is free to appraise the value of
clichés. However, it is also notable that each of the stories often stages a critical moment when a fault line introduces itself into the perception of reality and
confuses all familiar landmarks. One of the forms taken by this crisis is the revelation of a discrepancy between reality and its bidimensional image, be it a
magazine or a television picture. As was also the case in most of the stories from
other collections, stereotypes then cease to perform their reassuring function
for the characters, losing some of their power to transform the unknown into
the known. The stories, in fact, seem to exist on the fragile border that separates
ordinariness from the *uncanny.* Much of the stories' irrepressible comedy actually stems from such a coexistence. Contrary to other fictional characters who
might strive to escape ordinariness, Carver's characters usually suffer from an
acute desire to conform to the image of the "ordinary man" when they realize
that their lives do not correspond to the pretty and smooth pictures they had
formed for themselves. "Why can't we be like everybody else?" is their leitmo-
tiv when reality, made of loss, despair, conflict, and emptiness, contradicts the
flat surfaces of the television screens.

In "Menudo," for example, this desire to live in accordance with stereotypes
is clearly articulated as the narrator's vaudeville is punctuated by comments in
which he compares himself with the characters of televised melodramas,
finally taking on an even more pathetic—almost comic—turn: "I wish I could
be like everybody else in this neighborhood—*your basic, normal, unaccom-
plished person*—and go up to my bedroom, and lie down, and sleep" (62, my
emphasis). The banality of the narrator's plight appears both as a threat and as

a shelter from the unknown and from the possible tragic consequences of his inconsequence.

The same discrepancy between life and its ready-made image is emphasized in "Boxes" by the narrator and the other protagonists, exemplified by the narrator's description of Larry Hadlock: "He is a widower—a big fellow, mid-sixties. An unhappy man with a good sense of humor. His arms are covered with white hair, and white hair stands out from under his cap. He looks like a magazine illustration of a farmer. But he isn't a farmer. He is a retired construction worker who's saved a little money" (9). In this case, the negation of the stereotype is but one of the symptoms of the narrator's crisis: just as he does not fit the farmer's stereotype, Larry Hadlock, who might have become the narrator's mother's suitor, does not prove up to her expectations and is turned, instead, into the object of her acrimonious resentment. Regularly the mother expresses her distress by tragically acknowledging the gap between the oppressive stereotypes of happiness and her own chaotic life: "Other women my age can be happy. Why can't I be like the other women? All I want is a house and a town to live in that will make me happy. That isn't a crime, is it? I hope not. I hope I'm not asking for too much out of life" (20). Thus, stereotypes and ready-made images are the only forms in which the characters' desires can be expressed, and their negation usually marks a disappointment or, worse, the gradual loss of significance in their existence when their aspiration to "normality" is radically threatened. Images and sounds are suddenly voided of all significance, and conversations no longer fulfill their communicative value. The characters may be seized by a form of paralysis that prevents them from moving or talking. For example, in "Whoever Was Using This Bed," the narrator and his wife have a conversation about terminal diseases and dramatic decisions, which leads the narrator away from anything he knows: " I don't say anything right away. What am I supposed to say? They haven't written the book on this one yet. I need a minute to think. I know it won't cost me anything to tell her I'll do whatever she wants. It's just words, right?" (40).

Thus, Carver's text is always balanced on the threshold that separates language from silence, stasis from movement. How is it possible for the characters to make sense any longer? The strikingly frequent use of questions, whether in titles or in the course of the narrative, expresses the frailty of human speech: meaning is usually left suspended, unresolved, and often more so at the end of the narrative than at the beginning. On the contrary, Carver's writing usually deepens this sense of interrogation and doubt that exceeds the pure transcription of contemporary American idiomatic speech. For instance, at the end of "Menudo," the sense of an absence gradually invades the whole universe of the narrator: the tale of his failed attempt at tasting his friend Alfredo's dish called "Menudo" (because he slept through the party) after the breakup of his marriage is followed by his total disconnection from the world of signs: he first expresses doubts about the meaning of the birds' song: "At least I think they're calling to each other"; then the doubting spreads to all the signs around him: "He lifts his hand off the steering wheel. It could be a salute or a sign of dismissal. It's a sign, in any case. . . . I get up and raise my hand, too—not to wave, exactly, but close to it" (71).

Meaning emerges precisely in these gaps, when identity threatens to dissolve into a whirl of questions. It might be convenient—but erroneous—to conclude that in Carver's text "nothing happens," as some critics have stated,[3] simply because the reader fails to find the usual hermeneutic landmarks that signal the dawning of an epiphanic insight, albeit a negative one. In fact, if banality is not transcended, and transmuted into a meaningful insight for the character, it may not be the same for the reader. Ewing Campbell is right to take this ontological leap and to assert, in substance, that in Carver's texts the epiphany belongs to the reader: "From a disinterested vantage, the reader must see the patterns Carver has constructed and cross that threshold to understanding from which the character is barred" (*Raymond Carver*, 45). We are indeed summoned to find meaning in stories that constantly point to their evanescence if not radical disappearance.

The Banal Is the Real

According to Sami-Ali, an aesthetics of the banal tends to create defamiliarization through the very representation (and proliferation) of familiarity.[4] In other words, the real is made excessively "canny" as opposed to "uncanny." Moreover, in its pathological acceptation, the banal corresponds to a state of depression during which the subject fails to project himself or herself imaginatively. It seems to me that Carver's writing combines both acceptations analyzed by Sami-Ali (anesthetic and pathological).

A first instance is the effect that defamiliarization provokes by excessively familiar language. In "Blackbird Pie," an explicitly metatextual notation illustrates Carver's lexical conception right from the opening paragraph of the story:

> My name was written on the envelope, and what was inside purported to be a letter from my wife, *I say "purported"* because even though the grievances could only have come from someone who'd spent twenty-three years observing me on an intimate, day-to-day basis, the charges were outrageous and completely out of keeping with my wife's character. (91, my emphasis)

The use of the term "purported" is quite unusual for a narrator in a story by Carver, as it belongs to a more elaborate and precise register than what we are used to finding in the other stories. However, the emphasis on the word deliberately amplifies this discordance and dismisses other possible interpretations of the passage, making the narrator, who is a historian, less of a pompous erudite than he might have appeared at first. In the middle of his narrative, the narrator inserts another comment on the use of language: "Historians should use more words like 'tooted' or 'beeped' or 'blasted'—especially at serious moments such as after a massacre or when an awful occurrence has cast a pall on the future of an entire nation" (108). This reflection introduces confusion between triviality and seriousness. Moreover, in doing so, the narrator echoes Carver's conceptions of literary vocabulary that are expressed in several essays: notably in "Fire" and "On Writing" and in his interviews where he refuses preciosity and sophistication.

On the level of both sonorities and semanticism, Carver's privileged signifiers seem to participate in his overall aesthetics of banality, as confirmed by the study of the different manuscripts or successive versions of a story. It is as though the phonic and semantic density of Carver's language imposed themselves with a violence echoing that of the real represented in the stories. One observes a simplification between several versions of the same story, as is the case, for instance, between "Dummy" and "The Third Thing That Killed My Father Off" (second version of the same story), which brings the narrator's voice closer to that of other narrators in the work. An early and unpublished story entitled "Late in the Summer" also testifies to this orientation of the work. This unfinished piece relates the (probably autobiographical) experience of a young man who has just started his first job. Although the document is not dated, its appearance suggests that it is one of the first stories by Carver. Its main interest lies in the handwritten corrections and deletions. In the fragment "sometimes we would talk about the willow tree and my father would speculate how much longer we had before the tree roots strangled our pipes and did something bad to the septic tank," the verb "speculate" is deleted manually and replaced by "wonder," the common level of speech preferred over the more openly "literary" and educated one.[5] Right from the beginning of his writing career, Carver's voice asserted itself through this apparent trivialization of vocabulary. Such examples could be multiplied to show that simple generic terms are usually favored over specific ones in his prose, and that any temptation of "technicity" is systematically banned, erased, or replaced by basic, unpretentious terms. This refusal of specific or technical vocabulary is partially responsible for the referential indeterminacy of the stories, together with the proliferation of indeterminate forms and the spartan use of adjectives.

A second instance confirming the pertinence of Sami-Ali's analysis of banality in our context is provided by Carver's strategies of representation of avoidance. The theme of avoidance is to be found in "Menudo," enhanced by the paratactic structure of narration. The narrator of "Menudo" will never taste the dish made by his friend Alfredo, an episode that the title of the story invites us to read as a metaphor for all the other failures of his life, his relationships with women as well as with his parents. If there is a link between all of the anecdotes of his narrative, it is, paradoxically, that of rupture and absence, whose extreme figuration is death. Through an overwhelming use of juxtaposition, the narrative exhibits the arbitrariness of associations, the blanks and breaks that constitute the subjective experience of time. It is a temporality essentially dominated by discontinuity and absence of causality. Thus, the *inversion* of signs is emphasized in the description of the father's death: "For instance, that time my dad had his stroke. He woke up after a coma—seven days and nights in a hospital bed—and calmly said 'hello' to the people in his room. Then his eyes picked me out. 'Hello, son,' he said. Five minutes later, he died. Just like that—he died" (58–59). This "Hello" should in fact be "Good-bye," and the five minutes that elapsed between his awakening and his death have been reduced to nothing, as if the events were perfectly simultaneous. The temporal compression is underlined further in the narrator's final repetition: "Just like that—he died"; the instant of death, intangible but unavoidable, is typographically materialized by the dash.

The death of the mother, which is related later in the story, gives rise to another digression, just as brutal and absurd. With a mix of irony and faithfulness toward his former dishonesty, enabled by the narrative distance, he first recalls that he had refused to buy her a radio before evoking her death: "Then what happened? She died. She *died*. She was walking home from the grocery store, back to her apartment, carrying her sack of groceries, and she fell into somebody's bushes and died" (63). The succession of events, as told in this paragraph, is no doubt a figuration of the suddenness of death, but it also suggests a conception of time that is not progressive: death springs up without any buildup of signs to announce its coming. The repetition does not compensate the absence of causality for the narrator. On the contrary, it even enhances it by reinforcing the son's astonishment, which is perceptible through the italics. Moreover, the mother's death is trivialized by the mention of her fall into the bushes with her grocery bag in her hand. This detail (the grocery bag) prevents the text from falling into pathos and confers to it a grotesque dimension worthy of a cinematographic gag. In other words, in this text we are reminded that the real is always both banal and surprising, or even shocking *because of* its banality, its predictability. Rosset shows that what is the most shocking in the real is its coincidence with itself, with its preestablished program that we tend to forget or avoid at all costs, a fact that culminates in the experience of death because its event is both unpredictable and ineluctable.

Just as the characters are irremediably fixed upon themselves, Carver's language is concerned by a coincidence with itself, the ultimate form of which is repetition or tautology, as shown by the narrator of "Menudo": "I know Oliver. He's relentless, unforgiving. He could slam a croquet ball into the next block— *and has*" (59, my emphasis).[6] Along the same lines, the notorious absence of metaphors from the work can thus be reinterpreted as a denial of literature's traditional tools to create an illusion of alterity.

We find in "Errand" a good illustration of Carver's aesthetics of coincidence. The story, because of its tragic autobiographical resonances, may be read, in parts, as Carver's literary testament. The story opens with an extradiegetic narrator who feigns adopting a relatively neutral and factual tone of voice: "Chekhov. On the evening of March 22, 1897, he went to dinner in Moscow with his friend and confidant Alexei Suvorin" (111). It employs in its last sections successively the point of view of Chekhov's young wife Olga and of the young man from the hotel. Atypically for Carver, such narrative complexity results in the confusion of the different levels of "reality" represented in the story. In her speech to the young man, Olga urges him to "imagine" he is carrying a vase of flowers, which is what he is actually doing (in the reality represented in the diegesis):

> After securing permission to leave the hotel he was to proceed quietly and resolutely, though without any unbecoming haste, to the mortician's. . . . [He]was to behave exactly as if he were engaged on a very important errand, nothing more. He was engaged on an important errand, she said. And if it would help keep his movements purposeful he should imagine himself as someone moving down the busy sidewalk carrying in [his] arms a porcelain vase of roses that he had to deliver to an important man. (123)

Once again, the passage shows that the imaginary world is always folded back onto the real as though it could not offer any escape route. The reflexivity of representation that is here illustrated by Olga could well be applied to Carver as well: writing can only ever transform the real into itself.

The study of Carver's texts, whether the last stories or of previous states of published stories, shows that the density of verbal clichés, together with a restrained use of conventional imagery, leads to a denial of alterity, enabling the emergence of the banal. The stories are destabilizing because they rely on a mode of representation based on literalness and repetition. Thanks to Carver's original work on language, the banal shown in the stories seems to draw its fascinating powers from itself. The effect is that when the characters have to face a moment of "dissociation"[7] and their usual classifying categories appear to be dysfunctional, a different kind of "real" is apprehended, all the more threatening for being so familiar. This brings to mind the description of the real given by Clément Rosset, who equates the "real" with the absolutely "singular," that which, like death, combines absolute predictability with the power to create shock and surprise:

> The density of the real signals the plenitude of everyday life, that is the unicity of a world made not of doubles but always of original singularities

(even if they may resemble one another), which, as a consequence, is not accountable to any model—a philosophy of the real, which perceives in ordinariness and banality, or even in repetition itself, the originality of the world.[8] (*Le Réel*, 151)

Notes

1. All references to this collection are taken from Raymond Carver, *Elephant and Other Stories* (London: Harvill, 1988).

2. A generic term which includes all types of fixed patterns—whether ideological or linguistic.

3. See John W. Aldridge, *Talents and Technicians, Literary Chic and the New Assembly-Line Fiction* (New York: Charles Scribner's Sons, 1992), 31–32.

4. Sami-Ali gives the examples of the works by Andy Warhol in visual arts and Raymond Roussel in literature; see Sami-Ali, *Le Banal* (Paris: Gallimard, 1980), 23–74.

5. See manuscript from Raymond Carver papers and manuscripts, William Charvat Collection of American Fiction, Ohio State University Library Special Collections, Columbus.

6. The same phenomenon appeared in an earlier story: "Then I suppose we'd have to be somebody else if that was the case. Somebody we're not. I don't have that kind of supposing left in me. We were born who we are. Don't you see what I'm saying?" (Raymond Carver, "Chef's House," in Carver, *Where I'm Calling From* [New York: Vintage Contemporaries, 1989], 301).

7. See David Boxer and Cassandra Phillips, "*Will You Please Be Quiet, Please?*: Voyeurism, Dissociation and the Art of Raymond Carver," *Iowa Review* 10, no. 3 (Summer 1979): 74–90.

8. "La densité du réel signale au contraire une plénitude de réalité quotidienne, c'est-à-dire de l'unicité d'un monde qui se compose non de doubles mais toujours de singularités originales (même s'il leur arrive de se 'ressembler') et n'a par consêquent de comptes á render á aucun modéle—philosphie du réel, qui voit dans le quotidien et le banal, voire dans la répétition elle-même, toute l'originalité du monde" (Clément Rosset, *Le Réel: Traité de l'idiotie* [Paris: Minuit, 1977], 151).

Works Cited

Aldridge, John W. *Talents and Technicians, Literary Chic and the New Assembly-Line Fiction*. New York: Charles Scribner's Sons, 1992.

Amossy, Ruth, and Elisheva Rosen. *Les Discours du cliché*. Paris: CDU et CEDES réunis, 1982.

Applefield, David. "Fiction & America: Raymond Carver." *Frank: An International Journal of Contemporary Writing & Art* (Paris) 8/9 (Winter 1987–88): 6–15. Also in *Conversations*, ed. Gentry and Stull, 72–83.

Boxer David, and Cassandra Phillips. "*Will You Please Be Quiet, Please?*: Voyeurism, Dissociation and the Art of Raymond Carver." *Iowa Review* 10, no. 3 (Summer 1979): 75–90.

Campbell, Ewing. *Raymond Carver: A Study of the Short Fiction.* New York: Twayne, 1992.

Carver, Raymond. *Elephant and Other Stories.* London: Harvill, 1988.

———. *Fires: Essays, Poems, Stories.* Santa Barbara, Calif.: Capra, 1983.

———. *No Heroics, Please: Uncollected Writings,* ed. William L. Stull. New York: Vintage Contemporaries, 1992.

———. Papers and manuscripts. William Charvat Collection of American Fiction. Ohio State University Library Special Collections, Columbus.

———. *What We Talk about When We Talk about Love.* New York: Vintage, 1982.

———. *Where I'm Calling From: New and Selected Stories.* New York: Vintage, 1988.

Gentry, Marshall Bruce, and William L. Stull, eds. *Conversations with Raymond Carver.* Jackson:University Press of Mississippi, 1990.

McCaffery, Larry, and Sinda Gregory. "An Interview with Raymond Carver." In *Alive and Writing: Interviews with American Authors of the 1980s,* ed. Larry McCaffery and Sinda Gregory, 66–82. Urbana: University of Illinois Press, 1987. Also in *Conversations,* ed. Gentry and Stull, 98–116.

Rosset, Clément. *Le Réel: Traité de l'idiotie.* Paris: Minuit, 1977.

Sami-Ali. *Le Banal.* Paris: Gallimard, 1980.

Von Moos, Peter I., and Christian Plantin, eds. *Lieux communs: Topoï, stéréotypes, clichés.* Paris: Kimé, 1993.

William Kittredge

Bulletproof

It is often said that something may survive of a person after his death, if that person was an artist and put a little of himself into his work. It is perhaps in the same way that a sort of cutting taken from one person and grafted onto the heart of another continues to carry on its existence even when the person from whom it has been detached has perished. (Proust, *Remembrance of Things Past*)

The quote is no doubt a strange way to begin a story about traveling to visit Ray Carver, who had just missed dying, or, as it turned out, not escaped. In fact, he was dying. But, of course, we all are. That was what I told myself.

In December of 1987, just after Christmas, Annick and I drove the freeways from Montana to visit my children and grandchildren and some friends in Seattle. We ate fresh oysters; we played frivolity and cultivated the idea that it is possible to live without guilt amid the pleasures of paradise; we tried to ignore the idea that Ray was dying not so far away, or at least I did; and then Annick and I drove over to Port Angeles on the Olympic Peninsula, where Tess Gallagher and Ray were seeing to what was the end of his life.

The rhododendrons were flowering, and the azaleas (or so it seems in memory), and Ray was fragile (a large, awkward man gone breakable) but not at all what you would think of as killed. Annick and I bought cut flowers in a shop on the main street in Port Angeles, and took them up through the incessant rain to Ray's big old-fashioned two-story house on the hill above the harbor; Ray made us some of his good coffee (he'd gone to coffee when he quit booze; coffee was one of his specialties). We sat in the bright kitchen with the cut flowers on the drain board, and drank the coffee, and pretty soon we were talking. It was raining outside and quiet, and Ray told us his story about healing from the almost literally unimaginable operation, the removal of about two-thirds of one cancerous lung. He'd coughed up some blood one November morning in a kind of innocent, almost painless way, and the nightmare began. That was how he put it. "It was a nightmare," Ray said. Sunlight broke through, casting long streaks of gunmetal brilliance across the seawater toward Vancouver Island. He smiled. "But now we're all right," he said. Something like that.

What I was doing was watching Ray like he was in possession of some secret message I could read if only I could pay close enough attention. I realize this acutely now and knew it at the time. The thought did not last but a second, a sort of easily forgettable twinge I put away as if such self-interest while face-on with the oncoming death of a friend were shameful. And maybe it is. The message I was looking for had something to do with taking care of yourself by cherishing what there was to cherish, moment into moment, and not holding to it, something like that, some secret Ray knew, and I didn't, some story he had learned.

For a while that evening Annick and I were alone in Ray's house, and I sat in the chair where Ray sat when he read; I held his books and opened them to the place where he had closed them. There was a good tape deck, and dozens of classical tapes. I played some Vivaldi, trying to fathom this man who had been my friend in another life, before he was dying, trying to hear what he heard, as he heard it. He was reading mostly European poets—Milosz, some others I can't remember. I'm moved to think of something I know closer to heart, Philip Levine:

> Earth is eating trees, fence posts,
> Gutted cars, earth is calling in her little ones,
>
> . . . .
> They Lion grow.

Ray was a man who had stared himself down in the mirror of his imagination, and now he was dying without allowing himself to descend into any rattled bitterness, so far as I could discern. I was trying to see how he got to where he was; I was trying to understand how it could be that he could absorb the terrifying joke of this perfect metaphysical injustice into his calmness and turn it reasonable, at least into something no more unnatural than the running water which drowns some mother's sacred child.

Ray and I had been friends since the spring of 1970, and we liked to tell ourselves, as he said in one of his stories, that we had *seen some things.* We met one spring evening in the old Olympic Hotel in Seattle, perfectly by accident, and we fell for each other as inebriates will, like playmates in love with the same possibilities. There was some college Comp. class English teachers' gathering in the Olympic. The lobby was given over to a vast display of books, a hundred or so yards of publishers' booths. But it was empty when I wandered through in the early evening. Empty, that is, except for one scruffy fellow who was way down the line. As I was looking through a book called *Short Stories from the Literary Magazines*, this fellow came right up to my elbow and tried to look over my shoulder.

"I've got a story in there," he said.

"Yeah," I said. "I'll bet you do."

"'Please Be Quiet Please,'" he said.

I knew what he meant, but I didn't believe it.

"It is," he said. "It's mine. Curt Johnson put it in there. He printed it in a magazine called *December.*"

It was not a lie anyone would have bothered telling, at least in those days. It was clear this man was Raymond Carver, and I was one of the few people in the world who would have found significance in that fact. This stranger had written the story called "Please Be Quiet, Please." It was already a kind of famous story in my mythologies.

A couple of years before, I had read that story in a hotel room in Portland, sitting with my feet up in the bed and disengaged from the world and waiting for my second wife to come back from somewhere, and that story got me started again in my wondering if I had already ruined my life. "Please Be Quiet, Please" caused me to hang my head with heartbreak over my own situation in the world and yet to admire myself for even trying to confront those troubles as a writer.

However stupid it sounds, that is pretty close to what I thought right after I read "Please Be Quiet, Please" one rainy afternoon in the old Benson Hotel in Portland while I yearned to be actual at something. For a little moment that story led me to think I was doing the right thing with my life.

And here I was, better yet, in another hotel, with the guy who wrote the story. This was indeed the life; we were shy for some moments, and then we touched, we shook hands, we talked about a cup of coffee. Wait a minute, he said, why not a beer; I said why not a drink. A drink would be fine, maybe a couple of drinks, what the hell; all things lay before us. It was that moment between drunks which is known as Exchanging Credentials. Would you have a drink? Well, maybe, sure.

Even on the morning of this writing, a brilliant blue day which began with the temperature well below zero, after an evening of Christmas celebration and decency with family, I think of the old days and going down to the taverns in Missoula to join the people I know. They are still there, some of them, and I still love the thought of their company. There was a time when we would be drunk by noon.

The days after Christmas, in the taverns, were always splendid in their timelessness. At heart loomed that perfect irresponsibility, long hours when it was possible to believe we were invisible and shatterproof, walking on water for at least a little while, and beautiful in our souls.

But those afternoons are gone. Ray took a hard fall on the booze. Drink became his secret companion in a more profound way than anything, even love, ever really works for most of us.

We pulled our tricks. It was our only sport; it would never end; we were free, invulnerable. In June of 1973, running on getaway bravado and whiskey, I took a long run from Missoula and found myself at Carver's house in Cupertino.

My first day in town we made our way over to a literary party in Berkeley, in some public room on the campus. I found myself talking to a famous critic with a glass of white wine in my hand, thinking in my drunken self-pretense that I knew some never-before-revealed thing about *texts*. Ray lifted a sack of ice over his head, crashed it down on the corner of a trestle table, and three half gallons of gin danced off to shatter on the stone floor. We hired a graduate student to drive us back to Cupertino.

And we lived there a week in dreams, drinking two bottles of vodka every day, one for each of us. In the morning I would come out of my bedroom to find Ray in the living room with vodka, orange juice, ice, my drink mixed.

Toward the end of the week we wandered up to the little liquor store at the high end of Cupertino Road, and ordered a half gallon. "Christ," the clerk said. "You guys together?"

Crossing the twilight of a moving-picture six-plex parking lot on the west side of San Jose, I looked back to see Maryann looking back another fifty yards to the place where Ray stood beside their little yellow Japanese automobile. He had waited until we moved off toward the theater and then come up with a pint from under the seat, and now he was downing the last of it, chin to the China pink of the evening sky and oblivious to us in what he thought of as his selfishness.

That fall Ray was teaching full time in Iowa City, in the Writers' Workshop with the likes of John Cheever, feeling like maybe he was some semblance of the real thing since there he was with Cheever, who was damned sure the real thing and as much a drunk as anybody.

Every Friday afternoon Ray was supposed to meet a beginning poetry writing class at College V, UC Santa Cruz. It was possible; he could fly every Thursday afternoon, meet his class, and fly back in time to meet his workshop on Tuesday. And he had worked a deal with one of the airlines. Free tickets in swap for an essay (which of course never got written) for some airline magazine.

No problem. Two jobs, two paychecks, home every weekend.

And he showed up on the airplane each Thursday evening for a number of weeks. Always drunk. I had left my second wife behind in Missoula and was thrashing around in the single life again, temporarily, according to my plans anyhow, at Stanford with a Stegner Fellowship. So I was available and I drove him down the fifty or so miles to Santa Cruz, and he ceremoniously pinned a notice to the door of his classroom: *Can't teach. Sick.* And it was true.

The next week Ray lay down in the back seat of my car so no one could possibly see him, and it was my job to pin up the notice. The next week Chuck Kinder and I went down without Ray. The class was mostly hippies with no shoes. We faced a circle of their bare, grass-stained feet propped up around our conference table. Kinder refused to look. I carried on like some prideful pissant. That was the last of those classes; Ray stopped coming altogether.

That Christmas there was a great swaying in the warm winds; Ray flew to Missoula, then drove south with my second wife and Ed McClanahan, who was taking my place in Missoula. It sort of seemed like we all might couple up again and make peace and be lovey. And we kind of did, for a week or so.

Ray and Maryann looked to be bemused by happiness as they drifted off from a small party at McClanahan's house in Palo Alto. It wasn't until the next day that I got a full report. It was one of our sports in those days, getting the full report.

Ray had lost Maryann. I mean lost her. He got in the car and drove the twenty-some freeway miles from McClanahan's to his place in Cupertino, innocently, without Maryann. Ray left her standing at the curb, door locked on her side. Rather than come back into McClanahan's, Maryann hitched a ride with an old couple. There was lots of hitching rides in those days; people fell out, temporarily. The old couple drove Maryann right to her door. Ray was rummaging in the refrigerator, building a great sandwich. "Oh," he said, when Maryann came in the door. "I wondered where you were."

At least that was how it was reported. Ray said he was slicing a great sweet onion, a Walla Walla sweet, for a huge, thick sandwich. Later on he never ate. That was one way you told the beginning of the end; some people stopped eating.

Maybe Ray was the more easily wounded, maybe he was physically fragile, or maybe he was simply capable of taking all of what was happening more seriously than most of us; maybe he saw through our joke in a clearer way; maybe he was more open to certain kinds of wounding, to witnessing what became our war zone with a heart not so securely boarded up and barricaded as, at the least, was mine.

Maybe Ray recognized that in the long run we weren't reaping freedom after all; maybe we had been tricked.

I hope there is not anything about this recital of antics which sounds prideful. I hope these are not seen as the kind of stories you dine out on. Once they were, once I used them that way, I suppose. At least I recall telling them in bars while we all had a swell time, they had a certain currency.

Ray suffered some sight of chaos deep in his soul and turned away and sobered up in the middle 1970s, and moved up to McKinleyville on the coast of California just north of the little university town of Arcadia, where he had gone to school in the old days and friends like Dick Day could help see him through the drying out. I visited there a couple of times, on my way to San Francisco. I asked Ray if he was writing. By this time he had been sober for most of a year. "No," he said. "I could. But I'm not."

I asked him why.

"Because I can't convince myself it's worth doing." That was the first time he surprised me. I thought about that for days afterward. It implied a kind of consequence I had never anticipated. We had seen a lot of our things by then, but it had never seemed to me possible that even the fractured marriages and falling-down, bite-your-tongue convulsions in the streets could lead to this kind of seriousness. Ray must have witnessed some things I had not imagined.

The thing I had believed in was work, the stories, and if that was not worth doing, well, then, there was no way to make good on anything, there was no justifying anything in your life. I had let myself believe that good writing was like a license to steal; anything was forgivable so long as you were writing well.

Which is a line of bullshit a lot of people like me have used to excuse endless rudeness, selfishness, cruelty, and general cheapshit misconduct. It's a line so stupid and so demeaning I have to wonder if I believed it at the time.

This is what I think: No one thing justifies any other thing. Each thing you do stands alone; they don't add up, not in any direction; nothing accumulates; there is no magic; the work you do is the work you got done, good or bad, and it doesn't earn you any moral privileges, no points. If you have the good luck to do some good work, that's a fine thing. But it has nothing to do with making you anything but lucky.

A lot of the long-term Sunday afternoon sadness in taverns where I go, among people I know, has to do with wasted possibilities, fine and capable people who didn't do any work and collapsed into serving their own selves and pleasures, as I was so inclined, for so long. Drunk in the morning. Those were fine times, I have to say, with fine friends. I loved them dearly.

But it has been a good idea, for me, to attempt putting away the indulgence and make-believe, and try to identify some decencies to serve. I do not mean God or country, but community, which is a larger, extended version of our own selves. We are responsible; nothing is bulletproof.

All these were not thoughts I wanted to let myself dwell on in those days. Most of what I did was support a set of all-day excuses for seldom doing any work. I thought maybe Ray saw some visions; maybe that was his trouble. Maybe he had the heebie-jeebies and scared himself. But I was not scared.

And there we were, not so many years later; he was famous, and dying, and I was studying him for hints.

In the months before his affliction revealed itself, Ray had taken to inspecting condominiums on the downtown hills of Seattle overlooking Elliot Bay and shipping lanes to the Orient, right near the Public Market with its perfect produce and living geoducks you could kill and fry for dinner, and flowers picked just that morning. He liked to talk about living close to such amenities.

Just out the windows you could witness sunset over the Olympic Mountains. This was the saw filer's son from Yakima, and he was finally getting his chance at the world. He wanted properties.

A few years before, in the fall of 1982, while I was visiting southern Vermont, Ray showed up driving an immaculate new Mercedes. He had been going home to Syracuse from John Gardner's funeral, he said, and he had decided you might as well enjoy some things, if you could afford them. "So what the hell," he said. "So I bought this car. Who knows?"

And that was what we were all studying, on that visit to Port Angeles: "Who knows?"

What I was most concerned about, that last time there in Port Angeles, was watching myself as I watched Ray and wondered who to be, studying him like a stranger, envying his equilibrium. He had survived some series of transformations, and I wanted to share the wisdom, if it was wisdom. Ray was dying, and I wanted to know how he could conduct himself as he did; I wanted to see what he saw when he looked out from his seashore to the flow of his ocean. I wanted to hear his music as he heard it.

The summer before, I had gone to Port Angeles for some salmon fishing. It all seemed so very easy, that dream, and natural enough. We caught salmon, the day was brilliant, Ray was the generous center of it all, our prince of good fortune, proof that some rewards were justly rationed out by the way of things. And now his life was over, soon now, forever. Someone had canceled his ticket to the rest of the party.

On a bright chill morning Ray and Tess and Annick and I took a short hike on a downhill path to the edges of the beach, where we were stopped by driftwood logs. Ray was still healing from his operation and moving like an old man. He refused to go climb over the logs, and we turned inland along the soggy fairways of a little golf course bordering a tiny creek and looped back to a bridge over the river. It was a small expedition into the native world, but longer than we ever took before. Back at Tess's house, Ray opened a tin of canned salmon, we ate a little, and that is what there is to tell. There is no insight here, no moment, no recognition.

There is just my friend in his gentle patience with his terrible fate, and with us.

He could have been impatient; he could have thought we were exhausting what little remained of his life. And maybe he did. Or maybe he was glad of the company.

On August 3, 1988, in warm morning sunlight on a patio outside a mental health clinic in Aspen, Colorado, I was meeting with a fiction writing class. "I see in the paper," one of them said, "where your friend is dead." He was talking about *The New York Times*. Ray was dead at fifty, leaving the example of his conduct while dying.

In December of 1988, coming home from the beaches near La Push, Annick and I passed by a chaos of clear-cut logging near the little town of Forks, heedless wreckage, mile-long swatches of torn earth and the jagged, rotting stumpage of the great cedar trees, limbs crushed into the black mud. Imagine paradise perfectly violated.

We stopped in Port Angeles and visited the highland over the seacoast where Ray is buried. Tess had worn a little path around the grave. She went down there and talked to him, she said. I tell him the news, she said. Like all of us, Ray was given to a love of gossip and scandal. His eyes would gleam, and he would lean into the talk. But as I stood there by his grave I had nothing much in the way of things to say to the dead, except to make a game of my question. How is it, old sport? Maybe I was too scared for much fun.

I said to myself: how many happy, contented people there really are! What an overwhelming force they are! Look at life the insolence and idleness of the strong, the ignorance and brutishness of the weak, horrible poverty everywhere, overcrowding, degeneration, drunkenness, hypocrisy, lying— Yet in all the houses and on all the streets there is peace and quiet, of the fifty thousand people who live in our town there is not one who would cry out, who would vent his indignation aloud. We see the people who go to market, eat by day, sleep by night, who babble nonsense, marry, grow old, good-naturedly drag their dead to the cemetery, but we do not see those who suffer and what is terrible in life goes on everywhere behind the scenes. Everything is peaceful and quiet and only mute statistics protest: so many gallons of vodka drunk, so many children dead from malnutrition—And such a state of things is evidently necessary; obviously the happy man is at ease only because the unhappy ones bear their burdens in silence, and if there were not this silence, happiness would be impossible. It is a general hypnosis. Behind the door of every contented, happy man there ought to be someone standing with a little hammer and continually reminding him with a knock that there are unhappy people, that however happy he may be, life will sooner or later show him its claws, and trouble will come to him—illness, poverty, losses, and then no one will see or hear him, just as now he neither sees nor hears others. But there is no man with a hammer. The happy man lives at his ease, faintly fluttered by small daily cares, like an aspen in the wind, and all is well.

(Anton Chekhov, "Gooseberries")

Chekhov understood that stories, when they are most valuable, are utterly open in their willingness to make metaphor from our personal difficulties. Our most useful stories focus simultaneously on our most generous and betraying ways. These troubles could be yours, the story says, this unfairness *is* yours, and so are these glories.

Ray must have spent lots of time listening to Chekhov's person with the little hammer. It is easy to see that his most profound sympathies lay with the disenfranchised, the saw filers like his father, as did Chekhov's.

Ray's last story, "The Errand," is about the death of Chekhov, drinking champagne as you die, celebrating what there is to celebrate, which is this, what we have. It is one of his put-yourself-in-my-shoes, try-my-blindness stories, like the story in which a man stands before a mirror in his neighbor's bedroom in his neighbor's wife's lingerie, making a try at being *someone else.*

Ray gave the world all the strength and decency he could muster and died out of an unnaturally foreshortened life (and we do, each of us). By his time of dying Ray had come to what seemed a learned and objectified sense of his own beliefs; he found it to say, Sure enough, sadness all over town—but, like my man Chekhov, I'm going to forgive myself, and try happiness anyway.

However terrifyingly misguided our lives may have been, we have to pray they are ultimately forgivable. My culture has poured burning napalm on babies; they did it on purpose; I didn't think I had any politics; much of what we do is madness.

We know the story of civilization; it can be understood as a history of conquest, law-bringing, and violence. We need a new story, in which we learn to value intimacy. Somebody should give us a history of compassion which would become a history of forgiveness and caretaking.

Ray's best work continually suggests the need for attempting to keep decent toward one another while deep in our own consternations. His best stories are masterworks of usefulness; they lead us to imagine what it is like to be another person, which is the way we learn compassion. It is the great thing: In intimacy we learn to cherish each other, through continual acts of the imagination. Nothing could be more political.

Contributors

Abigail L. Bowers is a Ph.D. candidate at Texas A&M University in College Station, Texas. She is currently working on her dissertation, which focuses on addiction and identity in twentieth-century American literature. Recent projects include a study of erased gender lines in avant-garde American poetry as it relates to the anthology *The Maverick Poets* (1988), as well as an ongoing interest in postmodern culture and consumerism.

Tamas Dobozy is an associate professor of twentieth-century American literature at Wilfrid Laurier University in Ontario, Canada. His works on Mavis Gallant, Charles Bukowski, John Coltrane, and Philip Roth have appeared in publications such as *Canadian Literature, Modern Fiction Studies, Genre: Forms of Discourse and Culture,* and *Philip Roth Studies.* His first book of short fiction, *When X Equals Marylou,* was published in 2002, and his second, *Last Notes,* was published by in 2006.

Jo Angela Edwins is an assistant professor of English and assistant composition coordinator at Francis Marion University in Florence, South Carolina. Her poems have appeared in *Sojourn, CrossRoads: A Southern Culture Annual,* and *Migrants and Stowaways,* an anthology of poetry, fiction, and creative nonfiction devoted to the journey theme.

Claire Fabre-Clark is a *maître de conférences,* a teaching and research position, at the University of Paris XII. Her essay in this work, "The Poetics of the Banal in *Elephant and Other Stories,*" draws on her study of the Carver manuscripts at Ohio State University in Columbus and in the Charvat Collection of the Ohio State University Libraries. Fabre-Clark has published articles on David Foster Wallace, Grace Paley, Nicholson Baker, and Raymond Carver, and she contributed a chapter on Patricia Eakins in *Reading Patricia Eakins* (2002).

Tess Gallagher, Raymond Carver's widow, is the author of numerous books of poems, stories, screenplays, essays, and translations, including *Instructions to the Double, Amplitude, A Concert of Tenses, The Lover of Horses, At the Owl Woman Saloon, Portable Kisses, Moon Crossing Bridge, Soul Barnacles: Ten More Years with Ray,* and, recently, *Dear Ghosts,* a new collection of poems. Her work has been published in eight languages, including Czech, Norwegian, and Japanese. She is active in collaboration projects with Mexican painter Alfredo Arreguin and with Irish storyteller and painter Josie Gray, including *The Courtship Stories,* fictional adaptations of oral stories from the west of Ireland.

Paul Benedict Grant is an assistant professor of English at Memorial University of Newfoundland's Sir Wilfred Grenfell College, where he teaches nineteenth- and twentieth-century literature. He specializes in humor studies and is currently preparing a book on humor in the work of Vladimir Nabokov.

William Kittredge is the author and editor of more than three dozen books, including *Hole in the Sky: A Memoir* (1992), *Who Owns the West?* (1995), and, most recently, *The Nature of Generosity* (2000) and *Balancing Water: Restoring the Klamath Basin* (2000); in 1984 he published a collection of short stories, *We Are Not in This Together*, which was edited by his longtime friend Raymond Carver. A former rancher and creative-writing professor at the University of Montana, Kittredge is an active environmentalist and conservationist. "Bulletproof," his memoir-essay on Carver, was first published in *Ploughshares*.

Sandra Lee Kleppe currently teaches English language literature at the University of Tromsø, Norway, the northernmost campus in the world. She has published works on American literature in a variety of journals, including *Literature and Theology, Mississippi Quarterly*, and the *Flannery O'Connor Bulletin*. Her articles on Carver's verse have appeared in *Classical and Modern Literature* as well as *Journal of Medical Humanities*, and an essay on his fiction was included in a special Carver issue of *Journal of the Short Story in English* in 2006. She is currently the director of the International Raymond Carver Society.

William L. Magrino is the director of the Business and Technical Writing Program at Rutgers University, in New Brunswick, New Jersey. He is also a doctoral student in literature and criticism at Indiana University of Pennsylvania. His major area of inquiry involves a psychoanalytic examination of male subjectivity in late-twentieth-century American fiction. Specifically Magrino is interested in identifying the effects of media and technology on the commodified subject—and the resulting cultural and economic implications in contemporary society—through the work of Don DeLillo and Bret Easton Ellis.

Robert Miltner is an associate professor of English at Kent State University, Stark Campus, and is on the faculty of the Northeast Ohio M.F.A. program at Kent State University. Miltner has published on Richard Adams, Rane Arroyo, Raymond Carver, James Joyce, Jorie Graham, J. D. Salinger, Terry Tempest Williams, and Virginia Woolf, as well as works on media and literacy, visual and textual collaboration, and assembling poetry manuscripts. He is the author of ten poetry chapbooks, including *Against the Simple, A Box of Light, Canyons of Sleep*, and *Rock the Boat*, and is editor of the *Raymond Carver Review*.

Kirk Nesset, an associate professor of English at Allegheny College in Meadville, Pennsylvania, is the author of a book of short stories, *Paradise Road* (2007), and a nonfiction study, *The Stories of Raymond Carver* (1995). His essays on Carver have appeared in *American Literature, Essays in Literature*, and *Profils Americains*; his short stories, poems, and translations have appeared in the *Paris Review, Ploughshares*, the *Kenyon Review, Southern Review, Gettysburg*

Review, the *Sun, Prairie Schooner,* and elsewhere. Nesset has been writer in residence at the Chautauqua Writer's Conference and distinguished guest lecturer on American literature at the Bundesbank Institute in Frankfurt, Germany. He has received a Pushcart Prize in Fiction, as well as various stipends and grants from the Pennsylvania Council on the Arts, and he received the Drue Heinz Prize for Literature in 2007.

Marc Oxoby completed his undergraduate work at San Jose State University and received his M.A. and Ph.D. in English from the University of Nevada, Reno (UNR), and where he specialized in modern American literature and media. He currently teaches English and humanities classes at UNR and has worked as editor of the small-press literary journal *CRiME CLUb.* He is the author of *The 1990s* (2003) and has contributed to scholarly journals such as *Film & History* and *Critique,* as well as to *The St. James Encyclopedia of Popular Culture* and *The International Dictionary of Film and Filmmakers.*

Randolph Paul Runyon is professor of French at Miami University of Ohio. He is the author of *Reading Raymond Carver* (1992), as well as *The Taciturn Text: The Fiction of Robert Penn Warren* (1990), *The Braided Dream: Robert Penn Warren's Late Poetry* (1990), *Ghostly Parallels: Robert Penn Warren and the Lyric Poetic Sequence* (2006), and *The Art of the Persian Letters* (2005). He is currently working on a rhymed verse translation of La Fontaine's *Contes* and on a reading of the hidden fabric of Baudelaire's *Les Fleurs du Mal.*

William W. Wright is professor of English at Mesa State College in Grand Junction, Colorado. His research interests include the history of rhetoric, poetics, composition, and contemporary rhetorical practice. He has published on writing instruction, baseball, illness, classical rhetoric, and the academic workplace. Recent work includes guest editing a special issue, on rhetoric, of the journal *Nineteenth-Century Prose* and a special English and Norwegian poetry issue of the literary journal *Pinyon.*

Chad Wriglesworth is a Ph.D. candidate in the English department at the University of Iowa. He has published articles on Wallace Stegner, Frederick Buechner, C. S. Lewis, William Stafford, and Margaret Edson in publications such as *Literature and Theology* and *ISLE: Interdisciplinary Studies in Literature and Environment.*

Index